Neuropsychological Assessment of Children

Neuropsychological Assessment of Children
A Treatment-Oriented Approach

BYRON P. ROURKE
JOHN L. FISK
JOHN D. STRANG
University of Windsor and
Windsor Western Hospital Centre

THE GUILFORD PRESS
New York   London

ISBN 0-89862-676-5

For Aaron, Bernie, David, Damon, Mandy, Nicole, Philip, and Sean

Acknowledgments

We owe a number of debts of gratitude to individuals who have contributed substantially to this work. E. Damon Rourke and the Medical Arts and Graphics Services of Henry Ford Hospital took on the enormous task of designing and constructing the figures contained in this text; their contributions were substantial and we are particularly pleased to acknowledge them. We are especially grateful to Jerel E. DelDotto, Robin Morris, Edite Ozols, and Diane Russell who read and commented on the entire manuscript. The editorial contributions of Clare Brandys, John DeLuca, Marilyn Chedour, Gerald McFadden, and Mary Stewart were also of considerable assistance. Without the patience and persistence of Maria Lalli, who labored long and diligently over its typing, the manuscript would never have seen the light of day. Finally, it is with the utmost gratitude that we acknowledge the seminal contributions of Ralph M. Reitan to the development of clinical neuropsychology as a scientific and clinical discipline. Without his contributions this volume would not have been possible.

Of course, any limitations, errors, or omissions that remain in this work are the sole responsibility of the authors.

BPR
JLF
JDS

Preface

The favorable reception accorded *Child Neuropsychology: An Introduction to Theory, Research, and Clinical Practice* (Rourke, Bakker, Fisk, & Strang, 1983) by scientists and clinicians in areas related to applied developmental neuropsychology was accompanied by suggestions from some of these individuals regarding the need for a more extensive work focusing on clinical issues that would complement this introduction to the field. The present volume is our attempt to meet this need.

Our aims for this work are quite simple: (1) to provide explanations, discussions, and evaluations of many of the important assessment issues in the field of child-clinical neuropsychology within a coherent treatment-oriented framework; and (2) to present clinical case material in sufficient detail so as to illustrate how the practice of treatment-oriented neuropsychological assessment can be carried out. Thus we adopted a format (Chapters 3 through 6) that begins with a brief description and explanation of the particular clinical issue in question. This is usually accompanied by our attempt to place the relevant parameters of this issue within a framework that would do justice to the developmental neuropsychological dimensions involved. Then we present one or more case examples that involve assessment and treatment dimensions that touch upon these clinical issues. In most of these case presentations, we attempt to provide an amount of detail sufficient for the reader to appreciate rather more general issues relating to the practical, clinical features of the case in question. In others, our presentation is briefer and geared to more specific aspects of particular clinical issues.

That having been said, the fact remains that our principal aim in this work is to provide a thorough description, explanation, and evaluation of treatment-oriented neuropsychological assessment as it relates to the formulation, implementation, and evaluation of clinical intervention programs for brain-impaired children. The format within which we chose to do this was meant to provide, in addition, some broad outlines of a more general applied neurodevelopmental framework for these clinical issues (Chapter 1).

As in *Child Neuropsychology*, we have chosen to focus on clinical issues relating to children between the ages of 5 and 16 years. Although some material is presented regarding children below the age of 5 years, we feel that a quite separate and extensive treatment of the clinical neuropsychological issues germane to preschool children is necessary.

The intended audience for this volume includes those professionals who have some familiarity with the field of child neuropsychology and who wish to delve into its clinical aspects in a more thorough and extensive fashion. (In this connection, we would suggest that a perusal of the contents of the Rourke *et al.*, 1983, and Spreen, Tupper, Risser, Tuokko, & Edgell, 1984, volumes would be quite helpful as a background for this work.) The book was written primarily for child-clinical psychologists and neuropsychologists as well as for school psychologists whose work brings them into daily contact with brain-impaired yougsters. The concerns of general clinical psychologists, pediatricians, child psychiatrists, pediatric neurologists, and other professionals who deal with the problems posed by developmental deviations in central nervous system functioning in children were also uppermost in our minds during the writing of this volume. Finally, we were especially interested in providing sufficient detail in many of the clinical presentations so that speech pathologists, special education specialists, and others who are involved in the remedial teaching and training of brain-impaired children would be in a position to evaluate a neuropsychological perspective of these issues.

References

Rourke, B. P., Bakker, D. J., Fisk, J. L., & Strang, J. D. (1983). *Child neuropsychology: An introduction to theory, research, and clinical practice.* New York: Guilford.
Spreen, O., Tupper, D., Risser, A., Tuokko, H., & Edgell, D. (1984). *Human developmental neuropsychology.* New York: Oxford.

Contents

Neuropsychological Assessment of Children

1. Introduction

This chapter is intended to provide a developmental neuropsychological framework for the clinical issues addressed in this work. It also includes a brief overview of the book's contents. First, the model.[1]

A treatment-oriented model of neuropsychological assessment

In *Child Neuropsychology: An Introduction to Theory, Research, and Clinical Practice* (Rourke, Bakker, Fisk, & Strang, 1983) we presented a model that was referred to as a "preliminary developmental neuropsychological remediation/habilitation model." A pictorial representation of this model is contained in Figure 1-1.

This original model was couched in a series of steps leading from a specification of brain–behavior relationships (Step 1) to the formulation of a realistic, practical remedial plan (Step 6). We have added an additional step (Step 7) to this preliminary model that is designed to accommodate the ongoing relationship between neuropsychological assessment and intervention that we feel should obtain during the course of habilitative/rehabilitative therapy. What follows is a detailed examination of each of the steps in this expanded model.

Step 1: The degree of overlap between brain lesion and ability structure

The crux of this step is the specification of the interaction between the child's brain lesion(s) and his/her neuropsychological ability structure. Also implied is the determination of the impact of this interaction on the child's demonstrable levels and patterns of performance. Although such

1. Some reviewers of this work have suggested that Chapter 2 (Case Illustration) should be read before Chapter 1. We see some merit to this point of view, and would invite the reader with a sophisticated background in neuropsychological assessment to follow this suggestion. However, for those who are quite unfamiliar with neuropsychological assessment procedures and principles of interpretation, the material contained in Chapter 1 should probably be examined before studying the case illustration presented in Chapter 2.

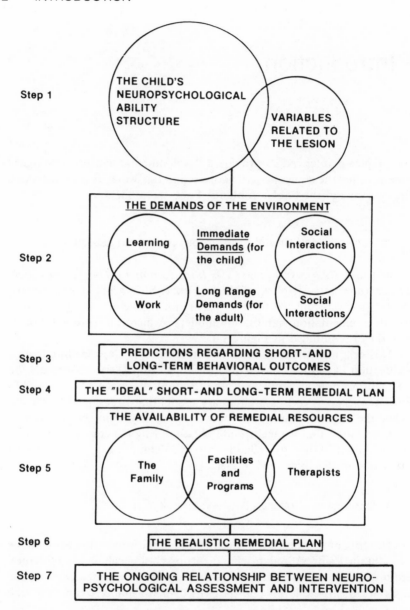

Figure 1-1. Formulating the remedial plan: A preliminary developmental neuro-psychological remediation/habilitation model.

interactions may seem to be straightforward, or even trivial, this is very often not the case. An example involving a comparison of two children suffering from brain lesions of quite different types and extents may serve to illustrate this point.

Recently we had occasion to examine a 10-year-old boy who presented with problems relating to blurred and double vision. It was subsequently determined that he was suffering from a very primitive type of brain tumor: that is, one that had been present since a very early developmental stage. This neoplasm occupied virtually all of the left frontal lobe of the brain anterior to the premotor strip. Prior to the development of his visual symptoms, there were no indications of problems in any aspect of his development or behavior that would have suggested, even to the careful observer, that this boy was suffering from a serious neurological affliction.

Indeed, in a neuropsychological examination carried out just prior to surgical removal of the tumor, this boy exhibited (among other things) Verbal and Performance IQs on the Wechsler Intelligence Scale for Children (WISC; Wechsler, 1949) that were in excess of 135. He also exhibited no problems in motor and sensory–perceptual abilities, and his psycholinguistic and concept-formation skills were at above-average levels. A second neuropsychological assessment that followed surgery for removal of the tumor revealed levels of psychometric intelligence and other adaptive abilities that were equal to or somewhat superior to those exhibited prior to the surgery.

In this particular case, the presence of a serious and extensive brain lesion appeared to have virtually no impact on the child's neuropsychological ability structure or his levels of adaptive behavior. This particular state of affairs can be contrasted with that experienced by a child of the same age whose demonstrable brain lesion was minuscule and chronic (i.e., a very small, static lesion in the temporal lobe), with adaptive consequences that were very serious (in this particular case, psychomotor seizures and profound memory and psycholinguistic disabilities). In this latter case, we see a very large intersect between brain lesion and neuropsychological ability structure with consequent serious ramifications for adaptive behavior.

A comparison of these two cases should suffice to demonstrate the point at issue, namely, that the impact of a brain lesion on ability structure and behavior is not a simple function of the extent or seriousness of the brain lesion. Rather, it is an interaction that must be specified through a comprehensive examination of the child's developmental neuropsychological ability structure and his/her adaptive behavior potentials. Although some recent neuropsychological research has begun to identify the prognostic and adaptive significance of various types, degrees, extents, and loci of brain lesions (e.g., Dennis, 1985a, 1985b), this genre of investigation is just beginning to shed some light on the multivariate nature of developmental brain–behavior interactions. For the present and foreseeable future, it remains necessary to formulate these specifications for the individual child on a case-by-case basis. Indeed, even were we able to specify with considerable accuracy many, or even most, of the relevant interactions between brain lesions, ability structure, and adaptive behavior through rigorous research, it would remain necessary for us at least to corroborate these interactions in the individual case.

It should be clear that the principal requirements for determining these interactions in the individual case are as follows: (1) a specification of the various details related to the lesion; (2) an accurate, comprehensive examination of the neuropsychological ability structure of the child; and (3) a determination of the impact of the interaction of (1) and (2) on the child's adaptive behavior. Each of these will be discussed in turn.

Variables related to the lesion involve the known or suspected etiology (and thus type) of the lesion, its level and extent, the age at which it was sustained, its chronicity, and the development of secondary degenerative processes. The sources for this information typically include data from a physical neurological examination, electroencephalographic recordings, and one or more image-enhancing techniques for visualizing brain structure, vascular function, and/or metabolism. Added to these as sources of information is the periodic availability of information gained as a result of exploratory or therapeutic neurological surgery.

We should be quick to point out that each of these methods of gathering information about the brain lesion is subject to problems in reliability and validity. Even in those cases where the results of many neuromedical evaluations are available, the fact remains that the concurrent validity of the conclusions drawn is almost invariably a function of the experience, perspicacity, and expertise of the professional who draws the inferences. That having been said, it is also the case that information gleaned from these various sources is most often quite helpful with respect to specifying those dimensions of the brain lesion in which we have particular interest. Each of these variables is discussed in turn.

KNOWN OR SUSPECTED ETIOLOGY OF THE LESION

The etiology of the brain lesion refers to its probable cause(s). For example, a particular brain lesion may be the result of a vascular anomaly, a mechanical injury, an infectious process, or any number of neoplastic and metabolic processes. Knowledge of the etiology of the brain lesion often throws some light on the likely course and ultimate prognosis in terms of brain–behavior relationships for a particular child. For example, knowing that a child has experienced a normal course of development up to the time that he/she sustains a severe head injury should remind us that some relevant facts are known about the posttraumatic course of adaptive abilities in such cases. One aspect of this situation is that one would not be inclined to place much confidence in the findings of a neuropsychological assessment that was carried out within hours of recovery from coma in, say, a 12-year-old child who has sustained a severe closed head injury (Levin, Benton, & Grossman, 1982). Rather, one would bide one's time until the child is sufficiently alert, orientated, and motivated to exhibit his/ her best possible levels of performance under this particular set of conditions. Ordinarily such a reasonably comprehensive examination is possible within 2 to 4 weeks following recovery from coma. However, even under these conditions, it must be borne in mind that subsequent examinations at intervals ranging from 3 to 4 months up to 2 to 3 years will undoubtedly be necessary in order to establish with any reasonable degree of confidence the relevant developmental parameters of the brain–behavior interactions for the individual child.

In the preceding example, the etiology of the lesion alerts us to the likelihood that the child will probably exhibit *progress* in adaptive abilities throughout some period of time following the brain trauma. Indeed, it is expected that the child will be much more adept at performance on many neuropsychological measures 3 months after recovery from coma than he/ she was at 2 weeks after recovery from coma. Some of these adaptive gains may be essentially *recovery* of previous skill levels, whereas other gains may reflect posttraumatic learning and/or maturational factors. In any case, increases in performance (from the acute to the chronic phases) on one or more neuropsychological tests are the rule rather than the exception when the etiology of the brain lesion is mechanical.

Such is not the typical occurrence in the case of children who are afflicted with progressive brain disease. Some neoplastic, demyelinating, and other progressive degenerative neuropathological processes are expected to yield, under most sets of circumstances, *deterioration* rather than advances in adaptive abilities following onset of symptoms (and diagnosis). Thus, the findings of a neuropsychological assessment during the early stages of a demyelinating disease would usually be expected to represent the *best* levels of performance (at least relative to age-based norms) that a particular child is likely to exhibit at any time during the remainder of his/her life. In this case, the etiology of the lesion should suggest that subsequent neuropsychological assessments are likely to reflect relative declines in adaptive abilities. Among other things, this should certainly serve as a principal and influential factor for the child-clinical neuropsychologist's consideration in formulating intervention plans, and especially in conveying information to parents and involved professionals regarding the probable future course of this child's adaptive abilities.

These two examples should alert us to the importance of etiological considerations in the formulation of prognoses and intervention plans. At the same time, it must be borne in mind that etiology per se may not be the most important or crucial feature that bears upon these two important clinical considerations.

LEVEL AND EXTENT OF THE LESION

Another potentially important neuropsychological consideration is the level and extent of the brain lesion. The term *level* refers to the common characterization of the central nervous system (CNS) as a hierarchically arranged set of systems and structures. For example, the spinal cord and its constituent structures are considered to be lower in level as compared to structures and systems within the midbrain and cerebellum; in turn, the midbrain and cerebellum are considered to be lower relative to the higher centers of the cerebral cortex. This is not meant to imply that there is a clear, undirectional, and agreed-upon ordering of centers within the CNS. Indeed, from the point of view of the maintenance of life itself, the intactness of the medulla oblongata (a lower center relative to the cerebral cortex) is essential, whereas most areas of the cerebral cortex are not. This is so despite the fact that the cerebral cortex is considered to comprise structures and systems that are higher than those within the medulla oblongata.

The important issue to bear in mind in this connection is that the hierarchical arrangement of the CNS is schematized by neuroscientists of different persuasions on the basis of various considerations that arise within embryological–ontogenetic development or phylogeny or particular views of the notion of "higher" and "lower" psychobiological systems as these relate to developmental skills and abilities. These theoretical differences can—and often do—serve to muddy the waters of scientific clarity in this field. Be that as it may, the level at which a lesion is sustained— however "level" may be defined in a particular case—can have considerable significance with respect to the present and future adaptive capacities of the individual.

For example, lesions that have a negative impact on motor and psychomotor performance may occur at a wide variety of levels within the CNS. Lesions at levels spanning virtually the entire hierarchy of the CNS (i.e., within and adjacent to the spinal cord, the medulla, the pons, the cerebellum, the midbrain, the basal ganglia and limbic system, and other subcortical and cortical structures) can have demonstrable and in most cases distinct effects on voluntary as well as rote, automatic, and reflexive movement. An analogous situation obtains with respect to the various sensory–perceptual systems. To make this matter more complex, even within the seemingly "simple" context of the various motor and sensory systems, there is very often a delicate and important interaction between lesions within the motor and sensory systems at each of these various levels. That is, the consideration of motor impairment must be evaluated within the context of sensory impairment and vice versa. Failure to do so may lead to grossly distorted and impractical conclusions.

But this is far from the whole story. It is also necessary to consider the extent of the lesion in question. The term *extent* refers simply to the number of structures and brain systems that are impaired. A simplified example may serve to illustrate the importance of this consideration.

In the case of cerebellar lesions in children, it is almost always crucial to determine the extent of the cerebellar structures that have been rendered inoperative. This is so because the prognosis and likely response to therapy for children afflicted with cerebellar lesions is usually a function of the amount and type of cerebellar tissue that has been spared. Indeed, knowing only that a child has a lesion at the *level* of the cerebellum conveys very little useful information, apart from the fact that there is likely to be some interference in fine motor control and that some specific aspects of kinetic steadiness are likely to be impaired. The adaptive potential of youngsters so afflicted is likely to be affected to a greater extent by the *number* and *type* of lesioned structures at this particular level. Hence the importance of determining the *extent* of the lesion.

Of course, many examples could be proffered to illustrate similar states of affairs with respect to other "higher" and "lower" CNS structures. The principal point of interest in all of this is that considerations of the level and extent of CNS lesions must be viewed within the context of our knowledge of the etiology and type of lesion that has been sustained. In turn, especially in the case of the developing child, considerations bearing upon age are crucial.

AGE AT WHICH THE LESION WAS SUSTAINED

For the developmentalist, the term *age* signifies little more than a gross, and often inadequate, marker for the important considerations relating to stage of ontogenetic development for a particular child. Furthermore, age becomes even less relevant as a marker for ontogenetic development when it is considered that there are various kinds of development that for an individual child may proceed (1) more or less out of pace with developmental norms for these abilities and (2) at varying relative rates across the brain–behavior systems of interest. That having been said, some general considerations with respect to the age at which a brain lesion is sustained are in order.

As pointed out previously, the interaction between the age at which a lesion is sustained in the developing brain and eventual levels of adaptive behavior is quite complex and not amenable to any simple or straightforward explanation (Rourke et al., 1983). Certainly, the so-called Kennard principle—to the effect that if one is to have a brain lesion, one should have it early—is a grossly oversimplified and under many circumstances completely erroneous statement regarding the probable outcome of early versus late brain lesions. Within the current context, we would simply note that brain lesions sustained during early developmental stages are likely to have the effect of preventing, limiting, and/or distorting the normal course of brain–behavior interactions within one or more areas of adaptive significance. This does not mean that early brain lesions are necessarily more pernicious in their effects than are later-occurring brain lesions, nor do we mean to imply that demonstrable negative impact on adaptive behavior is an *inevitable* consequence of early brain lesions. In fact, with respect to the latter point, many nonnormal alterations that take place in brain substance and function very early in life probably go undetected in later life because the individuals in question do not exhibit alterations in their behavior that are considered to be sufficient to occasion a neurological or neuropsychological workup. Issues such as brain and behavioral plasticity, familial and socioeconomic expectations, and a variety of other physiological and psychological factors can, and often do, have the effect of masking significantly deviant brain–behavior relationships, especially in young children (Rourke, 1983). At the very least, these factors often limit the generalizability of our research results in this area and render the determination of the long-term adaptive significance of early brain lesions in the individual case a difficult process.

With respect to the specific aspects of the developmental relevance of the age at which a lesion is sustained, a significant feature to bear in mind is that children who proceed through a normal course of development for some time (say, to the age of 9 or 10 years) before sustaining a behaviorally significant lesion to the brain have had these early years free of the potentially negative adaptive impact of an early brain lesion. One important upshot of this is that, given the presence of a reasonably supportive and multifaceted environment, such youngsters would be expected to have had what we usually refer to as a "normal" learning history. At first blush, one might hypothesize that such children should differ in some significant behavioral–adaptational respects from those who have sustained a brain insult during a very early developmental stage. In many instances this turns out to be the case. An example of the clinical significance of this point may serve to illustrate its importance for the matters under consideration.

The comparison of interest is between two children at the age of 9 years who exhibit significant psycholinguistic skill deficits. One of these children had the benefit of normal developmental experiences until she sustained a brain lesion at the age of 9 years. The other 9-year-old child experienced some anoxia and associated physiological disturbances during the perinatal period and, as an apparently direct result of the negative impact of these experiences on her brain, was consistently "behind" in the acquisition of psycholinguistic skills throughout her development. Although both of these youngsters exhibited very similar levels of psycholinguistic performance on a wide variety of tests, even a cursory qualitative analysis of their responses demonstrated very clearly that they were "obtaining" these scores in quite different ways.

For example, the girl who had experienced a normal period of development prior to sustaining a brain lesion typically exhibited unevenness of performance in that she would, for example, misread and misspell some simple words and then read and spell correctly some rather complex words. By contrast, the child who had experienced difficulties in the attainment of psycholinguistic proficiency since virtually her earliest days presented with a fairly even pattern of development across a large number of psycholinguistic skill dimensions, and was rarely seen to read or spell words that were beyond this general level of competence.

In subsequent chapters we will illustrate much more specifically that such qualitative differences in performance are the rule rather than the exception in the neuropsychological repertoires of children with these vastly different developmental histories. For the present, it is sufficient to note that the *pattern* or *configuration* of test results and the *quality* of responses were the dimensions of behavior that served to differentiate the two youngsters who exhibited similar, if not identical, levels of performance on many measures of psycholinguistic skill. To continue with variables related to the brain lesion, we turn next to the issue of chronicity.

CHRONICITY OF THE LESION

The term *chronicity* refers to a state of affairs that has continued for some time (most often, over a protracted period) and is currently in a "hardened" or stable condition. In this sense, *chronic* should be contrasted with *acute*. An acute brain lesion is one that began a relatively short time ago and is seen to be in a state of fairly rapid transformation rather than in a stable state. The important issue in this context is the celerity of change in the brain lesion: If the lesion is static, no matter how long ago it was sustained, it is referred to as chronic; if the lesion is fulminating at a rapid rate, even when such conditions have existed for some time, it is referred to as acute. However, there are some individual differences in the use of these terms; these differences relate to the relative balance between time and onset of the lesion and rapidity of change in the lesion itself.

For our purposes, it would be well to bear in mind that there is a clear difference between the chronicity of a brain lesion and the age at which it was sustained: that is, it is possible for a child to be suffering from an acute or chronic brain lesion, regardless of age. At the same time, many of the children typically seen by child-clinical neuropsychologists have sustained their brain lesions during very early developmental periods (e.g., those youngsters suffering from cerebral palsy). The fact remains, however, that the chronic phase of a brain lesion can follow the acute phase of such lesions even though they were sustained at very advanced developmental stages (e.g., in the case of a static brain lesion that has resulted from a closed head injury suffered during early adolescence).

The most important consideration in this context is that virtually all brain lesions have both acute and chronic phases. Also, it is important to know the difference between the two phases, especially as regards the termination of the acute phase and the duration of the chronic phase. It is, of course, also possible that a brain lesion can go through alternating acute and chronic phases, as is often seen in persons who are suffering from multiple sclerosis.

There are many dimensions of treatment-based neuropsychological assessment that relate to the relative acuteness–chronicity of the brain lesion in question. One of these very important dimensions is *prognosis*. For example, prognoses based upon assessments carried out during the acute phase of a brain lesion are in general open to many more sources of error than are those based upon assessments of youngsters who are suffering from chronic brain lesions. Long-term prognoses in the latter case are usually much more accurate than are those based on assessments of children that are carried out during the acute phase of their brain lesions. These inferior levels of predictive validity are often a result of the limitations imposed by less reliable measurement during the acute phase of the lesion, a point to which we shall return later in this chapter.

One corollary of the above is that it is often easier to determine with some confidence the method(s) of intervention that would be appropriate for youngsters who are suffering from chronic brain lesions than it is for those who are still in the throes of the acute phase of their disease. At the same time, it is also clear that questions regarding the clinical advisability of initiating treatment are not totally a function of the level of confidence one may have in either prognostic statements or the treatment programs themselves. Indeed, it is often preferable to begin a treatment during the acute phases of a brain lesion, even though confidence in the eventual outcome of the treatment–lesion–behavior interaction is much less than it would be for a youngster with a chronic brain lesion. In a word, the issues of confidence in prognostications and clinical efficacy are often not coextensive: that is, treatment may very often be instituted in the acute phases of the lesion because it is sometimes or often more effective than treatment initiated only during the chronic phase of the lesion. The clinical judgment to initiate treatment for a child with a particular neurological disease may be based upon the finding that some or all children with that disease benefit to a significant extent from therapy begun during the acute phase of the lesion, whereas few if any children exhibit therapeutically significant gains if treatment is delayed until the lesioned brain is in a chronic status.

These examples should serve to illustrate that the acuteness–chronicity dimension is a very important consideration, with respect not only to assessment, but also to clinically relevant dimensions of prognosis and the timing of treatment. Related to these dimensions is one final aspect of discussion in connection with variables related to the brain lesion, namely, the possible development of secondary degenerative processes that follow upon the primary brain lesion.

DEVELOPMENT OF SECONDARY DEGENERATIVE PROCESSES

As was pointed out in Rourke *et al.* (1983), there is some research to suggest that structures and systems of the brain that are remote from the primary brain lesion(s) may, with the passing of time, become less structurally intact (with concomitant diminution in function). This is felt to be the result of a lack of input from the primarily affected brain region. It is also possible that a similar state of affairs would obtain if the primary affected region plays an integral part in a complicated functionally interacting system involving the remote structure. In the latter case, both input and output considerations would play an important role in these secondary degenerative processes.

One very complicated aspect of this particular dimension of brain-behavior relationships is that functional adaptation may in fact become *worse* as a result of the development of secondary degenerative processes, even though such processes take place during the chronic phase of the primary brain lesion. For example, a child who seems to have recovered substantially, even fully, from a severe craniocerebral trauma may still be at risk for the development of seizures or other neurological complications as a direct result of the development of secondary degenerative processes. In this sense, actively debilitating (although not obviously acute) degenerative changes may take place during the chronic phase of the lesion that first brought the youngster to the attention of the child-clinical neuropsychologist. For these and a myriad of related reasons, it should be clear that there must be some ongoing relationship between assessment and intervention for the brain-impaired youngster—a point that we will explain in greater detail when we discuss Step 7.

Having reviewed in brief some of the more salient features of variables related to the known or suspected brain lesion, we consider next the dimensions of the child's neuropsychological ability structure. Our attention will be focused on determining the brain's capacities for adaptation. That is, we will attempt to demonstrate how one can gauge, through the use of neuropsychological assessment procedures, whether and to what extent known and available intervention methods will prove useful for (re)acquisition of functions that are thought to be crucial for adaptation.

In order to do this, we first must discuss briefly the parameters that are most relevant for a comprehensive treatment-oriented neuropsychological assessment.

NEUROPSYCHOLOGICAL ASSESSMENT: PSYCHOMETRIC CONSIDERATIONS

The primary evaluation criteria for any form of psychological assessment are reliability and validity. There are of course other dimensions, such as cost-effectiveness, practical suitability for particular clinical populations, and social psychological (including attributional) variables, to mention only a few, that should be considered. However, we will leave these to other sections of this volume, where their particular clinical significance will be illustrated in the context of individual cases. For now, we wish to consider rather narrowly defined aspects of reliability and validity. In this connection, the interested reader may wish to consult extended discussions of these topics as they relate to neuropsychological assessment (e.g., Rourke & Adams, 1984), as well as specific discussions within the context of the assessment of learning-disabled children (Rourke, 1976b, 1981), and rather more general considerations for the comprehensive assessment of the brain-impaired child (e.g., Rourke *et al.*, 1983, Chapter 5).

With respect to *reliability*, we need point out only that the clinical neuropsychologist is far more concerned with test–retest reliability than with considerations that are confined to issues of internal consistency. Although it is often very desirable to have internally consistent measures of particular skills, there are many more clinical considerations that relate to the consistency of measurement of particular skills from one time to another. Obviously, the time span of interest may be either short or long. For example, a very relevant consideration with respect to children who are suffering from deficits in attentional deployment is the consistency with which they respond to items of a similar sort and similar level of difficulty over fairly brief testing periods—say, only a few minutes. In the latter instance, we are very concerned that the test itself be reliable from the point of view of test–retest stability so that we can have confidence in the concurrent validity of the changes in level or quality of performance that are observed.

Such test–retest stability may be related to the internal consistency of the test itself, but this is far from a universally required or even desirable characteristic of tests used for neuropsychological purposes. Indeed, the common trade-off between complexity and internal consistency may have negative implications for the validity of tests used for neuropsychological purposes. This is the case because efforts to achieve internal consistency often involve item selections that lead to homogeneity of task demands and narrowness of ability spectra tapped by the test in question. Both of the latter attributes are sometimes undesirable in the neuropsychological assessment of a child, especially with respect to the elicitation of ecologically valid conclusions regarding adaptive behavior. That is, if the environmental challenges (current developmental tasks) that the child faces are themselves complex, both in changing task demands and in the wide variety of abilities and skills that must necessarily interact for their successful accomplishment, it should come as no surprise that narrow-band tests, although very internally consistent and stable, may be of little use for determining current and future brain–behavior-adaptive potential relationships.

While on the subject of reliability, we should also point out that longitudinal tracking of brain-impaired children as well as the requirements for gauging the effectiveness of particular forms of intervention often raise the need for parallel forms for various tests and measures. To date, little effort in the field of child neuropsychology has been directed to the construction of reliable parallel forms of commonly used tests. However, we anticipate that test and measurement batteries similar to the "repeatable battery" designed by Rennick and associates (Adams, Rennick, Schooff, & Keagan, 1975) will be constructed for use with children. In fact, a modification of the Rennick procedures has been used in the study of the effects of various types of medication on the performance (especially within the areas of attention, perception, and memory) of hyperactive children (Golinko, 1977). Such efforts need to be expanded and extended to tests and measures appropriate for children that deal with more complex psychomotor, linguistic, and cognitive tasks.

In summary, then, neuropsychological assessment procedures have in common with other psychological assessment procedures the requirement that they be stable and consistent. Reliability should be reflected in the internal consistency of homogeneous tests that are employed to determine the level of intactness of rather narrowly defined ability dimensions. In addition, we must be concerned with the test–retest stability of those complex measures that reflect more precisely the demands of the child's actual developmental milieu. Here we must often eschew internal consistency in favor of a level of complexity that mirrors the developmental demands of the child's immediate environment in a rather more precise fashion.

The degrees to which neuropsychological measures correlate with current and future events in the child's life are essentially questions of *validity*. In neuropsychological assessment, we are concerned with both concurrent and predictive validity as well as with many aspects of construct validity. Each of these merits some discussion in its own right.

Traditionally, neuropsychological measures have been evaluated in terms of their concurrent validity. That is, they have been assessed (1) in the light of their capacity to reflect the presence or absence of brain damage and (2) in terms of their psychometric relationships to other aspects of neuropathology such as locus, extent, type, severity, and chronicity of lesion. The evaluation of the relationship between various neuropsychological measures and such aspects of the brain lesion has not received the same degree of attention in children as it has in adults. Although there is a relatively long tradition of careful study of such variables in children (see, e.g., Reitan & Davison, 1974), it was not until recently that the degree of specificity required in this exercise has been attempted (e.g., Dennis, 1985a, 1985b).

Be that as it may, there is yet another dimension of the study of concurrent validity that relates to behavior rather than to the brain, that is, the *ecological validity* of neuropsychological tests. In this context, ecological validity refers to the power of neuropsychological measures to reflect the child's capacities for dealing with the current developmental demands that he/she faces. In a treatment-oriented approach to neuropsychological assessment, it is almost always found that the relationship of neuropsychological measures to both the current status of the brain and the child's current developmental agenda must be taken into consideration if meaningful, relevant treatment recommendations are the goal.

This particular point is sometimes easier to see in connection with *predictive validity*. Here we are concerned with the relationship between the child's test performances on neuropsychological measures and his/her future brain and behavior status. In particular clinical situations, the "future" may be a few weeks, a few months, or several years. We will discuss this point more specifically within the context of Steps 2 and 3. Of particular importance at this juncture is the fact that many aspects of variables related to the brain lesion must be seen within the context of the child's neuropsychological ability structure if confident and accurate predictions are to be made about eventual brain status and his/her capacities for adaptation in the future.

The *construct validity* of psychological tests is of little direct concern to most practicing child-clinical neuropsychologists. Since issues relating to concurrent and predictive validity tend to be uppermost in the clinician's mind, often the more theoretical—and in this case, the *most* theoretical—aspects of validity are relegated to the status of secondary considerations. This is understandable and appropriate, but perhaps shortsighted, because it is the clinician's input that often constitutes the most important contribution to studies of construct validity. This is so because construct validity is that aspect of statistical validation that refers most specifically to the exact nature of the psychological dimensions tapped by psychometric instruments. Although it is clear that principal components analysis and common factor analysis can be very helpful in determining the dimensionality of psychometric instruments, more sophisticated techniques such as confirmatory factor analysis usually require considerable input from clinicians, researchers, and theoreticians for the method to be appropriately applied (see Newby, Hallenbeck, & Embretson, 1983, for an example of the application of the latter technique to theoretical problems of clinical interest).

The fairly constant interplay that must take place between clinician and researcher in the process of establishing the dimensionality of a test or test battery may not on the face of it appear to contribute substantially to the multifaceted aspects of day-to-day clinical neuropsychological practice. However, nothing could be further from the truth. It is clear that clinical speculations regarding what tests measure must be subjected to rigorous testing with statistical methods that are appropriate to the task. Similarly, attempts to manipulate neuropsychological data in a theoretical–clinical vacuum often lead to nothing more than sterile, if not completely erroneous and counterproductive, results (Adams, 1985; Morris, Blashfield, & Satz, 1981; Rourke & Adams, 1984).

We hope that the latter points will become clear in the sections of this volume where we attempt to show how associations, disassociations, and configurations of test results of brain-impaired children serve to highlight the nature of the abilities tapped by the psychometric instruments employed in their assessment. For the present, it is sufficient to note that the long-range interests of the practicing child-clinical neuropsychologist are best served by devoting rigorous attention to the observational, methodological, and theoretical bases of the neuropsychological tests and measures that he/she uses. This mode of approach must be nurtured and developed if we are to gain more knowledge about the relationship between performance on these instruments and neuropsychological abilities.

We turn next to a consideration of the breadth of coverage that should obtain in the neuropsychological assessment of a child. This dimension of assessment has rather obvious relationships to the issues of concurrent and predictive validity discussed above, but its focus is on the actual content of the examination.

NEUROPSYCHOLOGICAL ASSESSMENT: COVERAGE

The principal clinical concerns of concurrent and predictive (including ecological) validity are constrained by another dimension of validity, that is, *content validity*. Within the present context, content validity refers to the degree of *coverage* of relevant neuropsychological abilities. The criteria for adequate coverage usually involve some combination of the following: (1) the ability domains tapped are sufficient to mirror the principal areas of human functioning that are thought to be mediated by the brain; and (2) the data gathered are sufficient to deal with the clinical (sometimes the referral) problems presented by the child.

Thus, just as the content validity of, say, a spelling test is measured by the degree to which it reflects the actual spelling words that the student was expected to learn, so too the content validity of neuropsychological assessment methods can be evaluated from the perspective of the degree to which they mirror the abilities that are thought to be subserved by the brain. Failing to do so—that is, having poor content (coverage) validity—can, and often does, severely limit our knowledge regarding the child's present neuropsychological status (concurrent validity), his/her probable prognosis with and without therapy (predictive validity), and the impact of the child's brain–behavior relationships on a reasonably broad spectrum of his/her developmental–adaptive task demands (ecological validity).

Furthermore, adequate coverage is, to a certain extent, a function of the referral question to which the neuropsychologist must address him/herself. For example, if the referring party is concerned with determining the presence or absence of brain damage, and the neuropsychologist is content to deal only with this issue (i.e., to answer yes or no to the referral question), then it is most often the case that relatively few observations, tests, and measures would be necessary to achieve the goal of adequate coverage. In most instances, a few moments of controlled observation of the youngster within any number of developmentally demanding situations would probably be sufficient for the experienced child-clinical neuropsychologist to determine the presence or absence of brain damage. Indeed, were this the only question to be answered by the reader in the vast majority of cases, he/she would be well advised to concentrate on very little of what follows in this volume.

More generally, we would be inclined to advise fledgling child-clinical neuropsychologists that they are probably wasting their time, energies, and talents if they concentrate on such a determination. The obvious reason for this position is that answering such a referral question is a trivial pursuit with a highly dubious potential for benefiting the child. As we have pointed out on numerous occasions previously (Rourke, 1975, 1976b, 1981; Rourke *et al.*, 1983), a determination of the presence or absence of brain damage is likely to have as many negative as positive effects—and the positive effects will probably be confined to the achievement of diagnostic accuracy (at a very gross level), which in turn will be of virtually no benefit to remediational programming for the child. At the risk of asserting the obvious, we would simply point out that there is no known treatment, program, or intervention strategy that has been shown to be better or worse for normal as opposed to brain-damaged children. Hence, treatment-oriented neuropsychological assessment of the sort we advocate must eschew this primitive level of analysis in favor of one that does more justice to the clinical imperatives of children in the real world.

Adopting a more reasonable perspective—for example, one that invokes criteria of probable therapeutic relevance for determining whether or not to embark upon a neuropsychological assessment—places the evaluation of coverage within a vastly different, and potentially more exciting, framework. Thus, the evaluation of content (coverage) validity within the context of ecological validity is tantamount to requiring that the content of the neuropsychological assessment (assuming for the moment that such content is adequately interpreted) must be fairly broad, pervasive, and comprehensive. Setting aside for now considerations that relate to the dimensionality of neuropsychological tests and test batteries (essentially an aspect of construct validity), it should be clear that such a goal will be achieved only through a reasonably painstaking analysis of a wide variety of functions, with attention being given to their interrelatedness and their dissociations.

To this end we would propose that the following ability and skill areas constitute a bare minimum with respect to the dimensions that must be addressed in order to provide reasonable, relevant, and comprehensive answers to developmentally important clinical questions for brain-impaired children. In each case, we provide the names of measures that we use routinely to aid in formulating what we hope will be therapeutically appropriate recommendations. The reader should bear in mind that the specific tests and measures mentioned are of secondary importance. The crucial issues in the present context are matters related to the ability and skill domains that are sampled, and developmental considerations that bear upon levels of performance and complexity; the actual tests and measures employed must be evaluated against these issues and considerations.

Table 1-1 contains a listing of the tests and measures that we typically employ in our neuropsychological evaluation of children. It should be noted that these tests have been divided into six categories that we have found useful for structuring our analysis of them. We should be quick to point out that this categorization system lacks a firm scientific basis; it is presented merely to facilitate discussion.

All of these tests and measures are described at some length in the Appendix. In addition, further data on them are available in the references at the end of this chapter. In this connection, the descriptions provided by Reitan and Davison (1974) and Wechsler (1949) are especially germane.

It will be noted that the first two categories of tests and measures include those that relate to tactile–perceptual and visual–perceptual functions, and that the third category contains those that relate to auditory–perceptual abilities. That the latter category also includes language-related measures reflects the view held by us and by most other child-clinical neuropsychologists that auditory–perceptual and psycholinguistic abilities are closely related, especially in children (Dennis, 1983; Tallal, 1976).

With respect to the measures noted within each category, it should be apparent that these vary across a considerable range of complexity. Furthermore, the complex measures, almost by their very nature, involve increasing contributions from systems other than those for which the category is named. For example, the constructional dyspraxia items of the

Halstead–Wepman Aphasia Screening Test require for their successful completion widely differing sets of abilities, including the following: visual–spatial analysis, organization, and synthesis; motor steadiness and agility; the capacity to benefit from both tactile and visual feedback; and organizational and planning abilities. In addition, the child must have some capacity to coordinate all of these activities within the demand characteristics of the testing situation so as to produce his/her drawings.

This outline of the ability and skill prerequisites for adequate performance on this particular measure should serve to highlight the necessity for appreciating the interactive aspects that obtain in the neuropsychologi-

Table 1-1. Tests included in neuropsychological test battery

Tactile–perceptual

1. Reitan–Kløve Tactile–Perceptual and Tactile–Forms Recognition Test
   a. Tactile Imperception and Suppression
   b. Finger Agnosia
   c. Fingertip Number-Writing Perception (9–15 yr)
      Fingertip Symbol-Writing Recognition (5–8 yr)
   d. Coin Recognition (9–15 yr)
      Tactile–Forms Recognition (5–8 yr)

Visual–perceptual

1. Reitan–Kløve Visual–Perceptual Tests
2. Target Test
3. Constructional Dyspraxia Items, Halstead–Wepman Aphasia Screening Test
4. WISC Picture Completion, Picture Arrangement, Block Design, Object Assembly subtests
5. Trail Making Test for Children, Part A (9–15 yr)
6. Color Form Test (5–8 yr)
7. Progressive Figures Test (5–8 yr)
8. Individual Performance Test (5–8 yr)
   a. Matching Figures
   b. Star Drawing
   c. Matching V's
   d. Concentric Squares Drawing

Auditory–perceptual and language related

1. Reitan–Kløve Auditory–Perceptual Test
2. Seashore Rhythm Test (9–15 yr)
3. Auditory Closure Test (Kass, 1964)
4. Auditory Analysis Test (Rosner & Simon, 1970)
5. Peabody Picture Vocabulary Test (Dunn, 1965)
6. Speech-Sounds Perception Test
7. Sentence Memory Test (Benton, 1965)
8. Verbal Fluency Test (Strong, 1963)
9. WISC Information, Comprehension, Similarities, Vocabulary, Digit Span subtests
10. Aphasoid Items, Aphasia Screening Test

Table 1-1. (*Continued*)

Problem solving, concept formation, reasoning

1. Halstead Category Test
2. Children's Word-Finding Test (Rourke & Fisk, 1976)
3. WISC Arithmetic subtest
4. Matching Pictures Test (5-8 yr)

Motor and psychomotor

1. Reitan–Kløve Lateral Dominance Examination
2. Dynamometer
3. Finger Tapping Test
4. Foot Tapping Test
5. Kløve–Matthews Motor Steadiness Battery
   a. Maze Coordination Test
   b. Static Steadiness Test
   c. Grooved Pegboard Test

Other

1. Underlining Test (Doehring, 1968; Rourke & Gates, 1980; Rourke & Petrauskas, 1978)
2. WISC Coding subtest
3. Tactual Performance Test
4. Trail Making Test for Children, Part B (9-15 yr)

Note. Unless otherwise indicated, these measures are described in Reitan and Davison (1974) or Wechsler (1949). All but one are described extensively in Rourke *et al.* (1983).

cal assessment of children. One must deal constantly with the interplay of many complex factors and systems in order to generate heuristic hypotheses regarding the neuropsychological significance of such seemingly simple performances. At the same time, deductions regarding the state of brain–behavior relationships in a particular child that are based upon observations within a very limited, albeit complex, set of circumstances are likely to result in oversimplified, if not completely erroneous, conclusions. Hence, hypotheses generated in one test situation must be tested in others. The manner in which this can be done will be outlined in subsequent chapters.

To return to the specific content issues at hand, the large number of measures included in the three categories under consideration mirrors the crucial role we feel that sensory–perceptual testing should play in the assessment of children who are suspected of having sustained brain impairment. As compared to adults who have experienced a fairly normal course of development before sustaining a brain injury, children who suffer such damage at virtually any time prior to middle adolescence must be examined with a view to very clear and precise delineation of their sensory–perceptual systems. By this we do not mean to imply that similar examinations of adults with acquired brain lesions would not be helpful. Quite the contrary: It is often by means of a thorough examination of such systems in the adult that meaningful and relevant diagnostic–assessment assertions are formulated. In the case of children, however, such examinations take on at least a double frame of reference: They serve not only to pinpoint significant brain–behavior relationships in the individual child; they may also highlight the potentially serious developmental consequences that can accrue if the child is suffering from impairments in one or more sensory–perceptual systems.

Although functional reorganization and brain–behavior plasticity may be "easier" for the child than for the adult, the fact remains that any diminution or distortion in basic perceptual processing is a potentially serious problem for the child. One obvious reason for this is the diminished, even seriously impoverished, reservoir of previous learned engrams which the child has available for use. A moment's reflection about this state of affairs will suggest that such a handicap, no matter how small or seemingly insignificant, may have seriously debilitating effects upon the child's capacity to discern and distinguish the panoply of sensory–perceptual input to which he/she is exposed daily.

An example of the interactive nature of basic sensory–perceptual functioning and factors associated with attention, memory, and higher-order information processing is the interrelationship of the various tests and measures included within the auditory–perceptual and language-related category.

After having assured ourselves that the child does not have a basic auditory acuity problem (through the administration of a Sweep Hearing Test or other similar measure), we then attempt to determine if there is any evidence of auditory suppression. The procedures involved in the Reitan–Kløve Auditory-Perceptual Test include the presentation of bilateral simultaneous auditory stimulation in order to determine if there is any evidence of auditory suppression. We are also concerned with the capacity of the child to make fine auditory discriminations under sustained attentional conditions; the Seashore Rhythm Test affords an opportunity to make observations along these lines. Since phonemic hearing, segmentation, and blending appear to be very important aspects of psycholinguistic skill development, we attempt to tap into these dimensions through the use of the Auditory Closure Test and the Auditory Analysis Test. The identification of words through the auditory modality and the capacity to match speech sounds with their appropriate graphemes are approached through an analysis of performance on the Peabody Picture Vocabulary Test and Speech-Sounds Perception Test, respectively. Immediate memory for meaningful and nonmeaningful auditory–verbal material can be examined through an analysis of performance on the Sentence Memory Test and the

WISC Digit Span subtest. Facility with verbal associations and elementary verbal concept formation may be reflected in performance on the WISC Similarities subtest. Word-finding skills can be reflected in a wide variety of analytic methods; we typically use a phonemically cued test of verbal fluency. This is sometimes supplemented by the use of semantically based tests of verbal fluency. In addition to a reflection of long-term storage of verbal information (WISC Information subtest), verbal comprehension of common problem-solving situations (WISC Comprehension subtest), and knowledge of word definitions (WISC Vocabulary subtest), these three WISC subtests involve the necessity of formulating and expressing word strings in answer to questions from the examiner. Thus, in addition to analyzing the subtest-specific content of the test items, one is in a position to analyze the phrase-generating capacity of the child. Finally, the linguistic items on the Aphasia Screening Test offer an opportunity to evaluate naming skills, auditory–verbal comprehension, and a number of other relevant features of the child's psycholinguistic repertoire.

When analyzing performance on the tests within this category, it is often necessary to juxtapose the results obtained on measures from various levels of this hierarchy. For example, the evaluation of some of the more complex tasks must be carried out in light of the limitations that are exhibited on simpler tests. In addition, it is the rule rather than the exception that performance on these measures themselves must be interpreted within the context of performance on other tests. For example, the limiting feature of the child's performance on the Peabody Picture Vocabulary Test may not be his/her receptive vocabulary, but rather difficulties in dealing with the identification of visual detail and/or visual scanning of the response alternatives. In order to determine if this may in fact be the case, it would be necessary to examine the child's performance on such tests as the Target Test, the WISC Picture Completion subtest, and the Underlining Test. By the same token, performance on various measures involving verbal expression (such as tests of verbal fluency, naming, or writing) may be poor because of oral–motor and other psychomotor problems rather than word-finding or other expressive verbal difficulties per se. When this state of affairs is suspected, it is necessary to obtain information regarding those simple and complex motor and psychomotor skills that are necessary for the actual type of verbal expression (e.g., speaking, writing) that is being examined.

These two examples should serve to show that the neuropsychological assessment of a child involves a constant interplay between hypothesis generation and hypothesis testing, both within and between various categories of tests and measures. Furthermore, this must all proceed within the general context of developmental considerations that go well beyond a simple comparison of the child's test results with developmental norms.

Indeed, some sophistication concerning the relative contributions of various component skills to performance at different developmental stages is a necessary prerequisite for engaging in this activity.

A fairly straightforward hierarchy of tests and measures is contained within the motor and psychomotor category. In this group of tests, we are interested principally in comparing the child's rather basic motor skills (i.e., force and speed) with his/her more complex psychomotor abilities (i.e., those tapped by the Motor Steadiness Battery). As would be expected in view of our previous discussions of measures that are arranged in terms of such a simplicity–complexity dimension, the more complex psychomotor measures in this spectrum of tests involve increasing contributions of skills that are not of an essentially motor nature. For example, performance on the Grooved Pegboard Test may be limited by problems in the capacity to benefit from visual or tactile input and feedback. Such forms of sensory ataxia (i.e., problems in movement that are the result of sensory–perceptual problems) may be elicited on any number of motor tasks, including some other measures within the Kløve–Matthews Motor Steadiness Battery.

As with all measures in the battery under discussion, the tests themselves are of secondary importance; the crucial issue is the design of a motor and psychomotor examination that will be sufficiently comprehensive and appropriate for the clinical problem to be addressed. For example, as suggested above, this particular battery would have to be supplemented with other measures (e.g., oral–motor examinations) when dealing with some clinical problems (e.g., some expressive verbal deficits).

It is essential too that we obtain an estimate of the level of motivation that the child exhibits throughout the examination. In this as in other areas of neuropsychological assessment, we seek to elicit the child's best possible, rather than typical, level of performance (Rourke et al., 1983). However, clearly this is not always possible, and difficulties of a socioemotional or motivational nature may arise during the examination that prevent optimal levels of responding. At the same time, it should be noted that this particular category of tests is one in which the majority of children referred for neuropsychological assessment typically exhibit very little in the way of untoward reactions of this sort.

This is particularly advantageous because we are often asked to make evaluations regarding the probable cause and course of difficulties in many aspects of psychomotor coordination (e.g., general clumsiness, marked difficulties in graphomotor skills). In the case of handwriting, for example, it is often found that a child who has considerable difficulty in this skill does not exhibit any problems on the Maze Coordination Test. Since this test involves an assessment of kinetic steadiness while using a stylus rather than a pencil, this dissociation in performance would tend to suggest that the child's problems in handwriting may be related to anxiety generated by persistent experiences of failure that are in turn due principally to the linguistic requirements of handwriting tasks. Such a hypothesis could be tested easily in conjunction with the systematic evaluation of other pairings of observations within this test battery.

The tests contained within the Problem Solving, Concept Formation, and Reasoning category, as well as some of the tests in other categories, have in common the necessity of engaging in abstract reasoning and various forms of either concrete and formal operational thought. For some of these measures (e.g., Matching Pictures Test), such requirements do not obtain until fairly advanced levels of the tests are presented; in the case of other measures (e.g., Children's Word-Finding Test), these requirements are fairly constant throughout the entire test.

The capacities for generating plans of action, testing hypotheses, and benefiting from positive and negative informational feedback are extremely important for adaptive functioning, even at fairly early developmental levels. Such capacities also tend to be interfered with by seriously debilitating lesions within most parts of the brain. Thus, although the localizing significance of impairment on such measures may be rather poor, the continuing presence of such deficits is of considerable prognostic—and hence rehabilitational—significance. It is important to determine whether and to what extent a child is likely to remain stable in the capacities to generate plans and strategies of action and the ability to test these against the adaptive requirements of his/her developmental environment. The child's level of competence in this area has wide-ranging ramifications with respect to the amount of structure and feedback that his/her habilitative–rehabilitative program should provide.

For these and other reasons, therefore, we are eager to obtain reliable estimates of the child's capacities to engage in such behavior under conditions involving *auditory–verbal* input (e.g., WISC Arithmetic subtest), *visual–spatial* input (e.g., Category Test), *tactile* input (e.g., Tactual Performance Test), as well as varying output modes (e.g., Children's Word-Finding Test: *verbal*; Tactual Performance Test: *nonverbal*).

As should be obvious from this discussion, the tests that are included in this category are certainly not the only ones that require such higher-level reasoning skills. Indeed, the WISC Coding subtest, the Tactual Performance Test, and a number of other measures within the visual-perceptual and auditory–perceptual categories involve similar skills. The availability of data from all of the measures within this battery—which may be supplemented from time to time with information from other measures such as causal thinking tests, maze performances, and tests of logical–grammatical reasoning—allow for systematic hypothesis testing regarding those environmental demand characteristics that tend to facilitate or hamper the child's performance in these important areas. Our own clinical work has suggested time and again that well-developed capacities in these areas can serve to compensate to some extent for problems that a child may have in other basic skills (e.g., phonological abilities). On the other hand, deficits in such abilities, despite the presence of many other well-developed capacities, can have rather devastating effects on the general adaptational potential of the child (Rourke, 1982b; Strang & Rourke, 1985a). These points will be illustrated extensively in the cases that follow.

The category labeled "other" contains tests that are difficult to classify even within the fairly broad boundaries of the other five categories. The subtests of the Underlining Test, for example, require a host of complex skills for their successful completion, including the following: sustained attention, complex visual discrimination, rapid visual processing and scanning, eye–hand coordination, sequencing abilities, and naming strategies. The neuropsychological analysis of performance on this test and on others included in this category requires that we have available indications of capabilities within these component skill areas on other rather more simple (homogeneous) measures of them. Nevertheless, as should be clear in view of the preceding discussion, developmentally appropriate levels of performance on such homogeneous tests do not *guarantee* successful performance on a task that requires the orchestration of these component skills under speeded or otherwise demanding conditions.

Before we conclude our discussion of the content of the neuropsychological assessment, it would be well to mention briefly the content of ancillary examinations for personality factors and socioemotional disturbance that we have found to be of considerable importance in the evaluation of brain-impaired children. These examinations are: Personality Inventory for Children (PIC; Wirt, Lachar, Klinedinst, & Seat, 1977); Activity Rating Scale (Werry, 1968); and Behavior Problem Checklist (Quay & Peterson, 1979).

The measures contained in these examinations are those that we routinely administer to the parents and/or caretakers of the children seen for neuropsychological assessment. The PIC is an empirically and rationally constructed instrument that seeks to provide comprehensive and clinically relevant personality descriptions of individuals primarily in the range of 6 to 16 years of age. The full version is composed of 600 true–false questions regarding the child's behavior, disposition, interpersonal relations, and attitudes, and is to be completed by one of the child's parents. There is also currently available a shorter, 280-question version of the PIC. The inventory itself is made up of three validity scales, one screening scale for general maladjustment, and 12 clinical scales. The clinical scales range from dimensions such as academic achievement through depression, anxiety, and social skills.

We have carried out a number of research projects in which the PIC has been used (e.g., Porter & Rourke, 1985; Strang & Rourke, in preparation). There is also a growing body of literature in which the PIC has been used and evaluated in populations of interest to the child-clinical neuro-psychologist (e.g., Breen & Barkley, 1983, 1984). In general, the results of these studies suggest that the PIC is of considerable utility in differentiating subtypes of learning-disabled children, in differentiating learning-disabled children with and without hyperactivity, and in differentiating among learning-disabled children with and without socioemotional disturbance and acting-out problems. Further specific information regarding the utility of the PIC will be discussed within the context of those cases in which information from the PIC is reported.

The Activity Rating Scale and the Behavior Problem Checklist are rather more direct rating scales that are meant to reflect the child's general level of physical activity in a variety of common situations and his/her usual behavior problems, respectively. Issues relating to the reliability and validity of these tests are discussed in their respective manuals. Our own clinical experience with these tests suggests that their results are likely to be helpful in a variety of situations, and that they very often reflect as much about the thresholds of tolerance that parents have for activity level and indications of "maladjustment" as they do the actual behavior of the child. In one recent investigation (Ozols & Rourke, in preparation) we found some relationships between patterns of abilities and deficits in subtypes of learning-disabled children at the ages of 7 and 8 years and their pattern of ratings on the Behavior Problem Checklist. However, there have been no extensive reports of the use of these scales with children suffering from well-documented brain lesions.

In addition to data about personality dimensions and socioemotional behavior derived from these three instruments, it is also our practice to conduct clinical interviews, when needed, in order to delve somewhat more deeply into parent–child interaction patterns, family dynamics, and perceived sources of conflict. At least one of the parents is also requested to fill in a medical history form, the data from which may very well require clarification during such an interview.

Finally, the child's behavior throughout the testing session(s) is monitored closely for such variables as motivation, activity level, tolerance for frustration, anxiety, difficulty in following directions, characteristic speech patterns, emotional lability, motoric balance and coordination, linguistic output, visual tracking, and a number of other behaviors that often contribute to understanding the child's characteristic patterns of adaptive behavior. These observations are made under conditions involving the administration of the comprehensive neuropsychological test battery described above, and hence involve ratings of these behaviors under a wide variety of circumstances. Our experience with this procedure is that indications of anxiety, resistiveness, and/or engaging in irrelevant activity are most likely to occur during those periods of the testing session in which the child has particular difficulty with the information processing and/or output demands of the task. At such times it is necessary to attempt to reduce the anxiety, resistiveness, irrelevant activity, and so forth in order to make some determination that the processing or output demands of the task are beyond the child's capability. Although not always successful, such efforts are very necessary in order to make some determination regarding the cause–effect relationship between ability and skill deficits on the one hand and untoward socioemotional behaviors on the other.

NEUROPSYCHOLOGICAL ASSESSMENT: DATA-GATHERING TECHNIQUES

There are a number of important issues regarding the manner in which neuropsychological assessment information is gathered. These issues are discussed at length in Rourke et al. (1983), and are summarized here.

First, with respect to the actual assessment of the child, it should be remembered that we always concentrate on obtaining the best possible, rather than the typical, levels of performance from the child. This is so for a variety of reasons, not the least of which is the fact that much is known prior to the initiation of the neuropsychological assessment about a child's disabilities. What is not known is whether, to what extent, and under what conditions these adaptive problems dissipate, remain stable, or worsen. Treatment-based neuropsychological assessment aims at specifying these variables in addition to determining current deficiencies in the skill areas that are needed for different forms of coping behavior, and the extent to which each of these component skills is remediable. In order to do all of this, it is essential that the child's best possible levels of performance be elicited.

All of this is done within the context of standardized testing procedures. It does little good, under a wide variety of circumstances, to alter standard testing procedures, since what we know with confidence about the concurrent, predictive, and construct validity of such measures is then no longer applicable. For this reason, we recommend that children be adequately warmed up and primed as much as possible for responding to the standardized administration of the tests. Thereafter, it may very well be illuminating to test the limits of the child's capacity on particular measures. In such situations, however, it is probably best to use other similar measures for this procedure, since one may wish to use the initial levels of performance as a baseline against which to measure subsequent forms of intervention (through readministration of the test). This becomes rather difficult to do when the child is exposed to the actual testing materials on a nonstandardized and repeated basis.

Another feature of data gathering that can be quite important is the potential influence of information from the developmental and medical histories of the child as well as knowledge of presenting problems. Although there are some valid reasons for suggesting that an examination of a child suffering from brain impairment should be undertaken only after an exhaustive history-taking and examination of presenting problems, such knowledge can also bias the examiner with respect to what he/she may selectively attend to during the examination. For this reason, we typically separate the gathering of relevant historical information and data concerning the presenting problems from the examination itself.

This is, of course, impossible to do in many situations, since the presenting adaptive problems (e.g., hemiplegia, various physical stigmata) are plain and obvious. In order to maintain some level of objectivity, therefore, we attempt to make an additional separation between the data gathering and the interpretational phases of neuropsychological assessment. That is to say, whenever possible we attempt to use "blind" interpretative strategies. More specifically, we attempt to employ a model in which the neuropsychologist who is to interpret the neuropsychological test data has no knowledge of the child's medical and developmental histories, and has furthermore not been involved in the direct examination of the child. Prior to writing the assessment report and formulating recommendations, of course, all of the available information on the child is taken into consideration. Indeed, it is at this point that very specific data regarding the child and his/her family may be required. The need for such information is often a direct result of the hypotheses generated on the basis of the neuropsychological assessment itself. Examples of this procedure and some of its ramifications are contained in the case analyses presented in other sections of this volume.

Step 2: The demands of the environment

In this and subsequent steps within our treatment-oriented model, we focus on varying aspects of ecological validity. In Step 2, we address the nature of the developmental tasks facing the child within both formal and informal settings. In addition, the unfolding developmental demands of the child's immediate and long-range environments are discussed.

For children in our society, the most formal environmental demands that they face between the ages of 5 and 16 are those posed by the school. Within the confines of the academic environment, the child is required to learn many skills. Some of these are rather *general* in nature, such as maintaining attention, control of impulses, general comportment, and due regard for the differing requirements of relationships with age-mates and with adult authority figures. These fairly general requirements may be very difficult for some brain-impaired children to meet. For example, children who have sustained rather serious closed head injuries that have resulted in extensive damage to the prefrontal cortex and the anterior portions of the limbic systems may very well present with extreme difficulties in impulse control. Outbursts of aggression, uncontrolled activity, inappropriate affectional responses, and a host of other deviations from expected social behavior may be common in such children. Such a child is viewed as having serious difficulties in learning the rather general skills that are necessary for continuing in the formal academic environment.

A more common example of failure to meet this particular set of task demands is the kind of behavior typically exhibited by a child who is thought to be afflicted with an attentional deficit. Although other aspects of his/her behavior may be quite acceptable, focusing and maintaining attention may constitute moderate to severe problems within the academic milieu, and may interact with other factors to lead to serious socioemotional complications (Barkley, 1981).

The *specific* demands of the academic environment are most often characterized as being co-extensive with the requirements for mastery of such academic skills as reading, spelling, writing, and arithmetic. Indeed, the enormous social importance ascribed to literacy in our society has led to intensive multidisciplinary investigation of one of these requirements (i.e., reading); there has been extensive neuropsychological examination of this problem as well (see Benton, 1975, and Rourke, 1978a, for reviews of research in this area). Relatively less attention has been directed to the neuropsychological analysis of spelling disabilities (e.g., Frith, 1983; Rourke, 1983; Sweeney & Rourke, 1978, 1985). There have been very few neuropsychological investigations of children who exhibit outstanding problems in mechanical arithmetic, although there are indications of more interest of late in arithmetic disabilities (e.g., Badian, 1983; Rourke, 1978b; Rourke & Strang, 1983; Strang & Rourke, 1985b).

Although these particular developmental problems (e.g., attentional deficit, learning disabilities) are of considerable neuropsychological importance, it should be emphasized that the principal framework within which they have been studied and to which clinical efforts have been directed is the academic situation. It is clear that this is not the only venue within which disordered information processing, deficient impulse control, strategy generation difficulties, and the host of other problems that brain-impaired children may experience will be exhibited. Indeed, most of the school-aged child's life is spent outside of the formal academic environment, and the demands of these other environments are no less specific and, in terms of long-term socioemotional development, of considerably more significance.

Thus, it is incumbent upon the child-clinical neuropsychologist to relate the brain–behavior relationships that are specified through the various diagnostic and assessment routines outlined in Step 1 to the child's informal as well as to his/her formal learning environments. Indeed, failure to recognize the necessity for dealing with the informal environment of the child may lead the practitioner to encourage the implementation of intervention programs that mirror an inappropriately heavy emphasis on the environmental demands of the academic situation. For example, we have encountered school psychologists whose quite legitimate concerns for seeing the brain-impaired child make advances in reading and other academic skills have led them to make recommendations (e.g., additional tutoring, supervised drills, extra homework, etc.) that have had the net effect of robbing the child of sufficient opportunities for engaging in normal peer interactions that would foster social learning. This becomes much more difficult when one must examine the normal social interactions of the brain-impaired child in order to appreciate those aspects of such situations that may have to be changed or for which the child may have to be specifically prepared if he/she is to reap any significant developmental benefit from them.

The long-range demands for the brain-impaired children are essentially the same as those for any child: It is desirable (1) that they become able to participate in some vocation that will allow them to live independently (i.e., apart from their primary unit), and (2) that they should be prepared to engage in fruitful, positive, and lasting interpersonal relationships. The attainment of both of these goals may be more difficult for the brain-impaired children than for normal children. But the crucial issue is that both should be kept in mind when planning intervention for brain-impaired children.

To illustrate this point, let us consider the case of a 14-year-old child with outstanding problems in various aspects of phonemic hearing and an associated severe reading disability who has very well-developed mechanical aptitudes and interests. Under most sets of circumstances, it turns out to be prudent to accentuate formal learning experiences for such a child that would engage his/her aptitudes and interests and not make great demands on his/her disability. This does not mean to say that one should necessarily recommend that he/she be denied access to the normal opportunities to make advances in reading (although one could conceive of some situations in which this would probably be beneficial). Rather, it would make good clinical sense to recognize that attempts to grapple with the serious acoustico-verbal and psycholinguistic deficiencies that appear to constitute the basis of this problem must take place within a developmental context of a child whose interpersonal environment now includes developmental conflicts surrounding issues of role definition, individual vs. group identity conflicts, and the other psychobiological changes of adolescence. For most adolescents facing this complex situation, formal educational requirements that do not have fairly immediate interest, perceived potential for success and development, and easily identifiable role relevance are, to say the least, scarcely attractive and hence are approached with something less than boundless enthusiasm. This being the case, a direct attack on the child's deficits is usually impractical. Even continued exposure to "normal" learning milieux—which leads almost inevitably to continuing failure—usually has counterproductive psychosocial results.

A very different set of interrelationships between information-processing capacities and environmental demands obtains in the case of some brain-impaired children who do very well in formal academic learning environments while faring very poorly in less structured situations. If such a child exhibits very deficient tactile–perceptual skills, visual–spatial–organizational capacities, problem-solving and strategy-generation capabilities, and bilateral psychomotor coordination problems within a context of very well-developed rote psycholinguistic skills, it is very probable that he/she will do quite well in rote academic tasks, such as word recognition and spelling, and very poorly in conceptually demanding tasks, such as arithmetic and unstructured learning situations (Strang & Rourke, 1985a). One particularly important developmental problem for such children is that their social interactional skills are often not perceived and acknowledged as deficient by most observers until late childhood or early adolescence. Such problems are predictable at much earlier age levels, and tend to be quite resistant to intervention at later age levels (Rourke, Young, Strang, & Russell, 1985). In this particular case, interventions aimed at dealing with what we have good reason to suspect will be a long-range problem should begin during early childhood, or at least as early as possible. In this instance, we would be recommending treatment for a problem that may be barely discernible in the 4- or 5-year-old child. However, since we are reasonably confident in the predictive validity of this particular confluence of symptoms, and since we know that treatment is very difficult to orchestrate and maintain at advanced developmental levels, it makes good sense to encourage at fairly tender ages interventions that are aimed at lessening the predictable impact of this set of disabilities.

These two examples should serve to illustrate some of the clinical ramifications of the interactions between formal and informal learning situations on the one hand and immediate and long-range environmental demands on the other. We turn now to a discussion of the implications of prognostication for various aspects of treatment–intervention for the brain-impaired child.

Step 3: Predictions regarding short- and long-term behavioral outcomes

As suggested in Step 2 above, some subtypes of children are characterized by particular patterns of information-processing abilities and deficiencies whose long-term prognoses have been investigated. Indeed, several investigations of learning disabled and brain-impaired children have yielded valuable information with respect to long-term outcomes (e.g., Fletcher & Satz, 1980; Peter & Spreen, 1979; Rourke & Orr, 1977).

However, there are a number of clinical imperatives within far broader areas of interest to the child-clinical neuropsychologist that have not been subjected to rigorous investigative efforts. That is, we have very little scientific information available to us that bears upon the issue of predictive validity for a variety of neuropathological syndromes. This necessitates rendering prognostic statements that are only the best estimates that we can make on the basis of our clinical experience. Often of considerable assistance in this regard are models of developmental brain–behavior relationships (e.g., Fletcher & Taylor, 1984; Rourke, 1982a) as these relate to the individual child's particular developmental history and his/her expected short- and long-term adaptational requirements.

In many cases, the neurological status of the child in the short and long term may pose no great obstacle with respect to prediction. This is certainly the case in the chronic phases of most types of brain impairment, such as cerebral palsy, and those classes of brain lesions that are degenerative in nature. However, in these situations the impact of the brain lesion on the child's developing ability structure, in addition to the impact of this interaction on developmental task demands in particular environments, is most often not known. Thus, the neuropsychological assessment question of import is one of attempting to determine the likely behavioral and adaptive manifestations of a neurological condition whose course is well known.

This situation becomes somewhat more complex when the course of the neurological condition is not well known. For example, rather little is known about the neurological consequences of various degrees of head injury in children of different ages. Such issues as the likelihood of posttraumatic seizure disorders, secondary neuronal degeneration, and related problems have not been well studied (Levin, Benton, & Grossman, 1982). Indeed, the general impression that has held sway for some time is that the neurological consequences of mild to moderate closed head injury in children are minimal or even nonexistent. At the same time, the neuropsychological investigation of children who survive head injury has been quite prominent of late (e.g., Gulbrandsen, 1984; Winogron, Knights, & Bawden, 1984). The results of these and other studies have suggested that there can be negative long-term behavioral residuals of moderate, and even mild, closed head injury in childhood. These findings of behavioral deficiencies should encourage more precise investigations of the neuropathology that would be assumed to underlie such deficiencies.

In any case, the child-clinical neuropsychologist is always left with the unavoidable task of formulating predictions, since any reasonable formulation of a short- or long-term remedial plan is contingent upon such predictions. In a word, if the neuropsychologist is not in a position to make some educated guesses about probable outcome(s), he/she should not presume to formulate short- and long-term remedial plans.

All of this should suggest that prognostications are essential, that they are often difficult to formulate, and that they should be subjected to rigorous case-by-case analysis in order to provide data that contribute to their refinement. We would like to emphasize the latter point. As in the case of construct validity, the practicing clinician can make a unique contribution to the advancement of our knowledge regarding problems of practical significance to the child-clinical neuropsychologist by scrutinizing carefully the natural history of children with brain lesions of various types and degrees. Such rigorous case-by-case analysis is often the most important foundation upon which significant large-scale applied research is based. Indeed, without it, it is difficult to conceive of how such research would yield much fruitful information.

In summary, therefore, we would suggest that child-clinical neuropsychologists should formulate their short- and long-term behavioral prognostications in specific written form so that these hypotheses can be tested sometime in the future. It may not be prudent to include such prognostications in clinical reports, but this does not lessen the importance of the exercise, nor the necessity for a rigorous testing of such hypothetical prognostications if they are to be refined in clinically relevant directions.

Step 4: The ideal short- and long-term remedial plans

At this point in treatment-oriented neuropsychological assessment, we feel that it is propitious to formulate an *ideal* remedial plan for the child that would be appropriate for his/her short- and long-term habilitative–rehabilitative needs. This plan, of course, should be formulated in light of the findings, impressions, and predictions formulated in Steps 1 through 3.

Since the short-term remedial needs of a child may differ markedly from his/her long-term needs, the overall plan must be formulated with these developmental considerations in mind. For example, a child with profound psycholinguistic deficiencies at the age of 7 years may be judged to be in need of very specialized training techniques designed to enhance his/her phonemic hearing. Eventually, however, it may very well be the case that this skill is learned to an extent sufficient to warrant attempts to enhance phonemic blending and phonemic segmentation. Hence, the overall remedial plan should contain allowances for the cessation of training in one area and the initiation of different or more advanced levels of remedial intervention in other skill areas.

Although such considerations may at first blush seem trivial, they can be quite important. An example may illustrate this point. It has been our experience that children who exhibit some of the skills necessary for reading (e.g., good phonemic hearing skills), but who lack other component skills necessary for age-appropriate progress (e.g., grapheme–phoneme matching skills) may persist in phonetic word-attack strategies, with attendant slow, laborious approaches to reading, when they should be concentrating on rapid whole-word identification, and eventually reading for comprehension (Sweeney & Rourke, 1985). This situation becomes compounded when well-meaning teachers persist in the encouragement of such approaches to reading as phonetic word-attack strategies on the assumption that they should favor and encourage the child's "strengths." By so doing, however, these teachers are essentially enhancing the likelihood that the child will not become adept at rapid reading with comprehension. This is an example of a remedial plan that may be beneficial in the short term but not in the long term. This point will be discussed further in conjunction with Step 7.

Step 5: The availability of remedial resources

After having formulated the ideal remedial plan, it is then necessary to evaluate the remedial resources that are available to the child. Of course, the most important set of resources to consider is that within the family.

Since youngsters are in many ways "captives" of their families, it is essential to make some evaluation of the remedial resources of the family. Some notions regarding family communicational patterns, typical ways of dealing with conflicts, ways of dealing with personal and social responsibilities, aims and goal-setting practices, patterns of child rearing, capacities for change, growth, and development, and tolerance of frustration and ambiguity are some of the more important attributes of the family system that have an impact on its capacity to play a role in the child's remediation. Practical matters such as socioeconomic status, language(s) spoken, linguistic facility, and any number of other factors can serve to enhance or limit the potential of its members for assistance in the remedial process.

Related questions must be raised with respect to the facilities, programs, and therapists that are available to the child. Indications of what actually happens in such programs and the specific skills and proclivities of available therapists are crucial considerations. For example, many children with various types of moderate to several psycholinguistic deficiencies are very much in need of language—rather than simply speech—therapy. In most settings, speech pathologists would be seen as those who are most likely to offer this sort of therapy. However, some speech pathologists are simply not prepared—or are disinclined—to offer developmental language therapy that meets the psycholinguistic needs of the child. By the same token, a child may need a form of psychotherapy that involves role playing, considerable social interaction, and learning to benefit from nonverbal feedback. If a particular psychotherapist is prepared to offer only insight-oriented verbal psychotherapy, it is clear that the child's psychotherapeutic needs would not be met by this therapist.

In all of this, an evaluation of the availability of remedial resources often leads the child-clinical neuropsychologist to the conclusion that the child's needs for remediation will not be even approximated. At this point, it may very well be necessary for the neuropsychologist to engage in attempts to bolster such resources through counseling, education, and other means. In this connection we have often found that families with initially low levels of resources for remediation can be encouraged rather easily to develop such skills. Very often a simple, straightforward explanation of the child's immediate and long-term needs is enough to begin the process of marshaling such resources. Analogous situations may obtain in the case of special education teachers, speech and language therapists, child care workers, and any number of other professionals involved with the care of brain-impaired children. In a word, once they are made aware of the child's abilities and deficiencies and perceive the important role that they can play in the short- and long-term plan for dealing with them, it becomes much more likely that they will adapt their therapies and programs to the needs of the child.

Step 6: The realistic remedial plan

All of this having been said, the fact remains that the realistic remedial plan (i.e., the one that is actually feasible in view of available resources) may fall quite short of the ideals formulated in Step 4. When this gap is very large, it should certainly signal that individual and/or community resources should be allocated to the improvement of those issues discussed in Step 5. It should be obvious that gaps in community services are usually identified by the difference between what actually can be done (Step 6) and what should be done (Step 4) for particular types of brain-impaired children.

Step 7: The ongoing relationship between neuropsychological assessment and intervention

Finally, in order to accommodate the ongoing changes that maturation and formal and informal learning experiences bring about in the child, it is necessary to point out that neuropsychological assessment may not be a "one-shot affair." Although we may have considerable confidence in our initial formulations of the short- and long-term remedial plans, we must acknowledge and make appropriate allowances for the vast lacunae in our knowledge of the developmental course of brain–behavioral relationships, especially as these interact with various types of remedial intervention. Hence, it should come as no surprise that repeated neuropsychological assessments are often required in order to fine-tune, or even grossly alter, remedial plans for brain-impaired children.

Follow-up neuropsychological assessments also afford an opportunity to evaluate the effectiveness of particular modes of remedial intervention. Leaving such evaluations to purely clinical impressionistic observations may be desirable in some instances. However, rigorous, objective, standardized assessment is likely to yield much more in the way of consensually validatable findings in this regard. Given our current state of knowledge, such an approach to evaluation of treatment plans would seem eminently desirable.

Summary and conclusions

The issues addressed in this chapter were dealt with in a summary—some might suggest superficial—manner. We referred to more extended treatments of them for the reader who finds our discussion somewhat incomplete; we attempted to spare the more sophisticated reader the monotony of repetition. In any case, most of the remainder of this work is designed to address specific problems that tend to arise in the practice of child-clinical neuropsychology. And with this chapter as background, we trust that the (now experienced) reader will be prepared to share our fascination with them.

Overview of subsequent chapters

The remainder of this work is divided into chapters that deal with specific clinical issues which the child-clinical neuropsychologist is likely to be called upon to address. Each chapter is constructed in terms of a common format that involves, to a greater or lesser extent, three principal components, as follows: (1) clinical issues emphasized; (2) discussion of these issues; and (3) case examples that illustrate the issues in question.

In each case presentation, more or less emphasis is placed on the seven steps involved in our working model. For example, some case presentations are designed to emphasize diagnostic and assessment issues and the relationship between brain lesion and behavior, whereas others are designed to address concerns regarding short- and long-term remedial planning. Although we have also attempted to point out and discuss all of the relevant steps in each case presentation, it was often necessary to sacrifice such completeness of coverage for the sake of in-depth consideration of the salient aspects of each clinical issue and the related neuropsychological assessment considerations.

It will be noted that, in the case presentations, a common format and a rather common set of test results are presented in the form of actual test scores, histograms, and verbal summaries. We have arranged these data displays on facing pages for each case so that the reader may engage in an inspection of this common test data and then attempt a "blind" analysis of it. Afterwards, he/she may turn to our comments on and impressions of these test results in order to determine how we have characterized them. In all cases, of course, there are many historical data on the child and his/her family, observations made during the testing periods, and psychometric data relating to other ability, personality, and socioemotional dimensions of the child that are presented in the text. Nevertheless, as discussed in an earlier section of this chapter, we have found it to be of considerable value for both training and actual clinical purposes to engage in a blind analysis of the types of data displayed in summary form for each child. Unfortunately, space did not allow us to include many actual examples of naming, auditory comprehension, reading, spelling, and other verbatim errors that we almost always have available for qualitative analysis. Nevertheless, thoughtful attempts to formulate, test, and expand hypotheses to the point of impressions regarding specific brain–behavior relationships based solely on the types of data displayed on the facing pages for each case (i.e., *before* considering the historical and other information contained in the text) can yield considerable dividends in terms of increased clinical perspicacity.

In order to familiarize the reader with the format for the case presentations that follow, we continue in the next chapter with the detailed analysis of a fairly straightforward set of neuropsychological test results that have rather clear implications for the clinical disposition and prognosis of the child who exhibited them.

References

Adams, K. M. (1985). Theoretical, methodological, and statistical issues. In B. P. Rourke (Ed.), *Neuropsychology of learning disabilities: Essentials of subtype analysis* (pp. 17–39). New York: Guilford.

Adams, K. M., Rennick, P., Schooff, K., & Keagan, J. (1975). Neuropsychological measurement of drug effects: Polydrug research. *Journal of Psychedelic Drugs, 7,* 151–160.

Aram, D. M., Ekelman, B. L., Rose, D. F., & Whitaker, H. A. (1985). Verbal and cognitive sequelae following unilateral lesions acquired in early childhood. *Journal of Clinical and Experimental Neuropsychology, 7,* 55–78.

Badian, N. A. (1983). Dyscalculia and nonverbal disorders of learning. In H. R. Myklebust (Ed.), *Progress in learning disabilities* (Vol. V, pp. 235–264). New York: Grune & Stratton.

Bakker, D. J. (1984). The brain as a dependent variable. *Journal of Clinical Neuropsychology, 6,* 1–16.

Barkley, R. A. (1981). *Hyperactive children: A handbook for diagnosis and treatment.* New York: Guilford.

Benton, A. L. (1965). *Sentence Memory Test.* Iowa City, IA: Author.

Benton, A. L. (1975). Developmental dyslexia: Neurological aspects. In W. J. Friedlander (Ed.), *Advances in neurology* (Vol. 7, pp. 1–47). New York: Raven.

Breen, M. J., & Barkley, R. A. (1983). The Personality Inventory for Children (PIC): Its clinical utility with hyperactive children. *Journal of Pediatric Psychology, 8,* 359–366.

Breen, M. J., & Barkley, R. A. (1984). Psychological adjustment in learning disabled, hyperactive, and hyperactive/learning disabled children as measured by the Personality Inventory for Children. *Journal of Child Clinical Psychology, 13,* 232–236.

Dennis, M. (1983). The developmentally dyslexic brain and the written language skills of children with one hemisphere. In U. Kirk (Ed.), *Neuropsychology of language, reading, and spelling* (pp. 185–208). New York: Academic.

Dennis, M. (1985a). Intelligence after early brain injury: I. Predicting IQ scores from medical variables. *Journal of Clinical and Experimental Neuropsychology, 8,* 526–554.

Dennis, M. (1985b). Intelligence after early brain injury: II. IQ scores of subjects classified on the basis of medical history variables. *Journal of Clinical and Experimental Neuropsychology, 7,* 555–576.

Doehring, D. G. (1968). *Patterns of impairment in specific reading disability.* Bloomington: Indiana University Press.

Dunn, L. M. (1965). *Expanded manual for the Peabody Picture Vocabulary Test.* Minneapolis, MN: American Guidance Service.

Fletcher, J. M., & Satz, P. (1980). Developmental changes in the neuropsychological correlates of reading achievement: A six-year longitudinal follow-up. *Journal of Clinical Neuropsychology, 2,* 23–37.

Fletcher, J. M., & Taylor, H. G. (1984). Neuropsychological approaches to children: Towards a developmental neuropsychology. *Journal of Clinical Neuropsychology, 6,* 39–56.

Frith, U. (1983). The similarities and differences between reading and spelling problems. In M. Rutter (Ed.), *Developmental neuropsychiatry* (pp. 453–472). New York: Guilford.

Golinko, B. E. (1977). *Hyperactive child syndrome: System to improve treatment with psychoactive medication.* Unpublished doctoral dissertation, Wayne State University, Detroit.

Gulbrandsen, G. B. (1984). Neuropsychological sequelae of light head injuries in older children 6 months after trauma. *Journal of Clinical Neuropsychology, 6,* 257–268.

Kass, C. E. (1964). Auditory Closure Test. In J. J. Olson & J. L. Olson (Eds.), *Validity studies on the Illinois Test of Psycholinguistic Abilities.* Madison, WI: Photo.

Levin, H. S., Benton, A. L., & Grossman, R. G. (1982). *Neurobehavioral consequences of closed head injury.* New York: Oxford.

Morris, R., Blashfield, R., & Satz, P. (1981). Neuropsychology and cluster analysis: Potentials and problems. *Journal of Clinical Neuropsychology, 3,* 79–99.

Newby, R. F., Hallenbeck, C. E., & Embretson (Whitely), S. (1983). Confirmatory factor analysis of four general neuropsychological models with a unified Halstead–Reitan battery. *Journal of Clinical Neuropsychology, 5,* 115–133.

Ozols, E. J., & Rourke, B. P. (1985). Dimensions of social sensitivity in two types of learning-disabled children. In B. P. Rourke (Ed.), *Neuropsychology of learning disabilities: Advances in subtype analysis* (pp. 281–301). New York: Guilford.

Ozols, E. J., & Rourke, B. P. (in preparation). Neuropsychological and behavioral characteristics of young learning-disabled children classified according to patterns of academic performance.

Peter, B. M., & Spreen, O. (1979). Behavior rating and personal adjustment scales of neurologically and learning handicapped children during adolescence and early adulthood: Results of a follow-up study. *Journal of Clinical Neuropsychology, 1,* 75–91.

Porter, J. E., & Rourke, B. P. (1985). Socioemotional functioning of learning-disabled children: A subtypal analysis of personality patterns. In B. P. Rourke (Ed.), *Neuropsychology of learning disabilities: Essentials of subtype analysis* (pp. 257–280). New York: Guilford.

Quay, H. C., & Peterson, D. R. (1979). *Manual for the Behavior Problem Checklist.* (Available from author.)

Reitan, R. M., & Davison, L. A. (Eds.). (1974). *Clinical neuropsychology: Current status and applications.* Washington, DC: V. H. Winston.

Rosner, J., & Simon, D. P. (1970). *Auditory Analysis Test: An initial report.* Pittsburgh: Learning Research and Development Center, University of Pittsburgh.

Rourke, B. P. (1975). Brain–behavior relationships in children with learning disabilities: A research program. *American Psychologist, 30,* 911–920.

Rourke, B. P. (1976a). Interactions between research and assessment. *Journal of Pediatric Psychology, 1,* 7–11.

Rourke, B. P. (1976b). Issues in the neuropsychological assessment of children with learning disabilities. *Canadian Psychological Review, 17,* 89–102.

Rourke, B. P. (1978a). Neuropsychological research in reading retardation: A review. In A. L. Benton & D. Pearl (Eds.), *Dyslexia: An appraisal of current knowledge* (pp. 141–171). New York: Oxford.

Rourke, B. P. (1978b). Reading, spelling, arithmetic disabilities: A neuropsychologic perspective. In H. R. Myklebust (Ed.), *Progress in learning disabilities* (Vol. IV, pp. 97–120). New York: Grune & Stratton.

Rourke, B. P. (1981). Neuropsychological assessment of children with learning disabilities. In S. B. Filskov & T. J. Boll (Eds.), *Handbook of clinical neuropsychology* (pp. 453–478). New York: Wiley-Interscience.

Rourke, B. P. (1982a). Central processing deficiencies in children: Toward a developmental neuropsychological model. *Journal of Clinical Neuropsychology, 4,* 1–18.

Rourke, B. P. (1982b). Child-clinical neuropsychology: Assessment and intervention with the disabled child. In J. de Wit & A. L. Benton (Eds.), *Perspectives in child study: Integration of theory and practice* (pp. 62–72). Lisse, The Netherlands: Swets & Zeitlinger.

Rourke, B. P. (1983). Reading and spelling disabilities: A developmental neuropsychological perspective. In U. Kirk (Ed.), *Neuropsychology of language, reading, and spelling* (pp. 209–234). New York: Academic.

Rourke, B. P., & Adams, K. M. (1984). Quantitative approaches to the neuropsychological assessment of children. In R. M. Tarter & G. Goldstein (Eds.), *Advances in clinical neuropsychology* (Vol. 2, pp. 79–108). New York: Plenum.

Rourke, B. P., Bakker, D. J., Fisk, J. L., & Strang, J. D. (1983). *Child neuropsychology: An introduction to theory, research, and clinical practice.* New York: Guilford.

Rourke, B. P., & Fisk, J. L. (1977). *Children's Word-Finding Test (Revised).* University of Windsor, Department of Psychology, Windsor, Ontario.

Rourke, B. P., & Gates, R. D. (1980). *Underlining Test: Preliminary norms.* University of Windsor, Department of Psychology, Windsor, Ontario.

Rourke, B. P., & Orr, R. R. (1977). Predictions of the reading and spelling performances of normal and retarded readers: A four-year follow-up. *Journal of Abnormal Child Psychology, 5,* 9–20.

Rourke, B. P., & Petrauskas, R. J. (1978). *Underlining Test (Revised)*. University of Windsor, Department of Psychology, Windsor, Ontario.

Rourke, B. P., & Strang, J. D. (1983). Subtypes of reading and arithmetical disabilities: A neuropsychological analysis. In M. Rutter (Ed.), *Developmental neuropsychiatry* (pp. 473–488). New York: Guilford.

Rourke, B. P., Young, G. C., Strang, J. D., & Russell, D. L. (1985). Adult outcomes of central processing deficiencies in childhood. In I. Grant & K. M. Adams (Eds.), *Neuropsychological assessment of neuropsychiatric disorders* (pp. 244–267). New York: Oxford.

Spreen, O., Tupper, D., Risser, A., Tuokko, H., & Edgell, D. (1984). *Human developmental neuropsychology*. New York: Oxford.

Strang, J. D., & Rourke, B. P. (1983). Concept-formation/nonverbal reasoning abilities of children who exhibit specific academic problems with arithmetic. *Journal of Clinical Child Psychology, 12*, 33–39.

Strang, J. D., & Rourke, B. P. (1985a). Adaptive behavior of children with specific arithmetic disabilities and associated neuropsychological abilities and deficits. In B. P. Rourke (Ed.), *Neuropsychology of learning disabilities: Essentials of subtype analysis* (pp. 302–328). New York: Guilford.

Strang, J. D., & Rourke, B. P. (1985b). Arithmetic disability subtypes: The neuropsychological significance of specific arithmetic impairment in childhood. In B. P. Rourke (Ed.), *Neuropsychology of learning disabilities: Essentials of subtype analysis* (pp. 167–183). New York: Guilford.

Strang, J. D., & Rourke, B. P. (in preparation). Personality dimensions of learning-disabled children.

Strong, R. T., Jr. (1963). *Intellectual deficits associated with minimal brain disorders in primary school children*. Columbus, OH: Columbus State School. (Mimeo)

Sweeney, J. E., & Rourke, B. P. (1978). Neuropsychological significance of phonetically accurate and phonetically inaccurate spelling errors in younger and older retarded spellers. *Brain and Language, 6*, 212–225.

Sweeney, J. E., & Rourke, B. P. (1985). Spelling disability subtypes. In B. P. Rourke (Ed.), *Neuropsychology of learning disabilities: Essentials of subtype analysis* (pp. 147–166). New York: Guilford.

Tallal, P. (1976). Auditory perceptual factors in language and learning disabilities. In R. M. Knights & D. J. Bakker (Eds.), *Neuropsychology of learning disorders: Theoretical approaches* (pp. 315–323). Baltimore: University Park Press.

Tallal, P., Stark, R. E., Kallman, C., & Mellits, D. (1980). Developmental dyslexia: Relation between acoustic processing deficits and verbal processing. *Neuropsychologia, 18*, 273–284.

Wechsler, D. (1949). *Wechsler Intelligence Scale for Children*. New York: Psychological Corp.

Werry, J. S. (1968). Developmental hyperactivity. *Pediatric Clinics of North America, 15*, 581–599.

Winogron, H. W., Knights, R. M., & Bawden, H. N. (1984). Neuropsychological deficits following head injury in children. *Journal of Clinical Neuropsychology, 6*, 269–286.

Wirt, R. D., Lachar, D., Klinedinst, J. K., & Seat, P. D. (1977). *Multidimensional description of child personality: A manual for the Personality Inventory for Children*. Los Angeles: Western Psychological Services.

2. Case illustration

Introduction

This case illustration is presented in order to familiarize the reader with the testing procedures and methods of inference that we usually employ in such instances. The sort of recommendations for intervention that flow from the type of neuropsychological assessment that we conduct are also presented. Other considerations include many aspects of Steps 1, 2, 3, 4, and 7 of the model introduced in Chapter 1. It is felt that a thorough study of this particular case will assist the reader in the interpretation of the rather more abbreviated assessment results that are presented in Chapters 3 through 6.[1]

Initial examination

This boy was seen initially at the age of 9 years, 10 months in order to carry out a brief evaluation of his levels of academic achievement and psychometric intelligence. School officials at the time reported that he experienced difficulty following instructions in the classroom and that they were concerned for his future academic progress.

This boy's early history in school was marked by several changes in academic programs and schools in addition to missing several months of school because of protracted illness.

Throughout the testing session, this boy was cooperative, talkative, attentive, and friendly. He exhibited an average level of physical activity, and rapport was easily obtained with him. He appeared to be quite well motivated, and there was no reason to believe that he did not try his best on all of the tasks presented to him. Throughout the testing session he exhibited some mild word-finding difficulties, and his use of grammar was not up to age-appropriate standards. On two of the subtests of the Wechsler Intelligence Scale for Children (WISC; Wechsler, 1949) he had some difficulty in understanding the instructions, which had to be re-

1. For readers who are unfamiliar with the tests and measurements typically employed in our neuropsychological assessment procedures, a perusal of the descriptions provided in the Appendix would probably be useful at this point. (For details on data presentation, see p. 57.)

peated. It appeared that we obtained a very reliable reflection of his abilities in this brief examination.

The WISC and the Wide Range Achievement Test (WRAT; Jastak & Jastak, 1965) were administered to him. As can be seen in Figure 2-1, he obtained a Verbal IQ of 100, a Performance IQ of 108, and a Full Scale IQ of 104 on the WISC. Subtest scaled scores on the Verbal section of the WISC suggested the possibility of a "warm-up" effect, in that he did rather poorly on the first three subtests administered to him (Information, Comprehension, and Arithmetic) and relatively better on the last three subtests administered (Similarities, Vocabulary, and Digit Span). Subtest scaled scores on the Performance section of the WISC were fairly uniform, ranging from lows of 10 on the Picture Arrangement and Coding subtests to a high of 13 on the Block Design subtest.

On the WRAT he obtained the following grade-equivalent (centile) scores: Reading, 6.5 (86); Spelling, 4.7 (50); Arithmetic, 3.2 (19). An examination of his errors in reading suggested very strongly that he was well able to use a phonetic word-attack strategy when attempting to read novel words (e.g., he read "and ever" for endeavor and "clariffee" for clarify). His misspellings were also largely of the phonetically accurate variety (e.g., "naicher" for nature and "ockuepie" for occupy). His level of performance on the Arithmetic subtest was quite poor relative to his performances on the Reading and Spelling subtests. The sort of errors that he made on the Arithmetic subtest are those usually made by children who have had irregular or insufficient tutoring in arithmetic calculation skills; that is, they may have reflected his rather uneven and inconsistent history of academic instruction.

Our conclusion on the basis of this available data was that this boy's principal drawbacks at the time of assessment were those that could be most adequately remedied by precision teaching aimed at the gaps in his academic experiences. We saw no reason to maintain that he had any information-processing deficiencies or that he was in need of any special remedial assistance over and above that which could be offered within the regular academic environment.

First posttraumatic neuropsychological assessment

Approximately 3½ years following our screening examination of him, this boy was admitted to the emergency ward of a local hospital in the early afternoon after having collapsed on a playing field. It was reported that he was hit on the neck or head by someone's hand while he was being tackled in a game of "pick-up" football with his friends. He reported that he tried to get up off the ground to retaliate for the "high tackle," but he fell unconscious.

Figure 2-1. Neuropsychological test results. Abbreviations for histograms in this and subsequent figures: R = right hand; L = left hand; T = timer; C = counter; SPEED = Finger Tapping Test; MAZE = Maze Coordination Test; HOLES = Static Steadiness Test; PEGS = Grooved Pegboard Test; SSP = Speech-Sounds Perception Test; AC = Auditory Closure Test; SM = Sentence Memory Test; VF = Verbal Fluency Test; AAT = Auditory Analysis Test; TPTD = Tactual Performance Test—dominant hand; TPTN = Tactual Performance Test—nondominant hand; TPTB = Tactual Performance Test—both hands; TAR = Target Test; MP = Matching Pictures Test; PF = Progressive Figures Test; TRA = Trail Making Test, Part A; TRB = Trail Making Test, Part B; CAT = Category Test; UL = Underlining Test; * = T score < 0; n/a = not administered.

Age	9 yr, 10 mo	14 yr, 2 mo	15 yr, 2 mo
WISC			
Verbal IQ	100	62	75
Information	8	4	4
Comprehension	8	4	5
Arithmetic	8	3	5
Similarities	15	7	8
Vocabulary	11	4	5
Digit Span	10	2	9
Performance IQ	108	94	96
Picture Completion	12	12	9
Picture Arrangement	10	11	11
Block Design	13	12	13
Object Assembly	11	9	10
Coding	10	2	4
Full Scale IQ	104	75	83
PPVT			
IQ		65	76
Mental Age		7–10	10–0
WRAT			
Reading (grade equiv.)	6.5	3.1	4.7
Spelling (grade equiv.)	4.7	3.6	3.6
Arithmetic (grade equiv.)	3.2	3.9	4.3

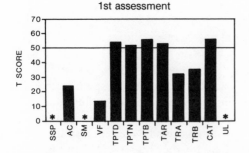

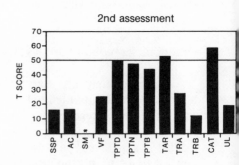

SENSORY–PERCEPTUAL ABILITIES

These functions were not examined in detail in the first (screening) assessment. In the second assessment, he exhibited marked tactile suppression with the right hand and right face, and marked auditory suppression with the right ear. There were no indications of simple tactile or auditory imperception, and he did not exhibit any difficulties in perceiving stimuli within the visual fields. There was clear and consistent evidence of finger agnosia and finger dysgraphesthesia on the right side. There were no indications of any disturbances within the left sensory fields on any of these measures. The examination for astereognosis for coins was marked by the influence of naming problems (see text for an explanation of these). He exhibited a moderate upper frequency (4,000 and 8,000 Hz) hearing loss with the right ear during the second and third assessments. Consistent, though much less marked, indications of tactile suppression with the right hand and right face and finger agnosia on the right side were evident in the third assessment. Marked finger dysgraphesthesia and astereognosis for coins with the right hand were also exhibited in this assessment. There was no evidence of sensory–perceptual disturbances on the left side, and there were no visual field defects and no indications of auditory suppression in this final assessment.

ASPHASIA SCREENING TEST

There were marked indications of dysnomia, spelling dyspraxia, dysgraphia, enunciatory dyspraxia, auditory–verbal agnosia, and problems in reading and arithmetic calculation exhibited in the second assessment. In the third assessment, aphasic signs were much less prominent, but still evident. However, there were no clear indications of dysnomia (although difficulties in word finding were quite prominent), dysgraphia, or simple word-recognition errors in this final assessment.

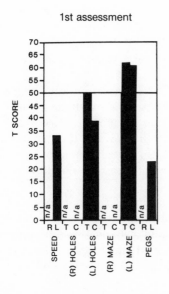

1st assessment

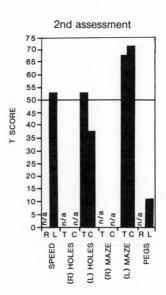

2nd assessment

At the time of his admission to hospital he was unconscious, his breathing was impaired, and he was paralyzed on the right side of his body. A neurological examination carried out once consciousness began to emerge (approximately 2 hours after admission) revealed some movement of the left extremities but not of those on the right side. There was, in addition, a marked facial weakness on the right side and no movements evoked by painful stimulation of the right extremities. The plantar response was extensor on the right side. Although pupil size in response to light was equal, the left pupil reacted in a somewhat sluggish fashion. The eye–ground examination revealed no abnormal finding.

Further neuromedical examinations suggested very strongly that this boy was suffering from some bleeding into the brain that was responsible for the right hemiplegia and associated symptoms. At the time it was thought that the most likely etiology was a ruptured aneurysm arising from a branch of the left middle cerebral artery.

A carotid arteriogram that was conducted shortly after admission showed a marked displacement of the anterior cerebral artery from left to right. A CT scan carried out subsequently contained findings suggesting rather strongly that the provisional diagnosis of a ruptured aneurysm within one of the branches of the left middle cerebral artery was correct.

Surgical intervention involved a left fronto-parietal osteoplastic craniotomy. The ruptured vascular malformation discovered was coagulated, and the hematoma was evacuated. It was apparent that bleeding was taking place from several thin-walled vessels situated near the Sylvian fissure; these vessels were being supplied by the parietal branch of the middle cerebral artery. The operative procedure proceeded well, with no undue complications.

Following the operation, recovery was slow but progressive. The boy regained full consciousness, but his right arm and leg remained paralyzed and his expressive speech was markedly impaired. Speech therapy and physiotherapy were initiated shortly after release from the Neurosurgical Department.

Approximately 2 months following this incident, he was seen by a rehabilitation psychologist who administered several psychometric instruments to him. It was recommended by this psychologist that the boy continue in an intensive program of speech therapy and that his physiotherapy be continued. The psychologist also noted that this boy was somewhat impulsive and that some behavioral measures should be instituted to help him to control his behavior.

The presenting reasons for our assessment of this boy included, of course, the problems noted above. In addition, it was thought that our involvement might be of some assistance in helping this youngster to return to a program of instruction in school. Following his release from hospital, he had been involved in a program of home instruction (two 1½-

hour sessions per week). This program did not appear to be meeting with much success and there was some concern about the level and type of instruction that would be most suitable for him in school.

Thus, our first comprehensive examination of this boy was carried out when he was 14 years, 2 months of age (approximately 9 months after the acute onset of his neurological illness). At the time of this assessment, this boy was receiving some speech and language therapy, physiotherapy, and home tutoring. Otherwise, he did little more than sit around the house, and his mother was quite concerned that he needed to get involved in some form of education and training that would prepare him for adulthood. She felt that her son wanted very much to learn, and that he was not being adequately instructed. In this sense, concerns of the mother and school authorities were quite similar: Both wished to institute an educational program that would be appropriate for the boy.

Following an initial interview with the mother, we discovered that this boy's therapy programs were not being well coordinated. Indeed, there were some suggestions that many of those who were working with him (with the exception of the speech and language pathologist) were aiming merely to achieve quite low-level goals of reasonable ambulation and self-help skills. These therapists seemed to be working from a kind of adult model in that they were not sufficiently aware of the potential short-term and long-term consequences of this sort of disabling condition. From our point of view, some of these potential consequences were emotional disturbance, including social withdrawal, and inadequate preparation for education and training opportunities now and in the future.

In the neuropsychological testing situation, this boy was alert and apparently well motivated. There was obvious weakness and clumsiness evident on the right side of the body, and he was unable to use his right hand to complete the majority of motor and psychomotor tasks ordinarily administered in our neuropsychological battery. He spoke slowly, with significant pauses between most words. Word-finding difficulties were quite evident, and he often used gestures to enhance his verbal communications. His responses on tests that did not require language processing, especially spoken language, were average. Throughout the examination he exhibited a high level of attentiveness and, in spite of his obvious verbal and motoric difficulties, he seemed to have a rather high level of tolerance for frustration. We completed the neuropsychological assessment over a 2-day period in order to ensure the elicitation of his best possible performances.

Figure 2-1 contains many of this boy's neuropsychological test results. The following is a summary of these results.

Although this boy was right-handed prior to his neurological illness, he now asserted that he preferred to use his left hand for all of the seven tasks contained in the Harris Test of Lateral Dominance. Strength of grip with the left hand was within the high average range, whereas strength of grip with the right hand was severely impaired. (As in Rourke, Bakker, Fisk, & Strang, 1983, we will use the term *mild impairment* to refer to performances that fall between 1 and 2 standard deviations below the developmental norms for each test in question; *moderate impairment* for performances that fall between 2 and 3 standard deviations below the mean; and *severe impairment* for performances that fall beyond 3 standard deviations below the mean.) His performance with the left hand on a test of finger-tapping speed fell toward the lower limits of the normal range. Similarly, foot-tapping speed with the left foot was low normal. He could not make progress on the finger-tapping test with his right hand, but he was able to use his right foot for the foot-tapping test. In the latter instance, his score was moderately impaired.

This boy was unable to do the three tests from the Kløve–Matthews Motor Steadiness Battery with his right hand. On the Maze Test of kinetic steadiness he performed quite well with his left hand, but it was clear that he sacrificed speed for efficiency in that he went very slowly through the maze in order to minimize the number of contacts with its sides. His performance on the Holes Test of static steadiness was marginally poor. He had considerable difficulty in making progress on the Grooved Pegboard Test; eye–hand coordination with the left hand under these speeded conditions appeared to pose considerable difficulty for him.

On the examination for sensory–perceptual disturbances it was clear that he had considerable difficulty with various aspects of tactile perception on the right side of the body. For example, although he was able to identify the right hand and the right side of the face when they were touched in isolation, he was never able to identify stimulation delivered to the right hand when the left hand or the left face was stimulated simultaneously; he was also unable to identify stimuli delivered to the right side of the face when the left hand was stimulated at the same time. Furthermore, he made errors on 16 out of 20 trials when asked to identify which finger on the right hand had been touched by the examiner. He made no errors on this task when asked to localize stimulation delivered to the fingers of the left hand. Similarly, he made 10 errors on 20 trials when asked to identify numbers written on the fingertips of the right hand; performance with the left hand on this task was error-free. On a test for astereognosis for coins he had considerable difficulty in identifying a penny, nickel, and dime when these were placed in the right hand. On such occasions it is interesting to note that he called a penny a pin, a nickel an eraser or a watch, and a dime a spoon. These types of response would suggest rather strongly that his evident problems in word finding and naming were posing additional difficulties for him in this sort of testing situation. Under such conditions, it is usual to adopt a form of examination for astereognosis for forms that reduces or eliminates the need to name the objects that are placed in the hand. However, it was clear from our examination of him up to this point that he had considerable difficulty in fine tactile perception with the right hand, and it was not felt necessary to extend this particular examination.

When the confrontation method for visual-field examination was carried out, this boy was quite attentive to the procedure, as he was throughout the examination, and there were no errors evident in his performance on it. That is, there was no evidence of visual imperception or suppression under conditions of unilateral and bilateral simultaneous stimulation conditions, respectively. When asked to identify clicks delivered to each ear separately, he performed in an errorless fashion. However, he was not able to identify such clicks delivered to the right ear when the same sound was delivered simultaneously to the left ear.

In summary, therefore, we see clear evidence of tactile suppression with the right hand and right face, considerable evidence of finger agnosia and finger dysgraphesthesia with the right hand, and marked auditory suppression with the right ear. These deficits were evident within the context of error-free performance on such tasks with the left hand, left face, and left ear. This set of test results would certainly be consistent with those expected of an individual of this age who is suffering from an actively debilitating lesion of the left cerebral hemisphere. The absence of visual imperception and suppression within the right visual field would suggest rather strongly that the optic radiations within the temporal and parietal lobes of the left cerebral hemisphere were not seriously affected by this neurological disease process.

Furthermore, the evidence of right-sided motor and psychomotor deficiencies, within the context of normal force with the left hand and normal motor speed with the left upper and lower extremities, would be consistent with the presence of an actively debilitating lesion that is confined to the left cerebral hemisphere. The significance of the problems on the Grooved Pegboard Test with the left hand and the other fairly minor deviations in performance on a test for static and kinetic steadiness with the left hand must be somewhat questionable at this point because this boy was exclusively right-handed prior to the onset of this debilitating lesion.

An examination of this boy's linguistic capacities sheds further light on the adaptive significance of his particular brain lesion. For example, he obtained a Verbal IQ of 62 on the WISC. Subtest scaled scores on this section of the WISC were outstandingly low on all of the subtests administered, with the exception of that on the Similarities subtest (which was only mildly reduced). In this particular case, we have the opportunity to assess the reduction in scores on the Verbal section of the WISC (from pre- to postneurological disease status), at least to some extent. Thus, relative to age-based norms, the reductions in subtest scaled score points were as follows: Information, 4; Comprehension, 4; Arithmetic, 5; Similarities, 8; Vocabulary, 7; Digit Span, 8. These results would suggest that this boy experienced a fairly general reduction in his linguistic capacities as measured with the WISC.

An examination of his performances on the Aphasia Screening Test adds some clarification of the rather marked psycholinguistic impairment which this boy was experiencing. For example, when asked to name a picture of a cross he said the following: "Square . . . [then he pointed to the cross] . . . Jesus . . . cross." When asked to spell the word "triangle," he said the following: "Z, no . . . RA, no, Rl 'n' NO . . . no." However, he performed quite well on a number of items of the Aphasia Screening Test. For example, he was able to name a picture of a square and a fork, he read "7 SIX 2" correctly, and in general he was able to follow simple commands. His enunciation of complex words was quite interesting in that it suggested rather strongly that he was able to hear the phonemic components of the words and deal with sound boundaries within the words. Thus, he repeated the word "Massachusetts" as follows (the spaces represent pauses of approximately 1 second): Ma sa chu sess. These findings would tend to suggest that this young boy has some residual auditory–verbal facility, and that his expressive verbal capacities are far from completely debilitated.

One other feature of his performance on this test was reflected in his attempts to name a picture of a triangle. In this instance, he said the following: "Sq . . . sq . . . cross . . . devil . . . water . . . ." Since he was asked to name a picture of a square and a cross before being asked to name the picture of a triangle, we are seeing evidence here of some perseveration of response. This is so in spite of the interpolated requirements for spelling and copying both the square and the cross. One might hypothesize on the basis of this information that there is some potential for advancement in his word-finding skills, but that his tendency to perseverate will have to be dealt with in a therapeutic fashion. Indeed, increasing demands for word finding within particular categories of response (e.g., plane figures) would be expected to result in progressively greater interference of the perseverative variety.

Further evidence for his psycholinguistic deficiencies includes his markedly impaired performances on the Verbal Fluency Test, the Sentence Memory Test, and the Speech-Sounds Perception Test. He also exhibited clear difficulties on the Auditory Closure Test. If anything, these results would tend to suggest that he had somewhat more difficulty with the expressive than with the receptive aspects of linguistic functioning. However, it is clear that he had considerable difficulty with very many aspects of psycholinguistic skills.

Finally, his performance on the Peabody Picture Vocabulary Test (PPVT) (Mental Age = 7 years, 10 months; IQ = 65) was in line with his

Verbal IQ (62) on the WISC. Since it would seem fairly safe to assume that this boy was capable of a normal level of performance on the PPVT prior to the onset of his neurological disease, this particular level of performance would suggest that there has been a dramatic decline in his general level of receptive vocabulary. This contention is reinforced by the fact that no verbal responses are required on the PPVT; all that this boy needed to do on this test was to point to one of four pictures that represented the word that he heard.

In contrast to his generally impaired psycholinguistic skills, this boy exhibited normal levels of performance on several tests requiring visual–spatial–organizational skills. For example, on the WISC he obtained a Performance IQ of 94, and all of the subtest scaled scores on this section of the WISC, with the exception of that on the Coding subtest, were well within normal limits. Indeed, he obtained subtest scaled scores of 12 on the Picture Completion and Block Design subtests; these subtests require attention to visual detail, complex visual discrimination, and visual–spatial–organizational skills of a fairly sophisticated nature. It should be noted in addition that his subtest scaled scores on the Object Assembly, Block Design, Picture Arrangement, and Picture Completion subtests of the WISC were either the same as or within one standard deviation of the subtest scaled scores that he obtained at the age of 9 years, 10 months. Thus, in contrast to his performance on the Verbal section of the WISC, these scores would suggest that he has made age-appropriate gains in the abilities tapped by these Performance subtests and that these abilities have not been affected adversely by his neurological disease.

The dramatic drop on the Coding subtest between the two administrations of the WISC would seem to suggest that the combination of requirements for rapid eye–hand coordination and the symbolic requirements of the task were the features that tended to interfere with his performance on it. This would seem to be a reasonable hypothesis in view of the fact that his performance on several other tests within this battery would suggest that he is well able to focus and maintain attention over a fairly protracted period of time and that the visual–spatial demands of the Coding subtest would not be expected to pose any limitations for him. That he was, at this point, learning to use his left hand for skilled activities, in addition to the considerable evidence of problems in symbolic usage and immediate memory for symbolic material, would suggest that these are the factors that posed considerable problems for him in the execution of this task.

Evidence of fairly well developed capacities for immediate memory for visual sequences was apparent in his normal level of performance on the Target Test. The fact that he performed at mildly to moderately impaired levels on the Trail Making Test, Parts A and B, within the context of the other findings of this examination, would suggest strongly that the very minimal symbolic requirements of the Trail Making Test posed considerable difficulty for him. Indeed, he made one error on Part A and three errors on Part B of the Trail Making Test, an unusually large number of errors on this test for a 14-year-old.

Evidence of this boy's fairly intact capacities for strategy generation, hypothesis testing, and concept-formation and problem-solving skills is not difficult to find. In addition to his average to high-average performances on four of the Performance subtests of the WISC, he performed very well on the Tactual Performance Test and on the Category Test. On the Tactual Performance Test all three trials were carried out with the left hand. It should be noted that his performance improved somewhat on each subsequent trial, as reflected in a decreasing amount of time necessary to insert the six blocks into the formboard. He also exhibited a normal level of incidental memory for the shapes of the blocks used on this task, although he had considerable difficulty in locating them on a drawing of the formboard. The latter problem may, once again, reflect his apparent difficulties in the verbal encoding of experiences.

On the Category Test his level of performance was almost 1 standard deviation above the mean. This level of performance stands in very marked contrast to his extremely poor performances on tests requiring symbolic and linguistic skills.

Finally, his levels of performance on the 14 subtests of the Underlining Test were mildly to severely impaired. It is noteworthy that he had considerable difficulty on subtest number 14, which simply requires speeded performance with no additional symbolic and discrimination components. This would suggest rather strongly that the speeded requirements of this test posed difficulties for him. In addition, there was some suggestion that he did particularly poorly on those subtests of this test that had a high symbolic content. For example, his performance was only mildly impaired on subtest 4, while it was severely impaired on subtest 10. Subtest 4 requires the capacity to deal with fairly subtle visual discriminations, whereas subtest number 10 is probably facilitated by the capacity to pronounce the target stimulus and the distractor items. Thus, it would appear that his overall level of performance on this task was limited by his problems in eye–hand coordination under speeded conditions, and that he had particular difficulty with those items that involved a linguistic component.

On the WRAT this boy obtained the following grade-equivalent (centile) scores: Reading, 3.1 (1); Spelling, 3.6 (3); Arithmetic, 3.9 (2). In contrast to his misspellings on the first administration of the Spelling subtest, his current misspellings were largely of the phonetically inaccurate variety. Similarly, he did not seem capable of sounding out words on this administration of the WRAT Reading subtest. For example, he read animal as "sounds," and theory as "that." In addition, his performance on the Reading subtest was quite uneven, as is often seen in youngsters who have enjoyed a fairly normal course of development for several years and then have experienced a brain insult. Examples of his uneven performance are manifold: He misread the letter *s* as *c*, the letter *t* as *d*, and the letter *q* as *k*, whereas he was able to read correctly such words as "himself," "between," "contagious," and "stretch." This extreme degree of irregularity would suggest very strongly that this boy was capable of at least normal levels of reading achievement prior to the onset of his neurological disease. In this particular instance, we have evidence that he was able to recognize words at the Grade 6.5 level (86th centile) at the age of 9 years, 10 months.

On the Arithmetic subtest it is notable that he made some simple errors within the context of successful performances on more difficult questions. For example, when asked to subtract 64 from 94, his answer was 40. However, when required to multiple 3 times $4.95 he answered correctly, $14.85. He also was able to add $2\frac{1}{2} + 1\frac{1}{2}$, and he carried out successfully a long division problem ($4527 \div 9 = 503$). As we have pointed out elsewhere (Strang & Rourke, 1985), youngsters of this age who exhibit very well developed psycholinguistic skills within the context of very impaired visual–spatial–organizational skills often have considerable difficulty with questions that require attention to visual detail and the successive application of arithmetical rules and procedures within a visual–spatial context. This boy exhibited no difficulties of this sort. Rather, his problems arose on those arithmetic questions that require the reading of words. There is no immediately apparent explanation for his difficulties on some of the other arithmetic questions except that he did work very slowly and, as mentioned several times above, he had difficulty in manipulating a pencil with his left hand.

Although clearly not diagnostic of any particular neuropathological condition, this particular pattern of neuropsychological test results would certainly be entirely consistent with the expected residual effects of a cerebral-vascular accident that has involved primarily the branches of the middle cerebral artery within the left cerebral hemisphere. The indications of tactile and auditory suppression on the right side, together with very clear indications of (1) finger agnosia and finger dysgraphesthesia with the right hand, (2) the absence of any evidence of tactile or auditory imperception or suppression with the left hand, and (3) no evidence of finger agnosia or finger dysgraphesthesia with the left hand would certainly be consistent with this hypothesis. In addition, these findings would suggest that the homologous structures within the right cerebral hemisphere are intact. Additional supporting evidence for the hypothesis of left hemisphere damage are the very marked psycholinguistic deficiencies exhibited by this youngster. Of course, the severe problems in motor and psychomotor skills with the right hand and right foot are also consistent with this formulation.

From the point of view of both remediation and the study of brain–behavioral relationships, it is essential to emphasize his normal levels of performance on the Category Test and most aspects of the Tactual Performance Test. In addition, his average to high-average performances on four of the Performance subtests of the WISC should be addressed. These average to above-average levels of performance were exhibited on tasks that primarily involve the following: (1) visual–spatial–organizational skills; (2) nonverbal concept-formation; (3) problem solving, hypothesis testing, and strategy generation abilities; and (4) the capacity to deal with positive and negative informational feedback of a nonverbal variety. Among other things, therefore, it would be reasonable to expect this boy to be able to benefit most from communications that are of this nonverbal sort, and that he would be expected to understand a great deal more about events that proceed in his presence than he is able to talk about.

One other feature of note in this protocol is the very characteristic quality and configuration of performances evident on the WRAT Reading, Spelling, and Arithmetic subtests. His performances on these subtests would suggest that this boy was experiencing profound difficulties in phonemic hearing within a context of fairly adequate problem-solving skills. In addition, there was considerable evidence of average to above-average premorbid levels of word recognition. In this instance, as was the case for the WISC, we have available premorbid data that would support these hypotheses.

Following this neuropsychological assessment, a Remedial Educational Conference (attended by this boy's mother, school officials, representatives from a children's rehabilitation center, a psychiatrist, a physiotherapist, and a speech and language specialist) was held to discuss the most optimal educational and therapeutic programs for this boy. Specific recommendations regarding academic instruction were presented. These included the following: (1) ways of providing immediate visual feedback (which we thought should be emphasized) when approaching new tasks; (2) ways of using a computerized word processor and/or a typewriter for spelling and writing tasks; and (3) procedures for instituting a morphographic ("word-chunking") approach to spelling and reading. The latter approach to spelling stresses the *visual* aspects of words; we felt that this would enhance the likelihood that this boy would remember such words. His continued involvement with a Big Brother was also recommended to provide additional social and emotional support for him, both individually and within the context of his family.

It was decided at this time that the conventional school programs available (e.g., "Opportunity Class" or "Learning Disabilities" class placements) were not appropriate for meeting his particular needs for intensive language and physical therapy. School personnel admitted that they were unfamiliar with concepts such as "recovery of function" and this boy's need for ongoing modifications and changes in therapeutic approaches. In short, they felt unequipped to deal with his unique rehabilitative needs. Therefore, a visit was planned for the boy to meet with teachers and therapists at a local rehabilitation center for children; shortly afterward, he was admitted into a full-time program there. A highly individualized program, involving occupational and language therapy as well as specialized methods of academic instruction, was instituted. In addition to individual language therapy sessions, he also participated in weekly sessions with adult aphasic patients. Although it was thought that this latter group situation might not be the best way to address his specific language difficulties, it was pursued on the grounds that he was in need of as much language training as it was possible to provide for him.

Second posttraumatic neuropsychological assessment

The third examination of this boy was carried out when he was 15 years, 2 months of age (i.e., 1 year after our second assessment of him). In this examination, we administered many of the tests from the Halstead–Reitan Neuropsychological Battery, the WISC, and several of the instruments that we typically include in our examinations of older children and adults. A comparison of the results of this examination with those obtained previously is instructive on a number of counts.

For example, it will be noted that the Verbal IQ–Performance IQ discrepancy on this administration of the WISC was somewhat less than was evident in the previous assessment. The reasons for this were due primarily to the rather dramatic increase in his subsequent scaled scores on the Digit Span subtest (i.e., 2 to 9). In all other respects, the pattern of subtest scaled scores on the Verbal section of the WISC was virtually identical to that obtained one year earlier.

This similarity of patterns was also exhibited on this administration of the Performance section of the WISC. Note that this youngster continued to have considerable and outstanding difficulty on the Coding subtest of the WISC. Except for a somewhat lower score on the Picture Completion subtest of the WISC, the pattern of subtest scaled scores on the Performance section was virtually identical to that obtained in our previous examination of him.

Other similarities in performance include his above-average levels of performance on the adult versions of the Halstead Category Test and the Tactual Performance Test. His total number of errors on the Category Test was 20, which is a score that is well within the superior range for his age. On the Tactual Performance Test he was able to place all 10 blocks into the board on each of the three trials with his left hand, and his successive levels of performance reflected very clear evidence of his capacity to benefit from experience with the task. His incidental memory for the shapes of the blocks used on this task was at an average level—a finding in line with his performance on the older children's version of the Tactual Performance Test. In contrast to the latter, however, he was able to locate properly 7 of the 10 blocks used on this task—a level of performance that was significantly superior to that exhibited in our previous examination of him.

Rather clear and consistent problems in psycholinguistic skills were still in evidence in this examination. In addition to the levels of performance already mentioned on the Verbal section of the WISC, this boy exhibited very impaired levels of performance on tests for verbal fluency, sentence memory, and auditory closure. His level of performance on the Speech-Sounds Perception Test was 2 standard deviations below the mean for his age, but this constituted a slight gain as compared to his performance on the older children's version of this task. It may very well be that he was, at this point, better able to deal with sound–symbol matching than had been the case previously, but that he continued to have very marked problems in those situations in which he was required to deal with auditory–verbal input and verbal output without the benefit of relevant visual cues.

On this administration of the Aphasia Screening Test he exhibited considerable improvement as compared to his previous performance on it. For example, this time he was able to spell the words "square" and "cross" correctly, and he was able to name the objects that were presented to him in pictorial form. However, in the latter case it is notable that he often spelled the word in question prior to naming it. For example, when shown a picture of a cross and asked to name it, he first said "c-r-o-s-s" and then, when questioned about the name of the picture, he said the word, "cross." Thus, we see continuing evidence of problems in word finding, and the particular adaptational strategy that he seems to have adopted in order to deal with this difficulty. (In this connection, it should be noted that in our first administration of the Aphasia Screening Test 1 year earlier, this boy repeated the word "triangle" as follows: "tri [pause] ang [pause] le." Note that the last syllable was pronounced in terms of its visual rather than its phonemic characteristics. This would suggest that this boy may have visualized the word that he heard prior to his initiation of its repetition—in effect, "reading" the visual image of the word in order to comply with the task requirements.)

Although auditory acuity (on a Sweep Hearing Test) was found to continue to be problematic with the right ear, there were no longer any signs of right-ear auditory suppression. The latter finding stands in marked contrast to the results of the examination one year earlier.

Although clear difficulties were still in evidence on a word-recognition task (WRAT Reading subtest), this boy showed a net gain of 1.6 grade-equivalent years (an increase from grade-equivalent scores of 3.1 to 4.7) over the 1-year interval between assessments. It was apparent in this examination that he was employing phonetic word-attack strategies in a more consistent fashion; his errors reflected an increased capacity to sound out words. For example, whereas he replied "that" to the word "theory," on his second WRAT administration, he was able to sound out "they-tho-thotto" on this third administration. His performance on this test often suggested that, despite concentrated efforts, his phonetic strategies deteriorated as a function of increasing time spent attempting to read a particular word.

Some improvement on a single-word receptive vocabulary test was in evidence (PPVT; increased from Mental Age 7 years, 10 months, to Mental Age 10 years, 0 months). This would suggest that his receptive language skills as well as his ability to attend to complex visual stimuli had improved somewhat.

Within the motor realm, this boy showed some quite marked improvements in motor speed with the left hand and foot. This finding was probably related both to continued practice using the nondominant upper and lower limbs and to some brain recovery phenomena. Complex eye-hand coordination skills (under speeded conditions) continued to be problematic for him. A pattern of response with the left hand similar to that noted in the first administration of a kinetic motor steadiness measure was in evidence: He continued to sacrifice speed for accuracy.

As alluded to earlier within the context of the Performance subtests of the WISC, this boy continued to exhibit relatively unimpaired visual-spatial skills. On the adult version of the Trail Making Test, Parts A and B, he showed some relative improvement. Although the symbolic requirements of this test (relying on numerical and alternating numerical and alphabetical cues) would seem to have hampered his overall levels of performance, he made fewer errors and his performance was only mildly to moderately impaired on Part B of the test. It would appear that this boy was able to perform better on a number of visual–motor tasks, probably as a result of increased practice with the left hand on writing tasks.

It is noteworthy that there was some diminution in tactile suppression and finger agnosia with the right hand, but no appreciable change in finger dysgraphesthesia with the right hand. Although the positive changes are encouraging, it is clear that this degree of tactile–perceptual deficiency is still very marked and suggests a very guarded prognosis with respect to further recovery of function for the affected regions and systems within the left cerebral hemisphere.

On the Underlining Test this boy also showed some significant net gains. Although his individual subtest scores reflected difficulties, he worked more quickly and accurately on this test. The previous finding, that verbal-type target items (e.g., "spot") posed more difficulty for him than visual–spatial items (e.g., a complex geometric shape), still obtained.

The quality of this boy's graphomotor performances remained relatively unchanged. When asked to draw complex visual–spatial shapes, the overall visual gestalt of the figures was preserved, but there was still a dearth of visual details in the drawings.

Shortly after this third assessment, this boy was placed in a special academic–vocational training program at the secondary school level. A follow-up visit to the school revealed that he was adapting well to this new program; he was reported to be an excellent student in nonverbal skill subject areas (e.g., shop class), but he continued to experience marked difficulties in linguistic skill subjects (e.g., English language and literature). His teachers questioned his level of motivation in the latter skill areas, but a rehabilitation counselor suggested that he may appear this way because of frustration when he is not given sufficient "wait" time to process language (i.e., extra time to answer questions so that he can find the words himself). We suggested strongly that this youngster's word-finding and other linguistic deficiencies were not the result of lack of effort or motivation, and we stressed that methods for circumventing his continuing problems in this area would have to be instituted and maintained for the foreseeable future. Methods for doing so were explained in detail, as were techniques for facilitating nonverbal communication.

Summary and conclusions

This detailed neuropsychological assessment was presented primarily in order to demonstrate the following: (1) the comparison of levels of performance with developmental norms for the various tests that we employed; (2) illustrations of the use of pathognomonic signs and how the qualitative analysis of performance can be carried out; (3) extensive comparisons of motor and sensory–perceptual performances on the two sides of the body and the inferences that can be drawn therefrom; (4) a comparison of pretest and posttest performances on the WISC and WRAT in order to demonstrate the effects of this type of brain lesion on measures of psychometric intelligence and academic achievement; and (5) the illustration of the course of recovery (or lack of it) from such a brain lesion through the analysis of follow-up assessment information.

Although some mention of the intervention strategies that arise from these sorts of analyses were mentioned, we chose to limit these in this particular case illustration so that the issues mentioned above could be highlighted. For the remainder of this work, our emphasis will be on the translation of neuropsychological assessment findings into intervention strategies and programs.

A note on data presentation

The presentation of test scores for this and the other cases in this work posed several difficulties, since the test battery produced in excess of 100 measures in addition to direct observations of behavior by the psychometrist(s). Although we wished to present as many data as possible, the limitations of space forced us to recognize that excessive data could produce more confusion than clarity. In order to simplify (but not distort) the presentations, we chose to provide data in graphic and tabular form, accompanied by brief narratives describing additional test results not included in the graphs or tables.

In each case, we present in tabular form the results of the WISC (Wechsler, 1949), the WRAT (Jastak & Jastak, 1965), and the PPVT (Dunn, 1965). The raw data for other neuropsychological tests were converted to age-based normalized T scores ($M = 50$; $SD = 10$), and these data were used to construct histograms. (In these histograms, the T scores were arranged such that good performance was represented above and poor performance below $T = 50$.) This procedure obviated the need to provide normative data for the many test measures in question. Normative data used in calculating the T score conversions are based on investigations by Knights and Moule (1967, 1968), Knights and Norwood (1980), Rourke and Gates (1980), and Rourke and Fisk (1977). Finally, the Aphasia Screening Test as well as the sensory–perceptual portion of the examination are presented in brief narratives outlining the major findings.

References

Dunn, L. M. (1965). *Expanded manual for the Peabody Picture Vocabulary Test*. Minneapolis, MN: American Guidance Service.

Jastak, J. F., & Jastak, S. R. (1965). *The Wide Range Achievement Test*. Wilmington, DE: Guidance Associates.

Knights, R. M., & Moule, A. D. (1967). Normative and reliability data on finger and foot tapping in children. *Perceptual and Motor Skills, 25*, 717–720.

Knights, R. M., & Moule, A. D. (1968). Normative data on the Motor Steadiness Battery for Children. *Perceptual and Motor Skills, 26*, 643–650.

Knights, R. M., & Norwood, J. A. (1980). *Revised smoothed normative data on the neuropsychological test battery for children*. Ottawa: Author.

Rourke, B. P., Bakker, D. J., Fisk, J. L., & Strang, J. D. (1983). *Child neuropsychology: An introduction to theory, research, and clinical practice*. New York: Guilford.

Rourke, B. P., & Fisk, J. L. (1976). *Children's Word-Finding Test* (Revised). University of Windsor, Department of Psychology, Windsor, Ontario.

Rourke, B. P., & Gates, R. D. (1980). *Underlining Test: Preliminary norms*. University of Windsor, Department of Psychology, Windsor, Ontario.

Strang, J. D., & Rourke, B. P. (1985). Arithmetic disability subtypes: The neuropsychological significance of specific arithmetic impairment in childhood. In B. P. Rourke (Ed.), *Neuropsychology of learning disabilities: Essentials of subtype analysis* (pp. 167–183). New York: Guilford.

Wechsler, D. (1949). *Wechsler Intelligence Scale for Children*. New York: Psychological Corp.

3. Common neurological disorders of childhood

Introduction

It is very probable that insult to the central nervous system (CNS) at any stage of development will be reflected, at least to some extent, in subsequent behavior. Although a "mild" concussion may have very minimal consequences in terms of day-to-day functioning for the youngster in question, an anoxic episode, a neurotoxic condition, or a disorder as a result of genetic anomaly can have significant negative impact on adaptive behavior.

Whether and to what extent brain damage results in serious maladaptive behavior in an individual so afflicted is determined by complex interrelationships among a host of variables. These would include, for example, (1) premorbid neurological and psychological status, (2) site, extent, and type of lesion, (3) demographic factors, such as age of onset and sex, and (4) the availability of appropriate treatment. These and other factors and their relationship to recovery of function have been dealt with in detail elsewhere (Chapter 1, this volume; Rourke, Bakker, Fisk, & Strang, 1983; Spreen, Tupper, Risser, Tuokko, & Edgell, 1984) and will not be elaborated upon in this context. However, we do want to repeat a point made earlier: namely, that simple rules of thumb, such as the Kennard principle, are clearly insufficient to explain the interactions in question, and are very often misleading in the clinical evaluation of the neurologically impaired child.

In this chapter we examine a number of cases of youngsters suffering from fairly common neurological conditions of childhood about whom the neuropsychologist is often called upon to render an opinion. Our focus is not specifically on diagnosis. Indeed, in clinical settings, diagnosis (quite properly) usually assumes a secondary or even tertiary role as far as the neuropsychologist is concerned. Rather, the principal role of the neuropsychologist is most often that of specifying the type and extent of the brain-impaired child's abilities and deficits for the purpose of developmental intervention planning. Obviously, the cases presented in this chapter do not represent an exhaustive list; however, we hope that they are sufficient to illustrate, among other things, the diversity of outcomes with respect to behavior and adaptation in neurological conditions that from a purely neuropathological point of view may appear to be quite similar, if not identical. In addition, we endeavor (1) to identify those variables which are likely to be most crucial with respect to assessment, prognosis, and treatment of the brain-impaired child, and (2) to illustrate the means by which the clinical neuropsychologist can interact with other professionals in the management of the brain-impaired child. Finally, we conclude by providing a summary of those principles which we have found useful in this enterprise.

Hydrocephalus

Hydrocephalus is one of the more commonly encountered neurological conditions of childhood. Technically speaking, hydrocephalus constitutes a symptom (increased volume of cerebro-spinal fluid [CSF] within the skull) as opposed to a unitary diagnosis, since it can result from, among other things, neoplasms arising in the ventricles; congenital conditions such as the Arnold–Chiari malformation; adhesions following meningitis, trauma, or hemorrhage; as well as reduced absorption of CSF asssociated with impaired venous drainage. The usual distinction between so-called "obstructive" and "communicating" hydrocephalus is worth noting. In the former there is an obstruction of the circulation of CSF that prevents the flow between one or more ventricles and the subarachnoid space. In the case of communicating hydrocephalus, there is no impairment in the flow from the lateral ventricles, although they are typically enlarged. In such cases, CSF pressure, as measured by routine lumbar puncture, is very typically normal. For more detailed discussion of this condition, the reader is referred to Milhorat (1972).

Infantile hydrocephalus can often be successfully treated via insertion of a silastic valve into one lateral ventricle with catheter drainage into the peritoneum or via a jugular vein into the cardiac atrium. Certain secondary complications can arise due to infection, thrombosis, embolism, or blockage of the shunt. Thus, it is very important that the neurological and neuropsychological status of such children be closely monitored. In cases where secondary complications arise, the consequences with respect to the development of the child's adaptive skills can often be quite serious. In our first case presentation, some of the issues in dealing with hydrocephalus and associated secondary complications are illustrated.

Case 3-1: Maurice

Maurice[1] had been diagnosed as suffering from hydrocephalus at 6 weeks of age, and a ventriculo-peritoneal shunt was performed at

4 months of age. Secondary complications (shunt blockage) resulted in subsequent shunt revisions at approximately 3 years and again at 5 years, 6 months of age. According to the child's mother, many aspects of her son's development were delayed. For example, he apparently did not walk until approximately 2½ years of age, and he was slow to learn how to use eating utensils. At age 4 he was enrolled in a preschool program where he received speech therapy and sensory–motor training. He remained in this program until entering elementary school at 6 years of age. At 6½ years of age, he was seen for neurological consultation, with the following diagnoses formulated: "hydrocephalus, constitutional small stature, hyperactivity, and developmental delay of nonverbal skills."

Upon entering school, it became clear that he was unable to cope with the kindergarten program and he was subsequently transferred to a "multiple-handicapped" class. Coincidentally, school personnel requested a neuropsychological evaluation to assist them in developing appropriate remedial plans for the boy.

In a preexamination interview, Maurice's mother reported that he was very active at home and that it was sometimes difficult to manage his behavior. Indeed, her major complaints centered around his very short attention span, high level of motor activity, and general restlessness. She understood that he exhibited similar behavior in the classroom. It was also discovered that a third shunt revision had been undertaken some 10 days prior to the neuropsychological evaluation, at which time the boy was 8 years, 4 months of age.

Throughout the examination this youngster was extremely distractible, active, and emotionally labile. Frequently he appeared frustrated by the tasks presented to him; on occasion, this produced uncontrollable crying. However, these episodes typically passed quickly and were followed by the exhibition of a calm, friendly, and cooperative demeanor. On the basis of observation, his balance and gross motor coordination appeared to be poor. However, his speech was clear and easily understood. A slight lateral deviation of the right eye was noted. From time to time he complained of headache, and toward the end of the testing session it was clear that he was quite fatigued. Physically, he was very small for his stated chronological age, measuring approximately 42 inches in height. The posterior right quadrant of his head was shaved and a recently healed vertical incision scar, approximately 2 inches in length, could be seen over the posterior aspect of the right parietal area.

Examination of the test results (see Figure 3-1a) revealed a broad range of deficient performances in the context of some relatively circumscribed strengths. Especially noteworthy were the problems that he en-

---

1. Throughout the remainder of this text we will assign common names to the children discussed; these names were chosen on an essentially random basis.

countered on tasks involving memory for and the perception and integration of visual–spatial information (i.e., Target Test, Matching Pictures Test, and the Block Design, Object Assembly, and Picture Completion subtests of the Wechsler Intelligence Scale for Children [WISC]). His drawing of a Greek cross was quite distorted from a visual–spatial standpoint (see Figure 3-1b), and his performance on the Progressive Figures Test suggested that he was experiencing difficulty in formulating flexible plans of action. In addition, he also exhibited clear and consistent difficulties on measures of static and kinetic motor steadiness and speeded eye–hand coordination. In short, it seemed that the planning, organizational, and integrational aspects of manipulatory tasks were quite difficult, if not impossible, for this youngster. In addition, he exhibited considerable difficulty on a task designed specifically for the measurement of higher-order concept formation, problem solving, and the use of informational feedback (the Category Test).

One might be inclined to attribute the aforementioned results to some sort of generalized attentional deficit. However, it is important to note that Maurice did exhibit some age-appropriate performances on tasks requiring concentration and attention. For example, the WISC Digit Span subtest, which is often thought of as a task sensitive to deficits in attentional deployment, was performed fairly effectively by this boy. He was able to recall a series of six digits forward and three digits in reverse order, yielding a subtest score of 11. Age-appropriate performances were also noted on the Auditory Closure and Sentence Memory Tests, which further supported the view that Maurice was capable of attending appropriately under certain conditions (i.e., when the information was presented via the auditory modality).

In any event, it is clear that this youngster was appropriately sensitive to the acoustical and phonological structure of spoken language. This inference was further supported by qualitative evaluation of his reading and spelling performances on the Wide Range Achievement Test (WRAT). His spelling responses suggested an emerging appreciation for sound–symbol relationships. For example, the word "watch" was spelled as "woch," "cook" as "cok," "make" as "mak," "order" as "odr," "dress" as "dres." Furthermore, it was clear from his responses on the Reading (word-recognition) subtest that he was attempting, with some success, to analyze the phonemic structure of the words presented to him.

In summary, the results of the initial examination indicated significant deficits in the processing of information presented via the visual modality as well as impaired simple motor and psychomotor functioning and poor problem-solving skills. These deficits were observed in the context of some reasonably well developed capacities to utilize psycholinguistic and language-related information. While the test protocol suggested relatively diffuse dysfunction at the level of the cerebral cortex, it appeared

Figure 3-1a. Neuropsychological test results—Case 3-1 (Maurice).

Age	8 yr, 4 mo	8 yr, 10 mo	9 yr, 10 mo
WISC			
Verbal IQ	74	85	77
Information	4	5	5
Comprehension	4	5	5
Arithmetic	3	5	4
Similarities	7	10	9
Vocabulary	6	8	7
Digit Span	11	13	8
Performance IQ	57	61	72
Picture Completion	5	8	6
Picture Arrangement	2	4	8
Block Design	4	3	8
Object Assembly	4	4	4
Coding	4	3	4
Full Scale IQ	62	71	72
PPVT			
IQ	113	93	88
Mental Age	9–5	8–3	8–5
WRAT			
Reading (grade equiv.)	2.4	2.4	2.7
Spelling (grade equiv.)	1.3	2.5	2.6
Arithmetic (grade equiv.)	K.9	1.9	2.3

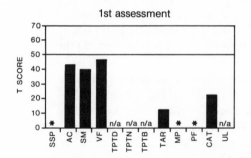

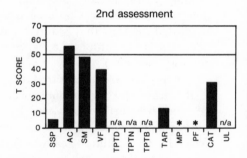

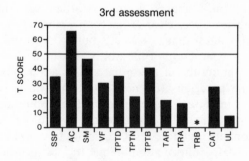

SENSORY-PERCEPTUAL ABILITIES

In the initial assessment, Maurice performed normally on the Sweep Hearing Test. However, on two occasions (out of four trials), he suppressed simple auditory stimulation delivered to the left ear when the right ear was simultaneously stimulated. Tests for visual field defects were negative. There was no compelling evidence of tactile imperception or suppression or of astereognosis for forms. There was evidence of a moderate degree of finger agnosia bilaterally. The results of the second and third evaluations were unremarkable except for some evidence of bilateral finger agnosia and very mild dysgraphesthesia.

APHASIA SCREENING TEST

In the initial assessment, there was evidence of difficulties in arithmetic calculation. However, he experienced no difficulty with the naming, reading, body orientation, or right–left discrimination items of the test. On repeat evaluation, he exhibited some (possible) right–left confusion, but otherwise performed quite well. On the final evaluation (older children's version) he was unable to spell correctly several (three oral; two written) age-appropriate words; he was unable to compute two simple arithmetic problems (one oral; one written); several simple words were misread in two short sentences; there was also some evidence of auditory–verbal agnosia. In all three examinations, there was evidence of constructional dyspraxia.

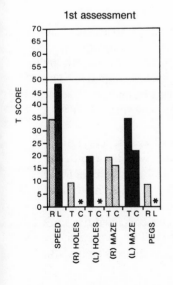

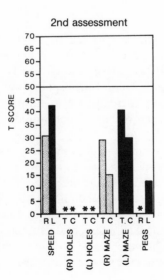

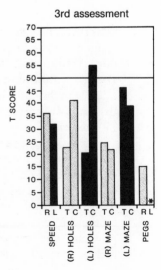

63

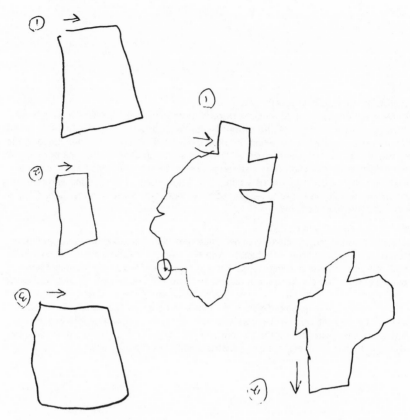

Figure 3-1b. Aphasia Screening Test drawings of Maurice—first assessment.

that there had been relative sparing of some of those structures and systems ordinarily thought to subserve certain aspects of language function. Abilities and skills ordinarily thought to be subserved primarily by systems within the right cerebral hemisphere were clearly impaired. The quality of his motor performances also raised the possibility of some degree of subcortical involvement, which would not be atypical in view of his medical history.

In developing a treatment plan for Maurice, there were several important factors to be considered. First of all, we interviewed the mother in order to explain in practical language how her son was experiencing difficulty in processing visual–spatial information and how this might lead to disorganized behavior. (In this connection, it became apparent that the mother believed that medical intervention should have corrected her son's problem. This being the case, her son's emotional lability, hyperactivity, and poor motor skills were a source of confusion and distress to her.) In our contacts with her we emphasized the need to establish consistent routines in all aspects of her son's day-to-day living. The mother was urged to contact the attending physician immediately if the boy exhibited headaches, nausea, or vomiting. The need for ongoing monitoring of his neurological status was emphasized as well.

Next, a conference was arranged with school personnel in order to elaborate upon our recommendations regarding his academic program. It was emphasized that Maurice would require a highly structured program in a "contained" classroom. The need to monitor the boy's activities suggested that the class should probably be one with a relatively low pupil/ teacher ratio. It was recommended that, as much as possible, extraneous stimulation be kept to a minimum, and that his work area be kept relatively free of nontask objects. Since Maurice exhibited fairly well-developed automatic language skills, it seemed reasonable to exploit these strengths. We suggested that some time be allocated to help him to develop more effective problem-solving strategies by using his verbal skills. For example, when beginning a particular task, he might be required to generate verbal statements describing specific steps in it. This would have to be closely monitored in order to ensure that his statements accurately reflected task demands. Then, he could be trained to tell himself what to do as he proceeded with the task in question. It was thought that, via verbal self-monitoring, he would be more able to maintain plans of action. It was also suggested that direct training of visual–spatial abilities should be undertaken. In this area as well, we emphasized the importance of having this boy talk about the specific activities in question while he was performing them. Finally, we suggested that Maurice be referred for an occupational therapy evaluation with a view to establishing a treatment program designed to assist him with the development of psychomotor skills.

A neuropsychological reevaluation was carried out approximately 6 months following the initial assessment. In examining these results (see Figure 3-1a), it was clear that his pattern of scores had not changed in any appreciable manner. There had been some modest improvement in his auditory–perceptual and language-related skills, but his poorly developed visual–spatial abilities, deficient psychomotor skills, and generally disorganized behavior remained as areas of concern.

At the Educational Conference following this second assessment, his teacher explained that Maurice continued to experience problems in organizing his behavior. Interaction with other children was sometimes problematic, as he seemed to require considerable structure, even in playtime activities. He continued to exhibit poor visual–spatial awareness, and graphomotor problems persisted. Academically, it was estimated that he was working at a Grade 1 level in reading, language arts, and arithmetic (although the WRAT scores that he obtained during our evaluation of him were somewhat higher than this). He seemd to be able to utilize basic phonics for reading, although some problems were noted with respect to the recall of vowel sounds. His understanding of basic operations in arithmetic was seen as weak, and his work very disorganized.

Shortly following the second assessment, in accordance with our original recommendation, the youngster was enrolled in an individualized occupational therapy program that involved two ½-hour sessions per week. The objectives of the program were to improve visual–spatial awareness, tactile discrimination, and motor skills. In working with Maurice, the therapist focused her efforts primarily on assisting him to structure tasks verbally along the lines we had previously suggested. After 10 months of this treatment, evaluation revealed gains in tactile discrimination and visual–spatial awareness. Modest improvements in his fine and gross motor skills were observed, although these skills remained quite deficient for his age. The therapist also observed that Maurice was a good deal less impulsive, and that he seemed able to approach tasks in a much more organized fashion. It was her opinion that the most important factor in this improvement was his ability to structure tasks in a verbal fashion. This endorsement of verbal mediation procedures, based on the clinical observation of the occupational therapist, supported our hypothesis that verbal mediation would be of considerable assistance to this boy in coping more efficiently with his environment.

Following termination of the individual therapy program, occupational therapy staff consulted directly with the child's teacher with a view to exploring remedial activities for use in the classroom. Follow-up meetings revealed that Maurice was responding well to explicitly stated expectations, and it was generally felt that he was coping adequately with the day-to-day demands of the classroom.

A final evaluation of this youngster was carried out when he was 9 years, 10 months of age. This assessment had been requested in connection with his enrollment in a special day-care program that was provided by a government agency. Coordination of his treatment was becoming difficult. In addition to daily attendance at school, he was seen for occupational therapy twice weekly at our hospital, and for weekly play group sessions at a local children's group therapy clinic. His travel schedule was complex, to say the least, and efficient communication among the various individuals working with him was problematic. It was agreed by all concerned that provision of an integrated program in a single location would be in Maurice's best interests.

At this juncture, we would draw the reader's attention to the fact that, in this particular case, the realistic remedial plan (Step 6) was essentially identical to the ideal remedial plan (Step 4), at least in terms of short- and intermediate-term goals. This fortunate circumstance does not always occur, as will become evident in subsequent cases presented in this text.

During the third testing session, he was quite cooperative and rapport was easily obtained with him. He was inclined to be somewhat talkative and required supervision in order to keep him "on task." His verbosity occasionally served to distract him, as he tended to interrupt instructions with information that was not always relevant to task demands. He required extra encouragement from the examiner in order to persist with some tasks. In general, he responded well to praise. All in all, the boy seemed to put forth good effort, and he did not exhibit the emotional lability and serious behavioral disorganization that had been characteristic of him in our previous testing sessions.

In reviewing the test results (see Figure 3-1a), it is clear that the pattern of adaptive strengths and weaknesses had remained quite stable over the 18 months since our first evaluation of him, although some modest gains were observed in circumscribed areas of functioning. As was noted previously, his receptive language skills, when he was required to deal with straightforward verbal information, were reasonably well developed. Specific tasks reflecting verbal expressive skills (e.g., the Verbal Fluency Test, and the Vocabulary and Comprehension subtests of the WISC) proved to be somewhat problematic for him, although some aspects of verbal expression seemed quite well developed. He was very talkative, and it seemed quite probable that in some cases he utilized speech as a way of avoiding tasks that he perceived as too difficult for him.

Maurice continued to exhibit very poor verbal and nonverbal reasoning. He performed poorly on tests that required learning via the sense of touch (note in particular the Tactual Performance Test scores), and clear visual–spatial organizational difficulties remained. Complex eye–hand coordination, as measured with the Grooved Pegboard Test, remained as a source of difficulty. Furthermore, examination of his printed letter formations revealed a tendency to exert uneven pencil pressure. This behavior is often seen in children who have difficulties with graphomotor coordination. At the same time, there was clear evidence that static motor steadiness was improved with both hands.

In presenting our recommendations to agency personnel, the need to provide Maurice with step-by-step verbal directives was emphasized, especially when he was to be confronted by novel or otherwise complex situations. Although there were indications of some improvement in his attentional skills, it was recommended that these continue to be a focus of treatment through continued training in verbal self-regulation techniques. Personnel at the center were urged to consult the "Think Aloud" program (Camp & Bash, 1981) for specific activities geared to his level of functioning.

While we had focused on the utilization of verbal abilities in Maurice's treatment, those working with him were also cautioned not to overemphasize this capacity. We felt that it was important not to reinforce extraneous, off-topic speech—a feature of his behavior that was character-istic in many day-to-day situations, especially when he was under any stress. We suggested that work with the speech and language pathologist focus almost exclusively on activities designed to improve the pragmatic aspects of his language, and that focused, task-oriented verbalizations be reinforced whenever possible.

In subsequent contacts, his mother reported that Maurice seemed happier and better adjusted with respect to school. She noted that at home he did not seem to be as easily upset, and that he was generally much calmer than had previously been the case.

It is difficult to make accurate prognostic statements with respect to the development of Maurice's adaptive skills. He had clearly benefited from the intensive treatment program provided for him. Indeed, the follow-up investigations of Maurice's neuropsychological status served to provide at least some index of the effectiveness of remedial intervention thus far (Step 7). Whether and to what extent he might lead a "normal" life in the future is difficult to ascertain. It is our impression that Maurice will require the support of some community services, at least for the forseeable future. Indeed, his continuing difficulties with concept forma-tion, problem solving, and strategy generation do not bode well for his ability to cope with the increasingly complex demands that accompany subsequent developmental stages.

Maurice's case does illustrate the potentially serious effects of hy-drocephalus, particularly when secondary complications occur. However, the effects of hydrocephalus can be quite variable, as the next case illus-trates.

Case 3-2: Jason

Structural abnormalities of the brain are sometimes relatively asymp-tomatic, and consequently remain undetected for considerable periods of time. Just such a case is that of Jason who was referred for neuropsycho-logical assessment because his kindergarten teacher reported a notable lack of participation in classroom activities. He was described as a timid, lethargic, noninvolved child who seemed content to sit and watch the activities of other children in the classroom.

In a pretest interview with his parents, it was learned that Jason had been diagnosed as suffering from hydrocephalus when he was approxi-mately 5 years of age. Apparently he had been seen just prior to this time by an ophthalmologist because of ocular–motor problems involving his right eye. The physician diagnosed a sixth cranial nerve palsy, at the same time noting that the boy seemed to have an unusually large head. Indeed, subsequent measurement revealed a head circumference at 5 years, 3 months in excess of the 97th centile. A CT scan was ordered; it revealed "marked hydrocephalus on the basis of aqueduct stenosis and a very small fourth ventricle."

We examined Jason at the age of 5 years, 3 months. The boy separated easily from his parents and during the first hour of the examination he was reasonably cooperative, seeming to put forth adequate effort. However, as the session progressed, he became increasingly recalcitrant and oppositional, often refusing to respond. In some instances, no amount of encouragement or prompting from the examiner was sufficient to elicit responses from him. His balance and gait appeared to be normal, although obvious hand tremors were noted when he was engaged in fine motor tasks.

Bearing in mind that we did not always obtain maximum performance from this boy, the following tentative generalizations were formulated on the basis of the results obtained (see Figure 3-2a).

1. Although this right-handed boy exhibited adequate speed and strength with the upper extremities, there was evidence of motor control difficulties, particularly within the static disposition. The poor quality of his drawings of simple geometric forms and his very poor performance on the Coding subtest of the WISC (scaled score of 3) indicated rather obvious difficulty with pencil control. His performances on the Grooved Pegboard Test were age-appropriate; however, in contrast to his apparent hand preference, performance with his left hand was superior to that with his right hand.

2. He exhibited some efficient performances on tasks of a visual–spatial and visual–constructional nature, provided that these demanded little in the way of graphomotor requirements. Especially noteworthy in this regard were his performances on the Picture Completion and Picture Arrangement subtests of the WISC, the Matching Pictures Test, and the Progressive Figures Test. In contrast, the Block Design and Object Assembly subtests of the WISC and the Target Test proved to be mildly problematic for him.

3. His performances on the Auditory Closure Test, the Auditory Analysis Test, and the Verbal Fluency Test suggested some appreciation for the phonological structure of words. In addition, he was able to identify correctly various upper-case letters of the alphabet (13 in all) on the Reading subtest of the WRAT.

4. His single-word receptive vocabulary (as measured by the Peabody Picture Vocabulary Test [PPVT]) was age-appropriate, as was his performance on the Information subtest of the WISC. His rather poor performances on the WISC Digit Span subtest and the Sentence Memory Test suggested difficulty with the immediate and/or short-term recall of verbal information. His performances on the WISC Similarities and Comprehension subtests were much poorer than those typically seen in children of this age. However, the rather uneven pattern of performances on verbal and

Figure 3-2a. Neuropsychological test results—Case 3-2 (Jason).

Age	5 yr, 3 mo	6 yr, 3 mo
WISC		
Verbal IQ	76	99
Information	10	7
Comprehension	3	7
Arithmetic	10	12
Similarities	4	7
Vocabulary	7	9
Digit Span	3	17
Performance IQ	89	107
Picture Completion	12	11
Picture Arrangement	13	12
Block Design	8	12
Object Assembly	6	9
Coding	3	11
Full Scale IQ	80	103
PPVT		
IQ	109	121
Mental Age	5–11	8–1
WRAT		
Reading (grade equiv.)	1.3	1.4
Spelling (grade equiv.)	P.5	1.3
Arithmetic (grade equiv.)	1.1	2.5

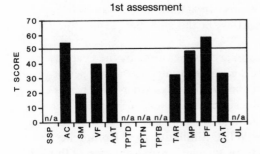

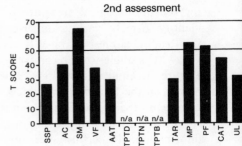

SENSORY-PERCEPTUAL ABILITIES

In the first evaluation, Jason refused to respond on tests for visual, tactile, and auditory imperception and suppression. Although administered, the results of the Tactile Finger Recognition and Fingertip Symbol-Writing Recognition Tests were probably invalid. Reevaluation revealed some evidence of tactile suppression with the left hand (when the right face was simultaneously stimulated), mild bilateral finger agnosia, and some finger dysgraphesthesia with the right hand. Otherwise, his performance on the sensory-perceptual portion of the examination was normal.

APHASIA SCREENING TEST

In the first assessment, Jason responded correctly to the naming and body orientation items. However, he experienced difficulty with the reading, arithmetic, and right-left discrimination items. There was also clear evidence of constructional dyspraxia. On subsequent reevaluation his performance was considerably improved, although he continued to exhibit some degree of constructional dyspraxia. He also failed to read the words in one simple sentence; instead, he opted to name the individual letters of the words, which he did correctly.

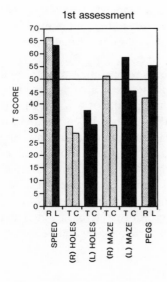

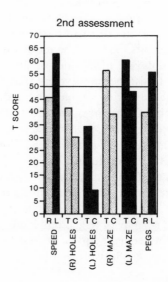

language related measures renders interpretation difficult. In other words, it was difficult to determine whether, and to what extent, his poorer performances reflected legitimate information processing deficits, untoward motivational effects, or both.

In summary, it was rather difficult to make any confident inferences with respect to the functional integrity of this child's cerebral systems. However, the sort of graphomotor and static steadiness problems observed suggested that subcortical dysfunction was quite probable.

Following this evaluation, Jason's parents were interviewed in order to apprise them of our findings and recommendations. It became evident that the parents were mildly defensive regarding their son's behavior. While they did acknowledge that he tended to be rather shy and timid with other children as well as adults, they were inclined to attribute this to a "personality" trait. They explained this by the fact that, during the first few years of Jason's life, they had lived in an apartment building populated primarily by adults and as a consequence he had little opportunity to interact with other children during his "formative" years.

Review of the developmental history revealed that pregnancy and delivery were normal, although he was born 22 days past the due date. According to his mother, Jason was walking by 1 year and spoke in sentences by the age of 2; in other ways his development was also quite normal. It was interesting to note that the results of the Personality Inventory for Children (PIC; Wirt, Lachar, Klinedinst, & Seat, 1977) completed by the mother yielded significant elevations on the Depression and Withdrawal scales (T scores of 86 and 96, respectively) and a moderate elevation on the Anxiety scale (T score 79). This particular profile (see Figure 3-2b) is typically seen in children who are inclined to be excessively shy, fearful, and isolated. Parents of such children often report problems with sleeping, eating, emotional lability, and a tendency to avoid group activities. In other words, the results of the PIC suggested that many of the statements made by the mother during the interview constituted a kind of downplaying of his "personality" problems.

It also became evident that Jason's parents were somewhat confused by the differing opinions regarding appropriate medical treatment that had been recommended for him. Based on the results of a CT scan, the attending neurosurgeon had recommended that the boy be considered for a ventriculo-peritoneal shunt. However, it was the opinion of a consulting pediatric neurologist that, because there was no symptomatology of increased intracranial pressure, aggressive intervention was contraindicated, at least until evidence resulting from careful monitoring suggested otherwise. We advised the parents to report immediately any changes in the child's behavior (e.g., complaints of headaches, unusual lethargy, etc.) and recommended periodic evaluations of both his neurological and neuropsychological status.

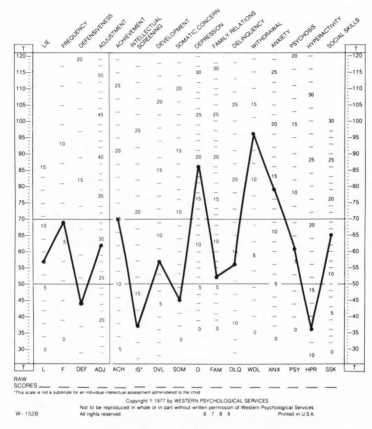

Figure 3-2b. Personality Inventory for Children profile—Case 3-2 (Jason).

A conference with personnel from Jason's school was convened. In this instance, the conference served to provide additional evidence that Jason was not dealing in an entirely appropriate fashion with the social interactional and some academic learning demands of the classroom environment (Step 2). His kindergarten teacher reported that his behavior was unpredictable. At times he was relatively cooperative and friendly, whereas on other occasions he became quite withdrawn and uncommunicative. It was very difficult for the teacher to predict his mood at any point in time. Although it was her opinion that he was making academic progress, he rarely demonstrated any desire to interact verbally with his classmates. Concern regarding his graphomotor skills was also expressed. It was recommended that efforts be directed toward encouraging greater social interaction through the use of behavioral modification techniques. It was explained that some experimentation would be required in order to determine which activities or concrete rewards would be beneficial in shaping his behavior in appropriate ways.

Jason was seen for reevaluation approximately 1 year following the initial assessment (at the age of 6 years, 3 months). On this occasion he was initially extremely resistant and uncooperative. He was quite uncommunicative, and simply refused to participate in any of the tasks presented to him. In an attempt to engage the child, it was decided to utilize concrete reinforcements (stickers of comic book characters) as a reward for a response. This procedure proved to be extremely successful. While he remained rather taciturn (speaking only when necessary) for the remainder of the examination, he did cooperate, and he worked assiduously for the aforementioned rewards. Indeed, by the end of the day-long session, he seemed to be much more animated and involved, to the extent that the need for concrete rewards was significantly reduced.

The results of the reevaluation (see Figure 3-2a) suggested a slightly different clinical picture (at least with respect to some auditory–perceptual and language-related skills) as compared to our initial findings. The following generalizations appeared to be warranted.

1. He seemed to have relatively well-developed visual information processing skills. He obtained a WISC Performance IQ of 107, with little intersubtest scatter in evidence. He also exhibited fairly good performances on the Matching Pictures, Category, and Progressive Figures Tests. As was noted previously, his drawings of simple geometric forms were poor, probably reflecting deficient motor control rather than problems with the visual–spatial elements of the task.

2. He continued to exhibit a rather prominent static tremor, especially during trials with his left hand. The quality of his drawings and printed letter formations also indicated some difficulty with intentional motor movements. As was noted previously, he was somewhat more proficient with his left hand as compared to his right hand on the Grooved Pegboard Test. However, his performance on the Coding subtest of the WISC was much better than he had exhibited in our first assessment of him.

3. His immediate memory for rote verbal material (digits) was outstanding and he seemed to have an adequate vocabulary, at least as measured by the PPVT and the Vocabulary subtest of the WISC.

4. There was some evidence to suggest that his capacity to utilize phonological information was somewhat less well developed than is typically seen in children of this age. Especially noteworthy were his poor performances on the Auditory Analysis Test, Speech-Sounds Perception Test, and Auditory Closure Test. Qualitative evaluation of his Reading and Spelling performances on the WRAT indicated only a limited understanding of sound–symbol relationships.

5. Although it is not readily apparent from the test scores presented in Figure 3-2a, closer evaluation of specific responses on the Category Test and the Underlining Test revealed that on occasion he exhibited some degree of "warm-up" effect. On both of the aforementioned tests he experienced difficulty with the initial, relatively easy, items and improved performance on more complex items presented later in the test. It is difficult to know whether or not this reflected difficulty in comprehending instructions, attentional factors, or both. In any case, it was clear that his performance improved as the result of experience with task demands.

Again, based purely on the test results, it is difficult to formulate confident inferences regarding cerebral dysfunction. While there was some suggestion of possible left temporo-parietal involvement, the general picture suggests intactness of cerebral cortical functional systems. However, the continuing evidence of static and intentional tremors did suggest some degree of subcortical involvement, possibly involving cerebellar tracts or basal ganglia. This would certainly seem to be consistent with what was known regarding his neurological status.

Our experience with Jason in the testing situation once again revealed a child who was somewhat reluctant to engage in verbal communication, at least with adults. Reports from school personnel indicated similar behavior in interactions with peers. In addition, there were "autistic-like" features to some of his behaviors. Whether and to what extent this behavior reflected some degree of limbic system dysfunction would need to be corroborated by other means.

Shortly following reevaluation of the child, we learned that the father had been transferred to another city in connection with his job. We arranged to put the family in contact with neurological and neuropsychological services in this new location. In subsequent follow-up 6 months later, we learned that the attending neurologist had undertaken another CT scan, which revealed aqueductal stenosis and enlarged ventricles. In the absence of symptoms of raised intracranial pressure and few indications of cognitive impairment, the opinion was rendered that surgical treatment was not warranted. Active follow-up of the child was left to the discretion of the parents after the neurologist briefed them regarding symptoms of increased intracranial pressure.

How well this child was developing socially was difficult to determine, since we no longer had direct contact with the family. For that matter, in light of the circumstances, any consideration of issues related to Steps 4 through 7 of our model was moot. The most that can be said is that Jason's neurological status appeared to be stable, but the prognosis remained unclear. Our observations of him clearly suggested that his behavior was not "normal," since he did display some atypical social behavior. Our impression in following similar children is that such behavior should be expected to constitute a source of considerable difficulty during subsequent stages of development.

Summary

Hydrocephalus can often be successfully treated by early surgical intervention. However, as the case of Maurice illustrates, secondary complications can result in serious consequences with respect to the subsequent development of cognitive and adaptive skills. Habilitation involved assisting the child to utilize intact skills in an effort to compensate for adaptive deficits. In Jason's case, hydrocephalus, being of the so-called "normal pressure" variety, was relatively asymptomatic, at least in terms of the pattern of neuropsychological test results. The concern in this case focused primarily around the atypical development of social skills. Be that as it may, both cases demonstrate the importance of monitoring the neurological and neuropsychological status of such children. Furthermore, these cases illustrate that hydrocephalus constitutes a symptom complex rather than a unitary clinical syndrome, and that the adaptational consequences of this condition can be quite diverse.

Traumatic head injury

Although it is difficult to make any confident inferences in matters such as this, it seems quite probable that head injury constitutes the most common source of neurological trauma in pediatric populations (Craft, 1972; Jamison & Kaye, 1974). Investigations (e.g., Hendrick, Harwood-Nash, & Hudson, 1964) have also indicated a lower mortality rate for children as compared to adults with head injuries, although the reasons for this phenomenon are not entirely clear. In any case, it has been a common belief for some time that early insult to the brain is less disruptive of adaptive functioning as compared to injury sustained in adult life. This belief, often referred to as the Kennard principle, is most often explained on the basis of greater plasticity in the developing brain. However, recent studies (e.g., Van Dongen & Loonen, 1977; St. James-Roberts, 1981) have raised serious questions regarding the validity of this notion. The fact of the matter is that a large number of variables appear to interact in the determination of behavioral outcome following head injury in both children and adults. Cerebral maturity (i.e., one aspect of developmental level) is only one factor in this complex relationship. The interested reader is referred to Levin, Benton, and Grossman (1982), Rourke et al. (1983), and Rutter, Chadwick, and Shaffer (1983) for a more detailed account of this complex topic.

In our clinical experience we find quite frequently that the traumatically head-injured child is assumed to have recovered once the "acute" effects of the injury have subsided. While the notion of acute effects of brain trauma is understood in some general sense, it is not entirely clear from the head injury literature what specific measurable signs or markers signal the transition from acute to chronic stage of injury. We would consider a patient to be, as it were, out of the acute stage when (1) coma has terminated, (2) general confusion and anterograde amnesia have resolved, and (3) posttraumatic amnesia (PTA) has stabilized. With respect to the latter, Chadwick, Rutter, Schaffer, and Shrout (1981) consider PTA to constitute a good prognostic indicator in children. However, Ewing-Cobbs, Fletcher, and Levin (1985) suggest caution in interpreting the length and characteristics of the initial recovery period, since the behavioral elements of PTA in children are not well defined, nor are there precise measures of PTA in children. The reader will also recognize that, in severe injury, the aforementioned characteristics may persist indefinitely.

In any case, Rourke (1983) has suggested that the "recovery" usually seen in the younger brain-injured child can very often be quite deceptive. Such children during the "acute" stage often manifest pronounced attentional problems; this phenomenon can serve to mask more focal impairments in adaptive skills. Follow-up of such children often reveals serious and debilitating deficiencies in cognition that become more obvious with advancing age. In addition, the work of Goldman (1976) and Goldman and Galkin (1978) would suggest rather strongly that problems resulting from very early damage to structures that are necessary for the subservience of more mature neurodevelopmental systems and behaviors will become manifest only several years later (i.e., when these structures are required for the mediation of more complex functions). For example, the so-called "executive functions" (Luria, 1973, 1980) thought to be subserved by systems within the frontal lobes (a very common site of childhood mechanical insult) may not be seen as disturbed until late childhood or early adolescence—that is, when the planning, direction, and initiation or inhibition of complex behaviors become crucial developmental demands (see Chapter 1 for an extensive treatment of this issue). The following case is instructive in this regard.

Case 3-3: Ronald

Ronald was involved in a motor vehicle accident at the age of 5 years. Upon admission to hospital he was unresponsive, although able to move his extremities. Investigation revealed a compound depressed left parietal skull fracture and a linear left frontal skull fracture. CT scan indicated a left parieto-occipital contusion and a small left frontal hemorrhage. Physical recovery was said to be rapid, but evaluation 12 days after hospital admission revealed emotional, cognitive, and language deficits. A speech and language evaluation indicated that his language comprehension and expression were severely impaired. There was evidence of word-finding difficulties, paraphasias, intrusive jargon, and perseverative behavior. Although generally cooperative and cheerful in the hospital setting, he was inclined to be easily agitated, and he exhibited a very low level of tolerance for frustration. His fine motor skills were somewhat impaired (e.g., he needed assistance to effect a pencil grip, and he experienced difficulty when asked to imitate various motor movements).

As to developmental history, Ronald was born 3 weeks early following an induced labor. His developmental history apparently followed a fairly normal course, although his mother stated that Ronald was somewhat slow to talk. He was also known to have a congenital heart defect. The precise nature of this problem was unknown to us at the time of our evaluation. However, we understood that, from a medical point of view, this condition was not considered life-threatening nor was treatment considered necessary.

Several weeks following his discharge from the hospital, Ronald was enrolled in a kindergarten program on a 5 half-days per week basis. His teacher rendered the following report at that time: "He displays immature language patterns, exhibits a very short attention span, and is not ready to tackle many of the readiness-related parts of the program." Approximately 2 months following his enrollment in school, he was seen for a speech and language evaluation. The results of this testing revealed his communication skills to be below age-expectancy in comprehension, auditory processing, and expression. Expressive skills were characterized by reduced length of utterance, perseveration, paraphasic errors, circumlocutions, and jargon. Although his articulation of speech sounds in the context of single words was age-appropriate, intelligibility at a conversational level was substantially reduced. It was recommended that he be enrolled in an intensive speech and language training program, and a complete neuropsychological evaluation was requested in order to evaluate the nature and extent of his adaptive deficits.

In a pretest interview, it was clear that Ronald's mother was in an agitated and anxious state. She seemed very reluctant to provide any information, stating emphatically that her child had made a perfect physical recovery and that there was no dramatic change in his behavior since before the accident. Although she agreed to the assessment, she stated quite clearly that she saw no purpose to it.

Ronald did not separate easily from his mother, and initially he began to cry and refused to enter the testing room. However, with reassurance and coaxing on the part of the examiner, he was eventually convinced to proceed, and for much of the time thereafter seemed to be relatively at ease.

Throughout the remainder of the day-long test session, he was somewhat emotionally labile, alternating between periods of cooperation and outright resistance. It was clear that he had a very low level of tolerance for frustration, often becoming upset when faced with tasks which he may have perceived as difficult. He engaged in little spontaneous conversation, and considerable prompting and encouragement were necessary in order to elicit verbal responses. His speech was characterized by some articulatory difficulties, which at times rendered it somewhat unintelligible. His balance, gait, and gross motor coordination appeared to be normal.

An examination of the test results (see Figure 3-3) reveals that Ronald performed poorly on many of the test measures. It was evident from his performances on the Verbal subtests of the WISC, the Verbal Fluency Test, and the Sentence Memory Test that his ability to deal with language-related information was particularly deficient. His understanding of words, phrases, and simple instructions was quite poor. However, it was interesting to note that he did obtain an IQ of 112 on the PPVT (possibly reflecting the training that he was receiving in word–picture pairings).

Some additional comment regarding the Verbal Fluency and Auditory Closure Test scores is warranted. The relatively positive T score (40) obtained on the Verbal Fluency Test is misleading. In fact, Ronald was unable to produce any correct responses (raw score $= 0$) on this test. Inspection of the normative data for 5-year-old children (Knights & Norwood, 1980) reveals a mean raw score of 2.90 and a standard deviation of 2.80. Thus, T score conversion yields a minimum score of 40, a spuriously good result in light of the actual performance.

Similarly, inspection of the 5-year-old norms for the Auditory Closure Test reveals a large standard deviation (4.00) relative to the mean (2.40). Again, this produces a somewhat misleading result when the raw score is converted to a T score. In addition, Ronald experienced marked difficulty on the Auditory Analysis Test (Rosner & Simon, 1970), which requires the child to reproduce spoken words while omitting specified phonemic elements of them. In all of this, we would caution the reader regarding the interpretative problems involved in the aforementioned scores.

Difficulties were also noted on tasks involving visual–spatial perceptual and organizational skills. It was clear from his performances on the Category Test, the Tactual Performance Test, and the Progressive Figures Test that he had considerable difficulty on any task that required him to formulate or maintain a plan of action. While some portion of this difficulty may have been related to his failure to understand verbal instructions, these results also suggested that his approach to problem-solving tasks was quite disorganized.

The results of the Harris Test of Lateral Dominance indicated that Ronald was exclusively right-handed. There was some evidence of mild bilateral static motor steadiness problems. However, he did obtain average

Figure 3-3. Neuropsychological test results—Case 3-3 (Ronald).

Age	5 yr, 2 mo	5 yr, 11 mo
WISC		
Verbal IQ	67	91
Information	6	10
Comprehension	3	11
Arithmetic	5	7
Similarities	6	9
Vocabulary	4	8
Digit Span	3	6
Performance IQ	79	92
Picture Completion	8	11
Picture Arrangement	7	11
Block Design	5	7
Object Assembly	7	9
Coding	8	6
Full Scale IQ	70	91
PPVT		
IQ	112	91
Mental Age	6–3	5–2
WRAT		
Reading (grade equiv.)	P.7	K.9
Spelling (grade equiv.)	N.8	P.5
Arithmetic (grade equiv.)	N.6	P.8

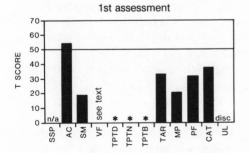

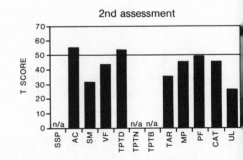

SENSORY-PERCEPTUAL ABILITIES

The results of a Sweep Hearing Test were negative. There was no evidence of auditory, visual, or tactile imperception or suppression. There were indications of finger agnosia and finger dysgraphesthesia on left-hand trials, and some suggestion of very mild bilateral astereognosis for forms. Reassessment yielded generally normal results, although there was some suggestion of mild difficulty on the Fingertip Symbol Recognition and Tactile-Form Recognition Tests.

APHASIA SCREENING TEST

Ronald was unable to respond correctly to the reading or arithmetic items. There was clear evidence of constructional dyspraxia and right-left confusion. However, he responded correctly on the naming and body orientation items. The second evaluation yielded similar results.

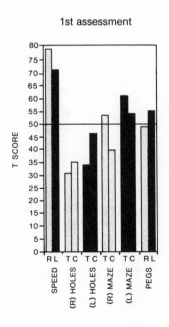

1st assessment

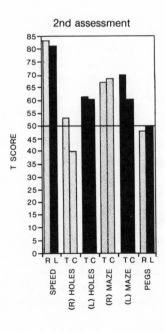

2nd assessment

to above-average scores on tests of motor speed, kinetic motor steadiness, and speeded eye–hand coordination. It was interesting to note that, for the latter two measures, performance with his left hand was superior to that with his right hand. There was also some evidence of finger agnosia and finger dysgraphesthesia (particularly with the left hand).

In summary, the pattern of test results obtained would be consistent with that usually seen in children who are experiencing the untoward effects of mild to moderate dysfunction at the level of the cerebral hemispheres. His generally poor performances on measures of both visual–spatial and language-related skills suggest relatively diffuse involvement of the cerebral systems. However, Ronald was more efficient with his left hand as compared to his right hand on several motor measures (e.g., static and kinetic motor steadiness, speeded eye–hand coordination), which would suggest somewhat greater involvement of the left cerebral hemisphere in this pattern of cerebral dysfunction. His outstandingly good score on the PPVT as compared to his generally deficient performances on the Verbal portion of the WISC is sometimes seen in children who have suffered a fairly recent trauma of the brain. Indeed, it would be rather unlikely that a child suffering from a developmental language disability who obtained a WISC Verbal IQ of 67 would exhibit an IQ-equivalent score of 112 on a measure designed to assess single-word receptive vocabulary. (This would be the case in spite of the frequently observed superiority of PPVT IQ over WISC Verbal IQ in youngsters who have undergone prolonged periods of language therapy that usually involve direct training in word–picture matching. In the latter instance, PPVT IQ is typically inflated somewhat as an apparently direct reflection of training in word–picture matching.)

Shortly after this assessment, an interview was arranged with Ronald's parents in order to apprise them of our findings and recommendations. As was the case at the time of assessment, the mother was extremely agitated, and she began the interview by stating emphatically that her son was quite "normal." It was her view that he had undergone complete recovery from his accident and, as far as she was concerned, he was the same as he had always been. The father did not comment on the mother's views, merely stating that he wanted to hear the results of the evaluation. Utilizing practical language, we presented the view that there was evidence that the child's language skills were very disorganized at the receptive, mediational, and expressive levels. The need for intensive therapy specifically designed to assist in the reorganization of his language capacities was emphasized. Some discussion ensued regarding how these services might be offered through the community hospital and local school board resources.

The father stated that it was his understanding from medical personnel who had attended Ronald following the accident that the boy would achieve complete recovery. However, he did acknowledge that he was willing to at least consider a contrary opinion. He stated that if it was believed that the child would benefit from more intensive treatment, then it should be provided. It was recommended that the parents consider our formulation of the problem and that we could review the situation at an upcoming conference.

In the conference that followed some time later, the parents agreed that the boy was in need of additional assistance, and he was subsequently admitted for language therapy on an individual twice-weekly basis in conjunction with his kindergarten program. After approximately 6 months of therapy, a speech and language evaluation was undertaken. The results indicated improvement in all areas tested as compared to the results obtained at the time of the initial assessment; however, his overall performance levels remained below age-expectation. School personnel felt that Ronald was not yet ready to progress to the Grade 1 program, and it was decided to have him remain in kindergarten for the time being. Outpatient language therapy was recommended to be continued on a weekly basis.

Ronald was seen for neuropsychological reevaluation when he was 5 years, 11 months of age. Throughout the assessment, he vacillated between periods of cooperative behavior and frank resistance. He seemed to be easily annoyed, and he was quick to respond "I can't" at the first sign of difficulty. He was inclined to be mildly distractible, and frequent prompting was necessary in order to maintain his attention to the task at hand. However, he was much more verbal than was the case in the previous evaluation. Indeed, at times he became quite chatty, often interrupting instructions to relate personal events, stories, and incidents. In contrast to what had been observed previously, his speech was clear and his conversation intelligible.

In reviewing the results of the second assessment (see Figure 3-3), it is immediately apparent there had been considerable improvement in his adaptive skills. Despite a generally broad range of improved scores, some specific difficulties remained. In particular, his capacity to retain and recall nonredundant verbal information as well as verbal information in context were clearly inferior to that typically seen in children of this age. For example, he obtained a scaled score of 6 on the WISC Digit Span test (three numbers forward and none in reverse order), and his score on the Sentence Memory Test fell close to two standard deviations below age-expectancy. In addition, the examiner noted that he often seemed to forget verbal stimuli presented on many of the tests, and that he required frequent prompting and reminders in order to stay on task. It was also apparent that Ronald was experiencing some word-finding difficulties. While he did obtain a scaled socre of 8 on the Vocabulary subtest of the WISC, a qualitative analysis of his responses revealed expressive difficulties. He was unable to generate meaningful responses to some relatively simple words (e.g., "letter," "cushion," "diamond," "join"). In some cases it was clear that he possessed some understanding of the words but could not provide precise definitions. In response to the word "nail," for example, he stated "hit into wood" with an accompanying gesture. These sorts of impoverished responses were typical of Ronald's performance throughout the testing session. In addition, he continued to exhibit deficits in skills that require various types of higher-order language skills (e.g., reading, spelling, verbal reasoning).

Following this assessment, we met with the parents in order to apprise them of the results. In describing the many encouraging improvements that we had noted in this child's adaptive skills, it was pointed out that difficulties with psycholinguistic and language tasks suggested that the development of academic skills might prove to be problematic. Ronald's mother, in particular, felt that the school system was not providing him with appropriate treatment for these shortcomings. For example, instead of attending kindergarten on a full-day basis (as was the case of the time of this assessment), she felt that he should have been promoted to Grade 1. We suggested that a meeting be arranged with school officials in order to evaluate the boy's progress and help deal with these types of concerns.

In all of our discussions with these parents, one important focus was to assist the mother to develop a more realistic appraisal of her child's adaptive abilities. This proved to be rather difficult. It was learned that the mother was driving the car involved in the accident in which Ronald was injured, and it seemed probable that she harbored considerable (unconscious) guilt regarding her son's condition. In our experience, this sort of reaction is not at all uncommon, even when, from a purely rational point of view, there is no reason for any blame to be assigned. This is a very important consideration in such cases, since enlisting parental cooperation is often crucial in the treatment of the child. In this regard, Klonoff and Low (1974), in a study of children 1 to 2 years following closed head injury, found that parents often reported apprehension with respect to brain damage in their children and were inclined to be somewhat overprotective of such children. Rutter et al. (1983) advise that parents be cautioned not to be unduly protective of head-injured children, since this attitude can serve to enhance or exacerbate psychiatric sequelae, a topic that we will examine shortly.

The subsequent conference with school personnel included the neuropsychologist, the child's speech pathologist, the school social worker, his remedial and classroom teachers, and Ronald's parents. The teacher provided a detailed account of Ronald's day-to-day school activities and outlined the specific skills typically exhibited by children who are likely to be successful in a Grade 1 program. Areas in which Ronald had met with success were highlighted, as were those activities with which he was continuing to encounter difficulty. Recommendations regarding language enrichment activities that could be incorporated in both home and school activities were presented by the speech pathologist. The parents were urged to maintain close contact with the school in order to develop a spirit of cooperation.

This case illustrates several important points with respect to the management and treatment of the head-injured child. We recommended that Ronald be monitored via yearly neuropsychological evaluations, since there was good reason to believe that he would meet with difficulty in the development of reading, spelling, and other skills requiring linguistic facility. With respect to his capacity to deal with other aspects of day-to-day living, we were quite optimistic since, on the basis of the reevaluation results, he appeared to have experienced considerable recovery of adaptive functions in these areas. However, with the increased demand for higher-order linguistic skills coincident with advances in academic demands, it seemed probable that academic problems would become more prominent if such skills did not continue to develop at a consistent rate.

In this case, our treatment recommendations focused primarily around activities designed to develop and enhance Ronald's language skills. His often disorganized approach to many tasks, including those of a nonverbal nature, suggested that he did not utilize language spontaneously in order to mediate and regulate his own behavior. Thus, to the extent that his general language skills could be improved, we would expect to observe more organized, coherent behavior in other realms of adaptive functioning.

Finally, this case illustrates the need to enlist parental understanding and cooperation in the treatment of the head-injured child. It is not at all uncommon to find that such parents are inclined to deny or otherwise fail to appreciate the adaptational consequences of their child's condition. Further, professionals often fail to recognize the devastating impact that the head-injured child can have on the integrity of the family (Polinko, Barin, Leger, & Bachman, 1985). For these and other reasons, in developing a treatment plan it is crucial to determine how parents feel about the situation and to have the means at one's disposal to deal with the implications of these feelings and any associated conflicts that may be present. Far too often there is a tendency to focus exclusively on the child's problems, without proper consideration for the parent's role in the rehabilitation of the patient.

In addition to the more obvious and frequently reported consequences of head injury in children (e.g., motor and psychomotor impairment, aphasic disturbances, memory deficits, etc.) there is also evidence that at least some head-injured children exhibit persistent social and emotional maladjustment well beyond what would normally be considered the point of recovery. A number of investigators (e.g., Flach & Malmros, 1972;

Klonoff & Paris, 1974; Klonoff & Low, 1974) have described various behavioral sequelae (e.g., impulsiveness, aggression, delinquency, etc.) in follow-up studies of samples of head-injured children.

While the relationship between behavioral disorder and head injury is not entirely clear, several factors do seem to have some bearing on the matter. For example, the literature contains a number of references to a higher incidence of parental mental illness, socioeconomic disadvantage, and unstable families in children experiencing head injury as compared with normal controls (Klonoff, 1971; Manheimer & Menninger, 1970; Partington, 1960). In reviewing this and other related literature, Rutter *et al.* (1983) conclude that such risk factors in addition to cerebral damage must be considered in evaluating the head-injured child. Related to this issue, Jennett (1972) has suggested that premorbid personality disturbance is a primary factor in such cases. However, other investigators (Black, Blumer, Wellner, & Walker, 1971; Brown, Chadwick, Shaffer, Rutter, & Traub, 1981) have provided evidence to indicate that premorbid disturbance is not a necessary condition to produce posttraumatic behavior disorder in at least some head-injured children. Relative severity of the injury does, however, seem to play an important role. Brown *et al.* (1981) found that the rate of psychiatric disorders was significantly increased in a 4-month follow-up of a severe head injury group (PTA of at least 7 days) as compared with mild head injury (PTA of less than 7 days) and non-brain-injured controls.

It is difficult to determine the relative contribution of familial factors or premorbid personality to psychiatric outcome following brain injury. However, we would suggest that behavioral disturbance in head-injured children cannot easily be separated from the perceptual and cognitive manifestations of trauma to the brain. As we have stated previously, recovery in the head-injured child can serve to obscure subtle cognitive deficits that become obviously debilitating, not only with respect to learning but also in terms of social and emotional adjustment as a result of increased environmental demands at subsequent stages of development. The following case serves to illustrate this principle.

Case 3-4: Allan

Allan was referred for a neuropsychological evaluation when he was 5 years of age. This referral had been initiated because of verbal receptive difficulties that had become apparent following a cranio-cerebral trauma sustained in an automobile accident at 46 months of age. Following the accident, ophthalmological examination, EEG, and brain scan were reported to be normal. However, during the period of time following his return home from the hospital, the mother had noted an increase in soiling and wetting accidents, general clumsiness, short attention span, and an inclination to temper tantrums. At 4½ years of age, he was enrolled in a preschool program. The teacher there had observed some difficulties with auditory perception and had raised questions regarding his audiological status. Poor attending behavior (at least for his age) was also identified as a major problem in the preschool setting. However, audiological examination conducted at 4 years, 9 months of age revealed normal bilateral acuity for pure tones and speech, and adequate discrimination efficiency.

The clinical history provided by the mother indicated that Allan was delivered at 8½ months gestation by caesarean section, weighing 7 pounds, 15 ounces at birth. Allan apparently experienced some respiratory distress and was subsequently incubated for his first 3 weeks, being finally discharged at 28 days of age in presumably good health. During his early developmental years he experienced several bouts of bronchial pneumonia, one requiring hospitalization at 29 months. In addition, there were reports of frequent occurrences of bronchitis and croup as well as a history of ear infections. His tonsils and adenoids were removed at 28 months. Otherwise, developmental milestones reported by the mother appeared to be within normal limits.

Allan was examined over two test sessions separated by six days. During both test sessions, his attention and cooperation waxed and waned. He was quite distractible, did not attend well to instructions, and often responded in an impulsive fashion. At times coaxing, encouragement, and redirection were necessary in order to elicit appropriate responses from him. It was noted that he often switched hands during paper-and-pencil tasks, and that his gross motor coordination appeared to be rather poor. His speech was characterized by mild misarticulations, although there was no difficulty in comprehending his verbal utterances. In light of his behavior during the examination, it seemed possible that the test results obtained did not represent his best possible performances.

Examination of the test results (see Figure 3-4a) revealed some adequately developed adaptive skills in the context of some specific deficiencies. His most serious problems seemed to center around motor skills. For example, he experienced considerable difficulty in maintaining steadiness in the static disposition (especially with his right hand) and on a test of speeded eye–hand coordination (Grooved Pegboard Test) with his right hand. There was also evidence of a mild kinetic tremor involving his left hand. In all of this, it should be noted that hand dominance did not appear to be well established. On a test of lateral preference in which he was required to demonstrate various actions (e.g., throwing a ball, hammering a nail, etc.) he consistently utilized his right hand. However, for purposes of paper-and-pencil tasks he spontaneously elected to use his left hand, although some switching of hands was noted during this sort of activity. His drawings of simple shapes were extremely distorted in terms of their visual–spatial characteristics, and he experienced difficulty in forming

Figure 3-4a. Neuropsychological test results—Case 3-4 (Allan).

Age	5 yr, 0 mo	6 yr, 5 mo	9 yr, 0 mo
WISC			
Verbal IQ	90	105	96
Information	8	10	6
Comprehension	8	10	7
Arithmetic	9	9	11
Similarities	8	15	11
Vocabulary	11	11	11
Digit Span	6	10	10
Performance IQ	96	107	107
Picture Completion	10	13	9
Picture Arrangement	13	7	11
Block Design	9	7	13
Object Assembly	9	13	13
Coding	6	9	12
Full Scale IQ	92	107	101
PPVT			
IQ	111	112	100
Mental Age	6–1	8–3	8–11
WRAT			
Reading (grade equiv.)	K.4	1.6	4.9
Spelling (grade equiv.)	N.8	1.9	4.5
Arithmetic (grade equiv.)	1.1	2.1	3.7

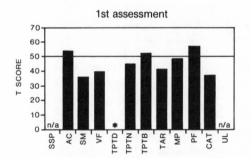

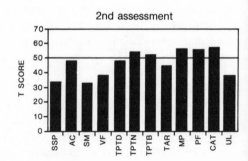

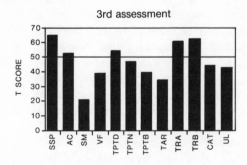

SENSORY-PERCEPTUAL ABILITIES

In all three assessments, Allan performed in an error-free fashion on tests of auditory, visual, and tactile imperception and suppression. For the most part, his auditory acuity for pure tones appeared to be within normal limits. However, he consistently exhibited mild finger agnosia and finger dysgraphesthesia.

APHASIA SCREENING TEST

Allan experienced considerable difficulty on this test in the initial evaluation. He was unable to read correctly numbers, letters, and simple words; his reproductions of simple geometric forms were quite distorted in terms of their visual-spatial characteristics; he failed to compute correctly one simple arithmetic problem presented orally. However, he responded correctly to the naming, body orientation, and right-left discrimination items of the test. Reassessment at 6½ years yielded some evidence of improved performance. His drawings, although slightly distorted and somewhat disorganized on the page, were much better than in the initial examination. He also experienced some difficulty with the reading items. Otherwise, his performance was unremarkable. On the final examination (older children's version) there was some evidence of auditory-verbal agnosia, constructional dyspraxia, dysnomia, and dyscalculia. He encountered no difficulty with the reading and spelling items of the test.

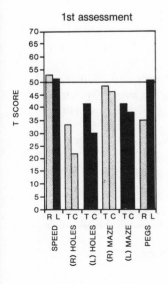

1st assessment

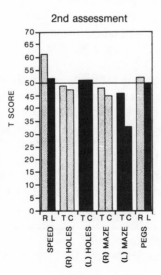

2nd assessment

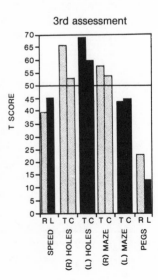

3rd assessment

recognizable letters or copying symbols. The possibility that he was switching hand dominance from right to left might explain some of his difficulties with graphomotor skills; that is, poor graphomotor performance could reflect lack of experience in addition to psychomotor inefficiency. The Tactual Performance Test also proved to be somewhat difficult for him. The initial trial using his left hand independently (he was assumed to be left-handed for purposes of this test) yielded a score in the impaired range. However, a robust practice effect was noted on repeated trials requiring (1) the use of his right hand independently and (2) both hands conjointly.

The test results also yielded evidence suggesting disturbances in the processing and expression of verbal material. For example, he performed very poorly on the Sentence Memory Test, the Verbal Fluency Test, and the Digit Span subtest of the WISC. There was also evidence of finger agnosia bilaterally. In most other respects, however, he seemed to exhibit fairly well developed adaptive skills. Tests involving basic visual–perceptual, visual–spatial, and visual–organizational skills (with the exception of paper-and-pencil tasks) were generally performed in an age-appropriate manner. He appeared to possess an adequate vocabulary (at least as measured by the Vocabulary subtest of the WISC and the PPVT), and he obtained a Full Scale IQ score within the normal range on the WISC.

These test results are consistent with those which we have come to expect from children who are experiencing the debilitating effects of dysfunction at the level of the cerebral hemispheres. This particular test protocol would tend to raise some question regarding the functional integrity of the fronto-temporo-parietal region of the left cerebral hemisphere. Evidence for significantly debilitating dysfunction within other cortical or subcortical systems was neither compelling nor consistent. This sort of hypothesized dysfunction is likely to be most debilitating with respect to the development of language-related skills, and it was felt that he was at some risk for significant difficulties in the formal academic situation.

We recommended that Allan be considered for placement in an academic setting with a relatively low teacher/pupil ratio in which his activities could be closely monitored. Those working with him were urged to exercise caution when providing him with verbal directives. We recommended that verbal instructions be kept relatively short and simple and that he be encouraged to paraphrase or repeat such instructions before engaging in a particular task. When and where it was possible, we recommended that supplementary visual and tactile–kinesthetic cues be used in conjunction with such verbal instructions.

With respect to motor skills, we suggested that an occupational therapy evaluation might be useful to specify more clearly the nature of his motor problems. We recommended that the school program concentrate on activities such as finger painting and cutting and pasting before introducing him to more complex pencil tasks that would require greater manual dexterity. Finally, we suggested that he be reexamined in one year in order to monitor the development of his adaptive skills.

Allan was reexamined when he was 6 years, 5 months of age. The battery was administered over two test sessions, during both of which he was quite talkative and friendly; rapport was easily obtained. However, from time to time his attention wandered and he frequently required encouragement in order to continue with the task at hand. It was clear that his tolerance for frustration was quite low. Allan exhibited a sort of shuffling gait, and he experienced difficulty when required to maintain his balance on one foot. Some minor problems with articulation were also in evidence. In all of this, his level of motoric activity was slightly elevated; indeed, he rarely sat on his chair. There was some question regarding the reliability of some of the results obtained. However, it was felt that his good performances could be viewed with confidence.

Examination of the test results (see Figure 3-4a) revealed that he had made a number of substantial gains in his adaptive skills since our initial examination of him 1½ years previously. He exhibited mild difficulty on tests for speech-sounds perception, memory for sentences of gradually increasing length, and phonemically cued verbal fluency. Otherwise, his psycholinguistic and language-related skills appeared to be relatively well developed. Similarly, most of his performances on tests involving visual–perceptual–organizational skills were within normal limits. However, he did exhibit some difficulty on the WISC Picture Arrangement subtest, which requires the child to arrange pictures into meaningful patterns of relationship. Poor performance on this sort of test sometimes reflects difficulties with respect to the appreciation of cause-and-effect relationships in general. At the same time, it is important to note that he performed quite well on this particular task in our initial examination of him, and thus it was certainly possible that this particular result was unreliable.

He also performed reasonably well on the Underlining Test, which requires rapid visual discrimination of various verbal and nonverbal target stimuli that are interspersed among similar-appearing distractor items. This relatively good performance suggested that, when he was motivated to do so, he was able to make fine visual discriminations, retain these discriminations in memory, and utilize these in conjunction with other skills in an adaptive fashion under time constraints.

On the WRAT he obtained the following grade-equivalent (centile) scores: Reading, 1.6 (66); Spelling, 1.9 (77); Arithmetic, 2.1 (75). These scores were at or above age-appropriate levels, and they appeared to be consistent with his grade placement. Qualitative evaluation of his reading performance suggested an emerging appreciation for sound–symbol relationships, and consequently word-attack skills. His spelling performances indicated that he was able to identify accurately the initial sounds of many of the words that he was asked to spell. On the Arithmetic subtest he seemed to have grasped the basic elements of simple addition and subtraction.

Allan's printing was rather sloppy and uncoordinated. However, in general his simple motor and psychomotor skills appeared to be somewhat improved as compared to our initial assessment of him. Tests for motor speed, static motor steadiness, and speeded eye–hand coordination all yielded normal scores. Some difficulties were noted with respect to kinetic steadiness with his left hand. Hand preference in the initial examination had been quite inconsistent, as exhibited by frequent hand switching when carrying out paper-and-pencil tasks. In the present examination, it was clear that he had developed a preference for his left hand with respect to carrying out most motor activities. In view of the absence of any outstanding motor, psychomotor, or visual–spatial difficulties, his rather poor printing suggested one or both of the following: anxiety surrounding the use of a pencil; problems attendant upon the switching of hand dominance from right to left. The latter appeared to be the more likely alternative.

To summarize, the results of the second evaluation suggested that the majority of Allan's perceptual and cognitive skills were intact. The only exceptions to this were some findings of isolated deficiencies in psycholinguistic skill development and printing, of fine tactile–perceptual deficits, and of some minor difficulties with respect to attentional deployment. The pattern of abilities and deficits obtained would be no more than marginally compatible with the presence of very mild cerebral dysfunction maximally involving the prefrontal regions of the brain. Any inconsistencies noted in the test findings seemed to be a reflection of a waxing and waning of his motivational level and his attentional deployment. These particular dimensions were undoubtedly the most problematic aspects of his behavior for his teachers and parents.

Examination of the results of the Activity Rating Scale (Werry, 1978) revealed that, out of a total of 27 items selected (the mother did not respond to five items having to do with activity level during homework), three "no," 12 "yes—a little bit," and 12 "yes—very much" items were endorsed. Thus, based on this particular rating scale, the mother viewed Allan as exhibiting a certain degree of restlessness and elevated motor activity in a variety of situations in the home, at school, and in other places in the community. Inspection of the PIC did not yield evidence of similar concerns (see Figure 3-4b). The primary dimension of concern on the PIC seemed to center around Allan's intellectual skills and academic achievement. However, in this context it should be noted that the Delinquency Scale was somewhat elevated, at least relative to other clinical scales.

All things considered, the prognosis for Allan seemed favorable. There was every reason to believe that he would meet with success in the

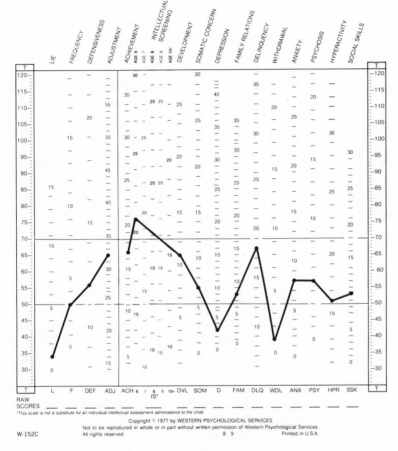

Figure 3-4b. Personality Inventory for Children profile—Case 3-4 (Allan), age 6 years, 5 months.

academic setting. To the extent that he could be assisted to improve his attentional deployment and level of motivation, it seemed reasonable to expect a positive outcome regarding most aspects of day-to-day functioning. With this sort of favorable prognosis in mind (Step 3), we formulated a number of recommendations for his teachers and parents, focusing primarily around ways and means of establishing a well-structured and organized environment for him.

Allan was referred for reevaluation when he was 9 years of age. This referral had been initiated in order to address behavioral difficulties; these were said to include acting out aggressively, failure to maintain his personal appearance, and being generally unmotivated. His classroom teacher reported that Allan was very easily distracted by extraneous stimulation, and she remarked that he tended to work very slowly because of fine motor difficulties. While his oral reading and vocabulary skills were adequate, Allan was said to experience considerable difficulty in drawing inferences and in recalling or verifying details in written comprehension questions. The teacher stated that Allan seemed to have great difficulty in organizing what he wanted to express in writing. With respect to mathematical calculations, he frequently failed to retain and apply steps used with "regrouping" in multiplication and subtraction. It was clear that he experienced difficulty in comprehending which mathematical operation to implement when attempting to solve word problems.

Allan's behavior during the test session was consistent with that which we had observed in our two previous evaluations of him. While he was friendly and cooperative, he was also talkative, and he was prone to distractibility and fatigue, especially during tasks that seemed to be challenging to him. While generally well motivated, he often needed encouragement and support from the examiner in order to obtain adequate responses. He exhibited consistent right–left confusion.

Examination of the test results (see Figure 3-4a) revealed that Allan's adaptive abilities had remained fairly stable since our previous examination of him approximately 2½ years earlier. Some evidence of isolated difficulties remained. For example, he did experience minor problems with respect to short-term visual memory (Target Test) and his performance on the Sentence Memory Test was clearly impaired. Motor strength and speeded eye–hand coordination were below age-expectation bilaterally, and he exhibited some mild tactile–perceptual deficiencies, enunciatory and articulation difficulties, and problems with right–left orientation.

In examining the results of the Activity Rating Scale, it was immediately apparent that Allan's mother now viewed him as much more motorically active than previously: 24 out of a total of 32 items were endorsed as "yes—very much" in reference to motoric and verbal activities in various day-to-day situations. Furthermore, examination of the PIC profile (see Figure 3-4c) completed by the mother revealed significant scale elevations on the Delinquency, Hyperactivity, Social Skills, Anxiety, and Psychosis scales. In short, Allan's mother perceived behaviors in her son that one would typically associate with rather serious acting-out psychopathology.

In subsequent discussion with Allan's mother, it became apparent that she was quite distressed by his apparent lack of concern regarding his personal appearance. She stated that it required great encouragement and effort to get him to wash his face or hair, brush his teeth, etc. She also reported that he seemed to be somewhat preoccupied with sexual matters. He often seemed to become sexually stimulated when watching television, and she stated that he was masturbating quite frequently.

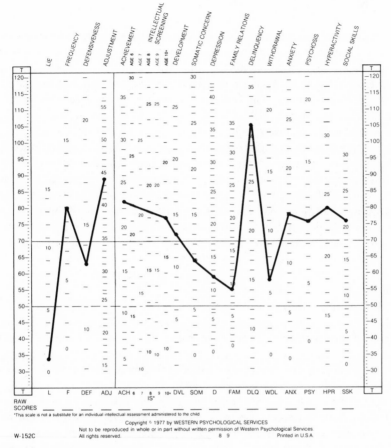

Figure 3-4c. Personality Inventory for Children profile—Case 3-4 (Allan), age 9 years, 0 months.

In summary, it was abundantly clear that, in contrast to the rather favorable prognosis formulated on the basis of our previous evaluation, Allan's behavior had deteriorated significantly to the point of constituting rather serious socioemotional maladjustment. This case clearly illustrates the need to exercise caution in formulating prognostic statements (Step 3). Indeed, the clinical neuropsychologist must be alert to the possibility that evidence of improved functioning in head-injured children between, say, the ages of 5 and 7 years may not be predictive of positive adjustment at later stages of development. This state of affairs is very similar to that illustrated by children who exhibit a so-called "later emerging" learning disability. For a more detailed discussion of this topic, the reader is referred to Case 5-4 (pp. 183–194).

Epilepsy

A detailed presentation of what is currently understood regarding the physiological basis of epilepsy is obviously beyond the scope of this text. Suffice it to say that epilepsy results from abnormal changes in the electrical potential of neurons or clusters of neurons that subsequently discharge in synchrony. The interested reader is referred to Corbett and Trimble (1983), Martin (1981), and Walton (1977) for a more detailed discussion of this complex topic.

So-called "seizures" may accompany a wide variety of neuropathological conditions, including cranio-cerebral trauma, vascular disorders, congenital abnormalities, and endocrine dysfunction, to name but a few. According to Martin (1981), in approximately half of patients no specific etiology is identified. In fact, seizures (although classifiable in terms of various typologies) are typically thought to constitute symptoms rather than diagnoses, since many differences with respect to known and suspected etiologies are ascribed to them. While there have been a number of attempts to classify the condition, none has been entirely satisfactory (Walton, 1977).

Behavioral symptomatology is quite variable, ranging from complete loss of consciousness, associated with chronic contractions and tonic spasms of the muscles, to a very brief loss of awareness (often measured in seconds) associated with minor motor movements such as an upward rolling of the eyes or a myoclonic twitch of the head or upper limbs. In the case of complete loss of consciousness, the symptoms are quite clear. However, the subtle manifestations of the latter type of seizure may elude even the careful observer; indeed, the patient him/herself may be entirely unaware that anything untoward has happened on such occasions.

Treatment of epilepsy very often involves the administration of anticonvulsant medication. In the typical situation, the physician will attempt to control seizures by using a single drug at moderate dosage. Dosage is then increased until seizure control is obtained or indications of toxicity occur. The latter often constitutes a problem, and far too often (perhaps more than is realized) the attending physician is not provided with sufficient information to make reasonable judgments regarding appropriate titration of dosage levels. For any number of reasons, parents and other caretakers may fail to alert the physician to subtle signs of toxicity and the patient may not exhibit symptomatology during the brief time-frame of a routine office visit.

The neuropsychologist may sometimes be of assistance in alerting the attending physician to some of the untoward side effects of such medication. Analysis of the pattern of neuropsychological test results, direct observation of the child during the examination, careful evaluation of behavioral descriptions by school personnel, and a structured interview with the parents can often provide information that is helpful in this regard. Furthermore, one of the advantages of a complete neuropsychological evaluation (our procedure usually requires a minimum of 4 hours) is the opportunity to observe the child's behavior over an extended period of time under a variety of conditions. Thus, data is obtained that is not always possible in a brief office examination. As an illustration of this, we present the following case.

Case 3-5: Louis

Louis, a 9-year-old boy, was referred for neuropsychological evaluation primarily because of academic difficulties. Indeed, his failure to progress academically had resulted in his placement in a Learning Disabilities program. His teacher reported that he seemed to require much individual attention in order to complete assigned tasks, and that he often appeared confused by changes in classroom routine. Academically, he was said to be very weak in phonics, reading, spelling, and other language-related skills. His cursive writing was described as slow and labored, and he performed poorly when required to copy from the blackboard.

In a pretest interview, Louis's mother reported that his behavior in the home was sometimes difficult to manage. According to her, he was inclined to variable moods, having "good and bad days." It was learned that Louis had been diagnosed as epileptic when he was 4½ years of age, and that phenobarbital had been prescribed for him by the attending physician. The mother stated that she was uncomfortable with the medication, since in her view it appeared to render Louis somewhat sluggish and irritable. Except for a bilateral myringotomy at 5 years of age, his medical history was otherwise unremarkable. It was also learned that the parents had separated approximately 1 year earlier. The family unit consisted of Louis, his mother, two older sisters, and an older brother. The father had maintained some contact with the two boys by means of weekend visits.

In the test situation, this youngster was very lethargic and hypoactive, and his tempo of response was very slow. He was extremely taciturn and very reluctant to engage in conversation. His verbal responses tended to be rather terse, and he seemed reluctant to elaborate verbally, even when specifically requested to do so. In short, the boy exhibited a decidedly low level of affect/arousal, and it was often difficult to determine his level of motivation to engage in the tests administered to him.

It was clear from the test findings (see Figure 3-5) that he fared rather poorly on tasks designed to evaluate his verbal, language, and psycholinguistic skills. In addition to a marked discrepancy between Verbal IQ (76) and Performance IQ (97) on the WISC, he also experienced difficulty on the Speech-Sounds Perception, Auditory Closure, and Verbal Fluency Tests. These tests reflect a capacity to discriminate speech sounds and his

Figure 3-5. Neuropsychological test results—
Case 3-5 (Louis).

Age	9 yr, 3 mo
WISC	
Verbal IQ	76
Information	4
Comprehension	3
Arithmetic	5
Similarities	10
Vocabulary	7
Digit Span	8
Performance IQ	97
Picture Completion	12
Picture Arrangement	9
Block Design	12
Object Assembly	7
Coding	8
Full Scale IQ	85
PPVT	
IQ	86
Mental Age	7–6
WRAT	
Reading (grade equiv.)	2.8
Spelling (grade equiv.)	2.5
Arithmetic (grade equiv.)	3.1

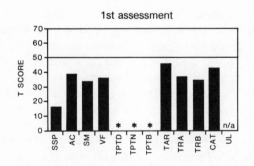

SENSORY-PERCEPTUAL ABILITIES

A Sweep Hearing Test revealed a 30- to 40-db loss at 4,000 and 8,000 Hz with the right ear. With the left ear, a variable level of hearing loss was in evidence, ranging from 30 db at 250 Hz to as high as 60 db at 8,000 Hz. He was able to detect simple auditory stimulation delivered to the right ear, but he failed to detect such stimulation delivered to the left ear under conditions of both unilateral and simultaneous bilateral stimulation. However, when this test was readministered using louder stimuli than are normally necessary, he performed in an error-free fashion. Tests for visual field defects were negative. There was no evidence of tactile imperception, although he suppressed such stimulation delivered to the left hand when the right facial region was simultaneously stimulated (three out of four trials). There was also evidence of bilateral finger agnosia and finger dysgraphesthesia.

APHASIA SCREENING TEST

Louis experienced considerable difficulty on this test. He was unable to spell correctly several relatively simple words (two oral; two written); he misread several words in two simple sentences; he was unable to compute two age-appropriate arithmetic questions (one oral; one written); he experienced difficulty in the enunciation of multi-syllabic words, and there was some evidence of auditory–verbal agnosia.

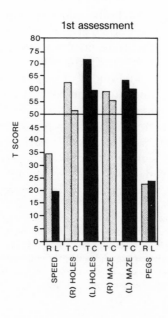

poor performances may in part have been a reflection of hearing loss. Based on the results of the Sweep Hearing Test,[2] it seemed that further investigation of his audiological status was warranted. His score on the WISC Digit Span subtest was low average (five numbers forward and three numbers in reverse order), and he performed poorly on the Sentence Memory Test. The latter result suggested that he was not especially adept at utilizing contextual cues as an aid to the recall of connected discourse. His Reading and Spelling performances on the WRAT were at least 1 year below age-expectancy, and detailed qualitative evaluation of these efforts revealed that his appreciation for sound–symbol relationships was somewhat poor. For example, on the Spelling subtest he responded "wich" to the word "watch," "grol" to the word "grown," and "dris" to the word "dress." His reading responses were characterized by a "best-guess" approach, probably based on the salient visual characteristics of the words presented (e.g., read "awake" as "away," "weather" as "water," "quality" as "question").

In general, he tended to perform more effectively (relative to verbal skills) on measures of visual–perceptual and visual–spatial skills. Indeed, on the surface, he seemed to possess the sort of ability profile that is most often seen in children who are thought to be "learning disabled." However, he did exhibit some rather curious performances that are not at all typical of such youngsters. On the Tactual Performance Test, for example, his physical movements were very slow and he seemed to develop no useful strategy. He was able to place only two (out of a total of six) of the blocks on the initial (right-hand) trial after 15 minutes. Furthermore, no meaningful practice effect was noted on subsequent trials involving the use of his left hand independently and both hands together. These performances were surprisingly deficient, particularly in view of his reasonably good performances on some other tasks involving manipulatory skills (e.g., the Block Design subtest of the WISC). Since the Tactual Performance Test requires that the child be blindfolded, it seemed reasonable to infer that this decreased level of stimulation (and hence arousal) was an important factor in his poor performance.

Evaluation of his motor skills did not reveal any deficiencies in static or kinetic motor steadiness. However, his performance on the Grooved Pegboard Test was very slow, and finger-tapping speed was reduced bilaterally. Thus, his speeded motor and psychomotor performances (i.e., Finger Tapping and Grooved Pegboard Tests) were noticeably inferior to

2. It is our practice to follow the procedures suggested by Northern and Derons (1974) in the administration of the Sweep Hearing Test. In reporting the data, it is our custom to use a term such as ". . . revealed a 40-db hearing loss at a frequency of 2000 Hz." This means that the *minimal* level of loudness that the child was able to detect (respond to) at a frequency of 2000 Hz was 40 db. Thus, stimuli presented at lower decibel levels (e.g., 30 db, 20 db, etc.) yielded no response from the child.

his performances on tasks where time pressure is not a factor (i.e., Holes and Mazes Tests).

There was also evidence of bilateral finger agnosia and finger dysgraphesthesia. A Sweep Hearing Test yielded evidence of a mild to moderate hearing loss with the left ear across the entire range of frequencies tested (250–8,000 Hz), and a mild loss at higher frequencies (4,000–8,000 Hz) with the right ear.

In evaluating the pattern of test results, it seemed quite probable that Louis's major processing deficiencies centered around poor auditory–perceptual and language-related skills. In this regard, it was recommended that he be referred for complete audiological and audiometric evaluations in order to clarify the status of his hearing. At the same time, concern regarding his general lethargy throughout the examination and our awareness of his medical condition raised the possibility that medication side effects were playing a role in some of his poor performances. Further discussion with Louis's parents and school personnel revealed that sluggish, lethargic behavior was quite typical of him in both the home and school situations. Indeed, the father stated quite spontaneously that "sometimes he acts as though he is drunk." (In cases of mild phenobarbital overdosage, the behavior exhibited often resembles alcohol intoxication.) His teacher also reported that in general he performed much more effectively on tasks that required active participation on his part. In contrast, on tasks requiring passive attention he was inclined to be somewhat distractible.

In view of the foregoing, we contacted the family physician and urged the reconsideration of Louis's medication. On the basis of this review, the physician decided to reduce the dosage gradually, with a view to considering alternate medication if seizure control could not be maintained. (This procedure was necessary since abrupt discontinuation of phenobarbital, even when daily dosage is low, may result in a dramatic increase in seizure activity or other very serious complications.)

In any case, some time later, on the advice of a consulting pediatric neurologist, the family physician decided to prescribe another medication that was thought to be more effective in the treatment of Louis's particular form of epilepsy. Subsequent contact with the mother suggested that, as a result of change in his medication, Louis was a more alert, active child. She stated that he did not seem so "dopey" and that his teachers had reported to her that he was much more alert in the classroom. His day-to-day academic performance was said to be improved, although he continued to experience difficulty in language arts.

In conclusion, let us consider what can be learned from this case. Disregarding for the moment Louis's performances on measures of psycholinguistic and language-related skills, it should be clear from the test results that he was capable of formulating effective plans of action on some tasks involving higher-order cognitive skills. For example, he exhibited age-appropriate performances on both the Category Test and on most of the Performance subtests of the WISC. On this basis, we would normally expect equally efficient responses on the Tactual Performance Test. This was clearly not the case. Instead, there was a dramatic disassociation between his level of performance on tasks that involve active participation and stimulation (e.g., responses on the Category Test are followed by a buzzer or a bell) and on those tasks for which stimulation is actually reduced (e.g., the child is blindfolded during administration of the Tactual Performance Test). In this regard, it is interesting to note that his teacher also reported generally better performance in the classroom when Louis was actively involved and stimulated. High dosage of a psychoactive drug such as phenobarbital might well serve to produce such a disassociation.

Thus, careful and detailed analysis of the neuropsychological test results led to the very specific recommendation that the child's level of medication be reviewed and, if possible, reduced. Subsequent changes in medication did seem to produce positive results, at least as observed by Louis's mother and his classroom teacher. However, it would seem quite probable that Louis would continue to experience deficits in his psycholinguistic and language-related skills, even after these positive gains are stabilized. If so, a neuropsychological reassessment of the child would be of benefit in clarifying the nature of his possible "learning disability" so that appropriate intervention could proceed on that front (see Chapter 5 for details regarding such interventions).

Neuropsychological evaluation often leads to recommendations for further medical evaluation. This course of action is reasonable when there is some suspicion of, for example, a metabolic disorder, a seizure condition, or some other sort of neurological problem. It has been our experience that, to the extent that the neuropsychologist can provide reasonable support for further medical investigation of the child, physicians are ready and willing to cooperate in arranging for such tests as might be suitably recommended.

Case 3-6: Jonas

As an example of this sort of activity, we present the case of Jonas, a 7½-year-old boy who had been referred for a neuropsychological assessment because of extreme distractibility, inattentiveness, and inappropriate verbalization in the classroom. With respect to the latter problem, his teacher had frequently observed what is best described as "tangential" thinking. His teacher stated: "Often Jonas's mind appears flooded with thoughts which, to those around him, seem unconnected and irrelevant." He was observed to echo or repeat his own utterances and he sometimes interrupted classroom activities with irrelevant remarks or questions. As a result of this behavior, he was seen by the school psychologist for a personality evaluation. On the basis of responses to projective tests, the psychologist reported the following: "Jonas views himself as helpless and easily overwhelmed by his environment. He is characterized as having poor inner controls associated with impulsive and disjointed thoughts, feelings, and reactions." A psychiatric consultation was sought with a view to determining the possibility that the child was experiencing a neurological disorder or alternatively, if the behavior reflected some sort of socio-emotional problem. The psychiatric opinion subsequently rendered was "specific delay in development related to minimal brain dysfunction." Medication (Mellaril) was prescribed for the boy, and it was also suggested that he be seen for neuropsychological evaluation.

In the test situation, Jonas was extremely verbal, although his conversation tended to be "off topic" and often unrelated to the task at hand. He seemed easily distracted by extraneous stimulation. Indeed, on occasion his own verbal utterances served to distract him from the presenting task. He was overly active, constantly moving about in the examining chair, squirming, swinging his feet, and so forth. On several occasions he exhibited what appeared to be a rather brief involuntary head tremor. On two occasions Jonas exhibited what can best be described as a "body shudder." These were very brief events, lasting only several seconds, and they appeared to be entirely involuntary. While it was difficult to judge his level of effort and motivation throughout the testing session, he was not antagonistic or unfriendly and he did create the impression of wanting to cooperate with the examiner.

The results of the examination (see Figure 3-6a) revealed a rather inconsistent pattern of performance. For example, he performed reasonably well on the Picture Completion, Block Design, and Object Assembly subtests of the WISC; in contrast, the Matching Pictures Test and the Target Test proved to be mildly problematic for him. His drawings of simple geometric forms on the Aphasia Screening Test (see Figure 3-6b) contained some visual–spatial distortions. While in general this right-handed boy's simple motor and psychomotor skills (with the exception of simple motor speed with each hand) appeared to be intact, he did exhibit some poor graphomotor performances. He also did somewhat poorly with his left (nondominant) hand and with both hands together on the Tactual Performance Test. With respect to measures of auditory–perceptual, psycholinguistic, and language-related skills, especially deficient performances were noted on the Comprehension and Information subtests of the WISC, and on the Sentence Memory Test. These deficiencies were exhibited within the context of relatively good performances on the Auditory Closure, Auditory Analysis, and Speech-Sounds Perception Tests.

Figure 3-6a. Neuropsychological test results—
Case 3-6 (Jonas).

Age	7 yr, 6 mo
WISC	
Verbal IQ	81
Information	6
Comprehension	3
Arithmetic	7
Similarities	10
Vocabulary	8
Digit Span	8
Performance IQ	96
Picture Completion	13
Picture Arrangement	7
Block Design	10
Object Assembly	13
Coding	4
Full Scale IQ	87
PPVT	
IQ	85
Mental Age	6–3
WRAT	
Reading (grade equiv.)	3.0
Spelling (grade equiv.)	2.6
Arithmetic (grade equiv.)	2.6

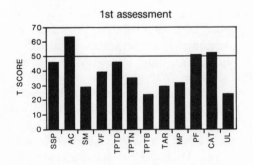

SENSORY-PERCEPTUAL ABILITIES
Performance on a Sweep Hearing Test was negative. There was no evidence of tactile, visual, or auditory imperception or suppression. He was able to discriminate simple shapes on the basis of tactile analysis in an error-free manner. However, there was evidence of mild bilateral finger agnosia and finger dysgraphesthesia.

APHASIA SCREENING TEST
Jonas encountered no difficulty whatsoever on this test.

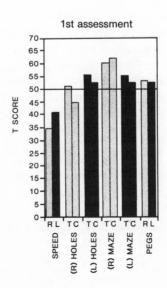

1st assessment

Figure 3-6b. Aphasia Screening Test drawings of Jonas—first assessment.

This rather variable and inconsistent pattern of performance is difficult to explain from a purely ability-based point of view. Often this sort of inconsistency is seen in children who are experiencing some form of socioemotional difficulty. It also seemed possible that Jonas was experiencing some sort of "absence" or seizure-like condition, one consequence of which might be periodic episodes of disorientation.

In any case, it was decided to meet with the parents in order to determine if additional information could be obtained that might shed light on this situation. During the interview, it was learned that an older brother had been recently diagnosed as having petit mal epilepsy. Medication (Dilantin) had been prescribed for him, and according to the parents this treatment was effective in the control of his seizures. The father also stated that there had been some suspicion that he (the father) was potentially epileptic, although this had never been confirmed by medical diagnosis. We discovered that the family was no longer administering the Mellaril which had been prescribed for Jonas; they had observed what they considered to be some untoward side effects, namely, that he was very drowsy and that on several occasions he had fallen asleep in school.

It was recommended to the parents that an electroencephalographic evaluation and neurological consultation be arranged. Although there was some resistance to these suggestions (from the father in particular, who expressed the view that there could be no possible connection between Jonas's medical condition and his problems at school), the parents agreed that this course of action would be in Jonas's best interest. The results of an electroencephalographic examination were interpreted as indicative of petit mal epilepsy, and a trial of phenobarbital was prescribed for Jonas by the attending physician.

Analysis of the test results in this case is instructive. Inconsistency was the most salient feature in the test protocol of this child. In other words, it was difficult to explain, from a purely ability-based point of view, how Jonas could perform so efficiently on measures such as the Picture Completion, Block Design, and Object Assembly subtests of the WISC, the Grooved Pegboard Test, and the Progressive Figures Test in the context of such poor performances on the Underlining Test, the Tactual Performance Test, and the Matching Pictures Test. Such inconsistency was also obvious on measures of psycholinguistic and verbal skills.

In such cases, we have often discovered, following further investigation, that socioemotional factors are playing a significant role in the child's presenting problems. At the same time, one must also consider the possibility that the child is experiencing periodic bouts of disorientation such as might be observed when subclinical seizures are occurring. As subsequent medical investigation revealed, the latter inference proved to be the more reasonable one in Jonas's case.

In concluding this section on seizure disorders, one point should be emphasized. In our clinical experience, there is no particular pattern of abilities and deficits that is characteristic of the epileptic child; this is illustrated in the cases of Louis and Jonas. In addition, a recent investigation by Camfield, Gates, Ronen, Camfield, Ferguson, and MacDonald (1984) would seem to lend some empirical support to this clinical inference. In this study, 27 children with a seizure focus restricted to either the right or left temporal lobe (as determined by EEG) underwent complete neurological and neuropsychological evaluations. The findings revealed no distinctive pattern of cognitive deficits in either the right temporal or left temporal groups. Furthermore, examination of individual children's test results revealed no clear relationship between severity of seizure symptoms and cognitive deficits. In other words, some youngsters with relatively severe seizure manifestations (e.g., frequent seizures that were poorly controlled by medication) exhibited little in the way of significant information-processing deficits. In contrast, some other children who had relatively mild symptoms were quite impaired in terms of their level of intellectual and cognitive functioning. These results suggest strongly that the prediction of cognitive outcome solely on the basis of the seizure disorder experienced by the child is not a useful enterprise.

Intracranial tumor

Recent advances in anesthesia and neurosurgical techniques have resulted in improved outcome for many patients afflicted with intracranial space-occupying lesions (Walton, 1977). Furthermore, the introduction of steroid drugs has been of immense benefit as a means of reducing intracranial pressure (Weinstein, Toy, Jaffe, & Goldberg, 1973). Radiotherapy has also played a significant therapeutic role in the treatment of tumors as well as serving to produce remission of symptoms in patients with intracranial metastases. This sort of treatment does, however, have side effects and with high radiation dosage, pathological degeneration of neurons and white matter has been observed.

Be that as it may, more children and adults are surviving such insults to the central nervous system than was previously the case. However, these patients are often left with rather serious and relatively permanent adaptive deficiencies. While applauding the efforts and success in prolonging life, it is also necessary to examine carefully the quality of such survival. In this regard, the neuropsychologist can often be of assistance to the patient, to his/her family, and to other professionals dealing with the child, especially with respect to formulating rehabilitation and treatment plans. If our recent experience is any indication, it would seem likely that future advances in the medical treatment of such patients will produce even greater demand for neuropsychological consultation of this type. As an example of the role that can be played by the neuropsychologist in the rehabilitation and care of such patients, we present the case of Joan.

Case 3-7: Joan

At the age of 8½ years, Joan was admitted to hospital with presenting symptoms of headache and vomiting. Investigation revealed a posterior fossa tumor, with pathologic diagnosis of medulloblastoma. The surgical treatment employed involved subtotal removal of the tumor and placement of a shunt. Following surgery, she was treated with radiotherapy and chemotherapy (Vincristine, CCNU, and Prednisone). Two months later, she developed seizures, which fortunately responded well to medication (Dilantin). Joan recovered slowly, but in a positive direction, over the next

18 months, at which time she experienced shunt obstruction. This was successfully treated on an emergency basis, but she was left comatose for approximately 2 days. This was followed by a period of complete paralysis, as well as loss of bowel and bladder control. During the next 3 to 4 weeks, she gradually regained control of these functions. Several months later, she was found to have hypothyroidism (thought to be due to primary thyroid failure) and L-thyroxin was prescribed. Subsequent endocrinological investigation, because of her short stature, revealed growth hormone failure, and appropriate medication was instituted. Finally, she was seen in the Cardiology Unit because of a heart murmur and she was found to have mitral valve prolapse. Prophylactic antibiotics were prescribed.

Her clinical history prior to the manifestation of her neurological disease was unremarkable. She was described as an excellent student, in the top 10% of her class through the third grade. Because of her subsequent neurological disease and attendant complications, Joan missed in excess of 300 days from school during the next 4 years. During this period of time she was seen regularly by a psychologist, who was attempting to assist her to adapt to her difficulties, which included, among other things, complete hair loss as a result of the radiation treatment. In any case, it was the psychologist's view that Joan was exhibiting some evidence of deterioration in her cognitive functioning. In addition, it was reported that she was experiencing problems with her academic program. Thus, a neuropsychological assessment was requested in order to obtain a more accurate picture of her level of adaptive functioning and to assist in the formulation of remedial and treatment plans in the school setting. At the time of the initial neuropsychological assessment, she was 12 years, 8 months of age. She was attending a regular Grade 7 class on a half-day basis. The school also provided home tutoring 2 mornings per week. It was hoped that she could complete the Grade 7–8 program over a 3-year time span.

In a pretest interview with the parents, it became evident that Joan's mother was not entirely pleased with the academic program provided for her daughter. It was clear that the mother had rather high academic expectations for her daughter. Joan's father, on the other hand, seemed much more realistic regarding any limitations that she might have. These differing expectations persisted in our subsequent contacts with the parents.

Testing was completed in two half-day sessions. On both occasions Joan was very pleasant, cooperative, and friendly. It was often observed that she did not appear to understand task requirements; she required a great deal of reinstruction at such times. Joan stated that she was having some difficulty in hearing verbal instructions; we were aware that she was being monitored because of a possible sensory–neural hearing loss, which was thought to be prominent with the left ear, and that she was being considered for the use of hearing aids. Although she did become fatigued toward the end of the sessions, it was clear that she was putting forth good effort and trying to cooperate as much as possible with the examiner.

Before considering the pattern of test results, we should first of all provide some additional observations regarding her problems with respect to her auditory acuity. On a Sweep Hearing Test, the following hearing losses were noted. Testing of the right ear yielded a 35-db loss at 2,000 Hz, 45 db at 4,000 Hz, and 60 db at 8,000 Hz. With the left ear, there was a 50-db loss at 500 Hz, no response at 70 db for 1,000, 2,000, and 8,000 Hz, and a 55-db loss at 4,000 Hz. Furthermore, on tests for auditory imperception and suppression, it was necessary to repeat all trials with louder stimuli than are usually required. Under such conditions she was able to detect simple unilateral stimulation presented to each ear. However, she tended to suppress such stimulation delivered to the left ear under conditions of bilateral presentation. Furthermore, it was abundantly clear from her responses to the various tests of auditory–perceptual skills that are delivered by means of a tape recorder (Speech-Sounds Perception Test, Auditory Closure Test, Sentence Memory Test) that she was experiencing considerable difficulty in discriminating auditory stimuli. In such instances, it was necessary to increase the volume of the tape recorder well beyond the level that is usually required. This increase in volume tended to distort the quality of the tape, and thus both the Auditory Closure and Sentence Memory Tests were also administered orally. This procedure served to improve her performance quite substantially, and we have reported her (best) results under these administrations.

In any case, evaluation of the quality of her responses on various measures of auditory–perceptual abilities indicated that she was not always hearing the stimuli accurately. At the same time, it was clear from evaluation of her Reading and Spelling performances on the WRAT that she did have some appreciation of the phonological structure of words. For example, many of her misspellings were of the phonetically accurate variety, and she appeared to utilize (with some success) a phonetic word-attack strategy in her attempts to decode longer and more complex words. Thus, even if we were unaware of Joan's medical history and were uninformed regarding her hearing difficulties, we would be drawn to the conclusion that her hearing loss and subsequent auditory–perceptual difficulties must have occurred at a relatively late stage of development that followed upon a fairly normal course of auditory–perceptual development.

Further examination of the initial test profile (see Figure 3-7) revealed that Joan's visual–spatial, visual–organizational, and nonverbal problem-solving skills were rather poor for her chronological age. Especially noteworthy in this regard were her deficient performances on the WISC Picture Completion and Object Assembly subtests and on the Target Test. Her performances on the Trail Making Test, Part B, especially in comparison to the score obtained on Part A, suggested that she experienced difficulty when required to shift psychological "set" on the basis of task demands. Her somewhat better performance on the Category Test (low average) may be an indication that she was capable of performing more effectively when informational feedback was provided.

While one might argue that her difficulty in the reception of verbal instructions was a component of the aforementioned performances, it should be clear that her problems with these tasks went well beyond those that would normally be expected as a result of poor auditory acuity. Indeed, it would seem quite probable that her primary difficulty in these problem-solving and otherwise complex situations was her relative inability to understand and/or synthesize all relevant elements of the task at hand. In short, it appeared as though her higher-order cognitive skills were quite impaired in a fashion that could not be explained entirely on the basis of her hearing loss.

Comparison of the performances on the two sides of the body on both the sensory-perceptual and simple motor and psychomotor measures did not reveal a consistently lateralized pattern of deficiencies. With respect to motor skills, it was clear that simple motor speed, strength of grip, and complex psychomotor abilities were deficient bilaterally. However, motor steadiness, within both the kinetic and static dispositions, was actually superior to the performances of most children her age. In view of her medical history, the excellent steadiness skills which she exhibited were somewhat surprising. This evidence, in addition to (1) her ability to benefit from repeated trials on the Tactual Performance Test (examination of the Tactual Performance Test raw score data reveals a positive practice effect over the three trials; this is not reflected in the T scores shown in Figure 3-7), (2) the absence of sensory imperception and suppression (except within the auditory realm), (3) her relatively good drawings of simple geometric forms, and (4) a consistent pattern of poor performances on more complex neuropsychological measures in the context of better performances on simpler measures, argues strongly against the presence of some type of acute lesion (subcortical or cortical) confined to a circumscribed area of the brain. Rather, the test results are consistent with the presence of rather diffuse and fairly static dysfunction at the level of the cerebral hemispheres.

A conference was convened with the parents and school personnel in an effort to develop a special program specifically designed to meet Joan's needs. In presenting our recommendations, we emphasized the requirement for a setting that would place a premium upon systematic, step-by-step instruction. Although it was necessary to bear in mind Joan's hearing difficulty, we advised that verbal directives (possibly including written instructions) would be the best starting point in teaching a particular task or skill. Following this, she should be provided with visual demonstrations and, finally, monitored practice.

Figure 3-7. Neuropsychological test results—Case 3-7 (Joan).

Age	12 yr, 8 mo	14 yr, 0 mo	16 yr, 4 mo
WISC			*WAIS*
Verbal IQ	85	79	79
Information	6	4	4
Comprehension	8	6	3
Arithmetic	6	4	3
Similarities	10	10	9
Vocabulary	8	7	5
Digit Span	8	8	9
Performance IQ	75	65	74
Picture Completion	5	4	6
Picture Arrangement	7	4	6
Block Design	8	6	5
Object Assembly	6	5	7
Coding	6	6	(Digit Symbol) 5
Full Scale IQ	78	70	75
PPVT			
IQ	85	81	75
Mental Age	10–7	10–5	10–5
WRAT			
Reading (grade equiv.)	5.4	6.8	5.9
Spelling (grade equiv.)	3.9	4.8	4.1
Arithmetic (grade equiv.)	3.3	3.6	2.7

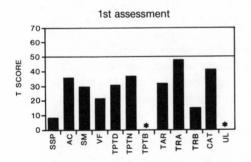

1st assessment

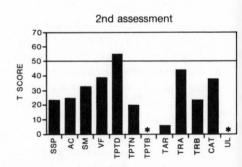

2nd assessment

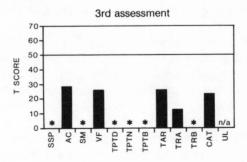

3rd assessment

SENSORY-PERCEPTUAL ABILITIES

In all three assessments of Joan, it was clear that auditory acuity was problematic. She appeared to have a rather severe (50 to 80 db) hearing loss with the left ear in the frequency range of 500 to 8,000 Hz. With the right ear, higher frequency (2,000 to 8,000 Hz) difficulties were noted, with the loss ranging from 40 to 80 db. Acuity for lower tones (250 to 1,000 Hz) appeared to be approximately normal. These results did not change in any significant way over the three testings (see also text). There was no evidence of visual field defects in any of the examinations. Although she experienced some bilateral difficulties (somewhat more pronounced on trials with her right hand) on the Fingertip Number Recognition Test in the initial examination, she performed in a normal manner on other tests of simple and more complex tactile- and kinesthetic-perceptual abilities.

APHASIA SCREENING TEST

In all three testings, Joan performed adequately on the spelling, reading, naming, and auditory-verbal agnosia items. However, she consistently encountered mild difficulty when required to enunciate complex multisyllabic words, and she was unable to compute correctly the arithmetic items. There was no evidence of constructional dyspraxia in any of the examinations.

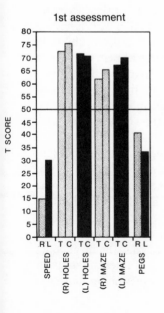

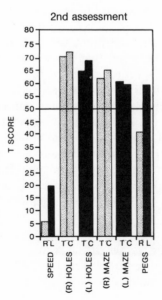

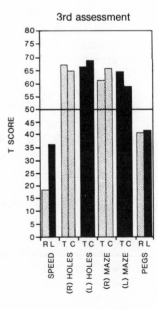

After a series of negotiations, it was decided that she would be best served by placement in a special residential treatment program. Following approximately 1 year in this program, we arranged to evaluate her (at which time she was 14 years of age) in order to monitor any changes in her ability structure. It was thought that this information would prove helpful in terms of modifying her program in a manner consistent with her level of development.

The results of the reassessment revealed that the general configuration of neuropsychological test results had not substantially changed since our previous examination of her. It was clear that Joan continued to suffer from rather generalized impairment of her cognitive abilities. She performed no better during this testing session than she had previously on the majority of the subtests of the WISC. In fact, lower scaled scores were obtained on all subtests of the Performance section, except the Coding subtest. This would suggest that she was experiencing difficulty in consolidating and utilizing general forms of information gained through everyday experiences. We also noted during our evaluation that she exhibited some periodic lapses of attention on measures that required sustained concentration. This raised some question as to whether or not she was experiencing some form of seizure disorder. Thus, we recommended that she be examined by a pediatric neurologist.

We met subsequently with personnel from the residential program in order to discuss our findings. Joan's teacher reported that she was working at a Grade 5 level in reading, spelling, and mathematics. However, the teacher also pointed out that her reading comprehension was weak relative to her word-recognition skills. While she was exhibiting some improvements in mathematics, she seemed to need excessive drill for the successful completion of calculations and simple word problems. She was described as rather quiet in the classroom, but it was felt that she had been exhibiting greater confidence of late, and that she was asserting herself with peers when required. With respect to residential routines, Joan had been somewhat uncooperative initially, but there were signs of definite improvement during the previous few months. It was the impression of those working with her that she was beginning to enjoy some of the social events, peer interactions, and other aspects of residential life.

Among our general recommendations, we emphasized the need to provide this child with as much structure and routine as possible. It was explained that she would require additional help as academic tasks became more complex. While she seemed very capable of benefiting from overlearning (by means of drill and repetition), those activities that required the integration and synthesis of information would probably continue to prove to be problematic for her. It was recommended that she be encouraged and trained to utilize verbal mediation strategies in her attempts to deal with the more complex aspects of day-to-day functioning and academic tasks.

A final reevaluation of Joan was undertaken when she was 16 years, 4 months of age. Several months prior to our assessment she had been discharged from the residential program and had entered a local secondary school, where she was enrolled in a special program.

At first blush, the test results (see Figure 3-7) would seem to indicate considerable deterioration in her adaptive skills. However, it should be noted that because of her age she was administered the adult versions of the Speech-Sounds Perception Test, Trail Making Test (Parts A and B), Category Test, and Tactual Performance Test. Therefore, we would expect relatively poorer levels of performance, given the generally greater complexity of the adult versions of these tests. Furthermore, evaluating her performances on measures of psycholinguistic abilities was complicated by the fact that her hearing remained impaired. She was virtually deaf in her left ear and despite a hearing aid auditory acuity with her right ear was somewhat less than optimal. Indeed, we learned that efforts to stabilize her hearing had thus far been relatively unsuccessful.

As reflected in her relatively stable motor, psychomotor, and sensory–perceptual (except auditory acuity) abilities, it was clear that overall there had been little significant change in Joan's adaptive ability structure. Furthermore, her level of psychometric intelligence, as measured by the Wechsler Adult Intelligence Scale (Wechsler, 1955), did not appear to be significantly different from that obtained in previous examinations using the WISC. Thus, at 16 years of age, Joan's primary problem centered around her marked difficulties in dealing with complex higher-order cognitive tasks. In contrast, she seemed quite competent when tasks involved only relatively concrete material that could be assimilated through overlearning and practice.

We arranged to meet with Joan's secondary school teachers in order to discuss with them any possible difficulties which they were encountering with her. Almost uniformly, their concerns centered around Joan's disorganized approach to tasks. She seemed to handle routines fairly well, especially when there was some opportunity for her to practice. However, any change in routine resulted in agitation, frustration, and confused behavior. Furthermore, it was felt that Joan did not always recognize that she was encountering problems, and as a consequence rarely sought individual assistance from teachers or other students. In short, while she was managing the academic requirements of her program quite effectively, there was considerable difficulty in terms of dealing with the more unstructured aspects of secondary school life. Based on our recommendations, it was decided to suspend her physical education program in favor of one-to-one daily sessions with a counselor. The purpose of these sessions would be to assist her to generate verbal recipes designed to deal with some of the problems that she confronted on a day-to-day basis. To provide some guidelines for these activities, we suggested the use of the "Think Aloud" program (Camp & Bash, 1981). It was also arranged for one of our staff psychologists to meet on a bimonthly basis with Joan and her counselor in order to monitor her progress in this and related programs.

This case illustrates the sort of adaptive difficulties that are frequently observed in school-aged children who experience an intracranial tumor or other space-occupying lesion, and who have undergone the varieties of therapy that are typically employed in such situations. However, the complexity of her medical history does not allow us to make confident inferences with regard to specific and direct effects of her neurological conditions. Indeed, one would be hard-pressed to distinguish the particular effects associated with the tumor itself, the consequences of Joan's subsequent shunt obstruction, the effects of radiotherapy, or the contributions of secondary pathology (e.g., endocrine dysfunction). However, it is clear that the cumulative effects of the various insults to the CNS that she sustained had resulted in significant impairment in Joan's higher-order cognitive functioning and adaptive capacities. It was these deficiencies that needed to be focused upon in her programs of remedial intervention.

As is illustrated in the case discussion, analysis of the neuropsychological test results does provide clear evidence that Joan's premorbid cognitive and adaptive skills were quite intact. The results of subsequent neuropsychological evaluations would seem to indicate that her abilities and skills failed to develop much (if at all) beyond a level consistent with her chronological age at the time of neurological insult. One would suspect that, had Joan experienced a similar insult to her brain at an earlier stage of development, the consequences in terms of her level of adaptive functioning would have been much more serious. In any case, the neuropsychological test results did provide information that was useful in the development of programs designed to assist her to compensate for her adaptive limitations.

It is very difficult to formulate an accurate long-term prognosis for this youngster. However, in the absence of any further complications or recurrence of her brain tumor, there is no compelling reason to believe that her neuropsychological status will deteriorate. In our opinion, Joan should be viewed optimistically and encouraged to complete her education, to develop her social skills, to find meaningful employment, and ultimately to lead an independent, productive life.

Summary and conclusions

In this chapter, we have examined the neuropsychological profiles of six children known to be experiencing the effects of specific neuropathological conditions. It should be recognized that the pattern of test scores in each case, while reflecting the specific condition, should not be viewed as necessarily typical. Unlike the case discussed in Chapter 2, the patterns of perceptual and cognitive skills associated with the neurological conditions discussed in this chapter showed considerable variability. Indeed, it is quite likely that considerable interindividual variability will be exhibited by children with the same neurological syndromes. Be that as it may, we will conclude by attempting to summarize some of the major points or principles illustrated by the six cases.

1. It is clear that substantial insult to the young brain is very likely to result in some long-term deficiencies in adaptive abilities. However, this assertion does not carry the implication that recovery from and/or adaptation to early brain insults do not occur. Nor does it imply that the development of abilities ordinarily ceases after such insult. Quite the contrary: Some degree of recovery, adaptation, and development are the rule, rather than the exception, following early brain insult. The principal issue in this context is the *degree* to which the various adaptational capacities of the child can be expected to develop, and this is the focus of concern for the child-clinical neuropsychologist.

2. In the absence of the information that the child-clinical neuropsychologist can often provide, it is often the case that parents, teachers, psychologists, and other professionals working with the child are led to believe that complete recovery of function has occurred when in fact the condition has merely stabilized, at least from a neuropsychological point of view. In some cases, the untoward effects are not readily apparent in the young child because the higher-order systems that have been compromised are not yet required for the developmental tasks in which a particular child is expected to engage. It is not unusual to discover deficits at some later stage of development that would not necessarily have been predicted on the basis of a cursory assessment at an earlier point in time. This suggests that it is essential to carry out a comprehensive neuropsychological evaluation of any child who has experienced significant neurological disease early in life, and to continue to monitor the subsequent development of that child's skills and abilities.

3. We should like to emphasize the point that diagnosis per se is rarely the primary objective of a neuropsychological evaluation. This is not to suggest that such diagnostic inferences may not be helpful. Indeed, such an effort on the part of the neuropsychologist may well lead to the discovery of other brain-related difficulties that have not previously been identified via specific medical procedures. However, all too often we have observed clinicians who feel satisfied merely because they have, as it were, identified the lesion, or, stated another way, interpreted test material consistent with neurological findings. For the child-clinical neuropsychologist, this exercise constitutes at most only one important beginning point. The much more important and demanding requirement is to utilize the test results in a manner that will lead to the development of a realistic treat-

ment plan designed to lessen the impact of adaptive deficits and to assist the youngster to take advantage of his/her intact realms of functioning.

4. As several of the cases in this chapter demonstrate, treatment of the child suffering from neurological disease very typically involves an attempt to utilize intact realms of functioning in order to assist the child to compensate for particular adaptive deficits. This approach is not intended to imply that rehabilitational efforts aimed directly at specific deficits are not warranted. For example, during the acute stages following closed head injury, it seems likely that such efforts do pay dividends in terms of recovery of function. Although it is very difficult to distinguish precisely the specific treatment effects from the "natural" process of healing, it would seem prudent to make a concerted effort to attack the deficit in a concerted, sensitive fashion. Indeed, those working with and planning for such children would do well to adopt, as a working hypothesis (that will hopefully be tested at some point), that the stimulation afforded by various direct treatment methods does play a positive role in recovery.

5. As has been pointed out in Chapter 1 and will be emphasized throughout this text, it is as or more important to know what the brain-impaired child can do as it is to know what he/she cannot do. Thus, evaluation aimed only at the delineation of deficient areas of functioning is quite insufficient. It is very difficult, if not impossible, to formulate meaningful treatment and remediational plans and goals in the absence of specific knowledge regarding the skills and abilities possessed by the brain-impaired child. In addition, some notion of the circumstances (i.e., with and without therapeutic intervention) under which he/she can be expected to be able to employ these skills and abilities in an adaptive fashion is very desirable.

6. It is extremely important to consider parental attitudes as well as other aspects of the social milieu in developing a treatment plan. For example, treatment may need to include ongoing supportive counseling in order to assist family members to develop a realistic attitude regarding the potentials of their brain-impaired child. As in the case of Maurice, there may be considerable affect associated with the child's condition, and as a consequence, parent(s) may be inclined to deny obvious symptoms or problems in the child's attempts at adaptation. It is crucial that these issues be identified and dealt with properly to ensure that appropriate treatment goals are not unwittingly sabotaged.

7. Finally, the clinician should always carefully evaluate how neuropsychological information is communicated to others working with the child. While we would never advocate avoiding full discussion of the child's presenting problem, it has been our practice to focus primarily on what the child can and cannot do, the conditions that would be likely to maximize effective coping, and the implications of the foregoing with

respect to treatment planning. The specter of "brain damage" often leads to inappropriate inferences by those who are not trained in the neurosciences. Speculation regarding possible neuropathological processes in children is rarely of value to those who are required to deal with the child on a practical, day-to-day basis. However, concrete aspects of the prognosis may be of considerable interest and importance to caretakers in their ongoing interactions with, and treatment of, the child.

References

Black, P., Blumer, D., Wellner, A. M., & Walker, A. E. (1971). The head-injured child: Time-course of recovery, with implications for rehabilitation. *Proceedings of an international symposium on head injuries* (pp. 131–137). Edinburgh: Churchill Livingstone.

Brown, G., Chadwick, O., Shaffer, D., Rutter, M., & Traub, M. (1981). A prospective study of children with head injuries: III. Psychiatric sequelae. *Psychological Medicine, 11,* 63–78.

Camfield, P. R., Gates, R., Ronen, G., Camfield, C., Ferguson, A., & MacDonald, G. W. (1984). Comparison of cognitive ability, personality profile and school success in epileptic children with pure right versus left temporal lobe EEG foci. *Annals of Neurology, 15,* 122–126.

Camp, B. W., & Bash, M. S. (1981). *Think aloud: Increasing social and cognitive skills.* Champaign, IL: Research Press.

Chadwick, O., Rutter, M., Shaffer, D., & Shrout, P. E. (1981). A prospective study of children with head injuries: IV. Specific cognitive deficits. *Journal of Clinical Neuropsychology, 3,* 101–120.

Corbett, J. A., & Trimble, M. R. (1983). Epilepsy and anticonvulsant medication. In M. Rutter (Ed.), *Developmental neuropsychiatry* (pp. 112–129). New York: Guilford.

Craft, A. W. (1972). Head injury in children. In P. J. Vinken & G. W. Bruyn (Eds.), *Handbook of clinical neurology* (pp. 445–458). New York: Elsevier.

Ewing-Cobbs, L., Fletcher, J. M., & Levin, H. (1985). Neuropsychological sequelae following pediatric head injury. In M. Ylvisaker (Ed.), *Head injury rehabilitation: Children and adolescents* (pp. 71–89). San Diego: College-Hill.

Flach, J., & Malmros, R. (1972). A long-term follow-up of children with severe head injuries. *Scandinavian Journal of Rehabilitation Medicine, 4,* 9–15.

Goldman, P. S. (1976). The role of experience in recovery of function following orbital prefrontal lesions in infant monkeys. *Nerupsychologia, 14,* 401–412.

Goldman, P. S., & Galkin, T. W. (1978). Prenatal removal of frontal association cortex in the fetal rhesus monkey: Anatomical and functional consequences in postnatal life. *Brain Research, 152,* 451–485.

Hendrick, E. B., Harwood-Nash, D. C. F., & Hudson, A. R. (1964). Head injuries in children: A survey of 4465 cases at the Hospital for Sick Children, Toronto, Canada. *Clinical Neurosurgery, 11,* 46–59.

Jamison, D. L., & Kaye, H. H. (1974). Accidental head injury in children. *Archives of Disease in Childhood, 49,* 376–381.

Jennett, B. (1972). Head injuries in children. *Developmental Medicine and Child Neurology, 14,* 137–147.

Klonoff, H. (1971). Head injuries in children: Predisposing factors, accident conditions, and sequelae. *American Journal of Public Health, 61*, 2405–2417.

Klonoff, H., & Low, M. (1974). Disordered brain function in young children and early adolescents: Neuropsychological and electroencephalographic correlates. In R. M. Reitan & L. A. Davison (Eds.), *Clinical neuropsychology: Current status and applications* (pp. 121–178). New York: Wiley.

Klonoff, H., & Paris, R. (1974). Immediate, short-term, and residual effects of acute head injuries in children: Neuropsychological and neurological correlates. In R. M. Reitan & C. A. Davison (Eds.), *Clinical neuropsychology: Current status and applications* (pp. 179–210). New York: Wiley.

Knights, R. M., & Norwood, J. A. (1980). *Revised smoothed normative data on the neuropsychological test battery for children.* Ottawa: Author.

Levin, H. S., Benton, A. L., & Grossman, R. G. (1982). *Neurobehavioral consequences of closed head injury.* New York: Oxford.

Luria, A. R. (1973). *The working brain: An introduction to neuropsychology.* New York: Basic Books.

Luria, A. R. (1980). *Higher cortical functions in man.* New York: Basic Books.

Manheimer, D. I., & Menninger, G. D. (1967). Personality characteristics of the child accident repeater. *Child Development, 38*, 491–513.

Martin, J. H. (1981). Properties of cortical neurons, the EEG, and the mechanisms of epilepsy. In E. R. Kandel & J. H. Schwartz (Eds.), *Principles of neural science* (pp. 461–471). New York:: Elsevier/North-Holland.

Milhorat, T. H. (1972). *Hydrocephalus and cerebrospinal fluid.* Baltimore: Williams & Wilkins.

Northern, J. L., & Derons, M. P. (1974). *Hearing in children.* Baltimore: Williams & Wilkins.

Partington, M. W. (1960). The importance of accident-proneness in the aetiology of head injuries in childhood. *Archives of Disease in Childhood, 35*, 215–223.

Polinko, P. R., Barin, J. J., Leger, D., & Bachman, K. M. (1985). Working with the family. In M. Ylvisaker (Ed.), *Head injury rehabilitation: Children and adolescents* (pp. 93–115). San Diego: College-Hill.

Rosner, J., & Simon, D. P. (1970). *Auditory Analysis Test: An initial report.* Pittsburgh: University of Pittsburgh Learning Research and Development Center.

Rourke, B. P. (1983). Reading and spelling disabilities: A developmental neuropsychological perspective. In U. Kirk (Ed.), *Neuropsychology of language, reading, and spelling* (pp. 209–234). New York: Academic.

Rourke, B. P., Bakker, D. J., Fisk, J. L., & Strang, J. D. (1983). *Child neuropsychology: An introduction to theory, research, and clinical practice.* New York: Guilford.

Rutter, M., Chadwick, O., & Shaffer, D. (1983). Head injury. In M. Rutter (Ed.), *Developmental neuropsychiatry* (pp. 83–111). New York: Guilford.

Spreen, O., Tupper, D., Risser, A., Tuokko, H., & Edgell, D. (1984). *Human developmental neuropsychology.* New York: Oxford.

St. James-Roberts, I. (1981). A reinterpretation of hemispherectomy data without functional plasticity of the brain: I. Intellectual function. *Brain and Language, 13*, 31–53.

Van Dongen, H. R., & Loonen, M. C. B. (1977). Factors related to prognosis of acquired aphasia in children. *Cortex, 13*, 131–136.

Walton, J. N. (1977). *Brain's diseases of the nervous system.* New York: Oxford University Press.

Wechsler, D. (1955). *Manual of Wechsler Adult Intelligence Scale.* New York: Psychological Corp.

Weinstein, J. D., Toy, F. J., Jaffe, M. E., & Goldberg, H. I. (1973). The effect of dexamethasone on brain edema in patients with metastatic brain tumors. *Neurology, 23,* 121.

Werry, J. S. (1978). Developmental hyperactivity. *Pediatric Clinics of North America, 15,* 581–599.

Wirt, R. D., Lachar, D., Klinedinst, J. K., & Seat, P. D. (1977). *Multidimensional description of child personality: A manual for the Personality Inventory for Children.* Los Angeles: Western Psychological Services.

4. Diseases of childhood that may affect higher nervous system functioning

Introduction

In addition to those cases involving well-documented CNS dysfunction, the clinical neuropsychologist is sometimes called upon to render opinions regarding the adaptive abilities of children who present with other medical problem(s). This sort of referral reflects increased awareness that diseases arising in other organs and systems of the body may have significant consequences with respect to the integrity of the brain, and hence adaptive functioning.

In this chapter, we examine the neuropsychological profiles of six children who present with relatively well-defined diseases of an essentially non-CNS nature. It is our primary intention to illustrate by means of these case studies some of the ways in which the child-clinical neuropsychologist can contribute to the management of pediatric patients for whom the primary clinical responsibility rests largely with the physician. As illustrative cases, we have chosen examples of muscular dystrophy, Turner's syndrome, renal dysfunction, and cardiovascular disease. We can only offer speculations regarding the likelihood and extent of direct or indirect CNS involvement in these cases, although this would seem highly probable in some instances. Some tentative conclusions regarding assessment and treatment issues are highlighted at the end of each section.

Muscular dystrophy

One of the most commonly encountered neuromuscular disorders known to afflict children is that of Duchenne muscular dystrophy (MD). This disease is due to a sex-linked recessive gene (Walton, 1977). Muscular weakness and motor difficulties usually become evident at about 4 years of age, followed by progressive deterioration of muscle fibers and resulting confinement to a wheelchair by age 11 or 12, and death from either respiratory infection or cardiac failure in the late teens. According to

Walton (1977), most of the evidence suggests that primary muscular dystrophies are diseases of the muscles, although associated neural dysfunction cannot be entirely ruled out.

Investigations of MD children have produced some evidence suggestive of retarded or diminished intellectual and/or cognitive capacities (Dubowitz, 1979; Karagan, 1979). However, it is not entirely clear whether and to what extent these phenomena reflect nervous system dysfunction. Furthermore, there has been little agreement with respect to the actual developmental course of this diminished functioning. Some investigators have reported an increase in psychometric intelligence coincident with increased age (Karagan & Zellwager, 1978; Knights, Hinton, & Drader, 1973), whereas other studies have found no differences in IQ across age (Leibowitz & Dubowitz, 1981; Worden & Vignos, 1962). At least one investigator (Black, 1973) has reported an actual decline in IQ coincident with advancing age.

These discrepant findings make it difficult to state any firm conclusions regarding levels of psychometric intelligence in children of different ages who are suffering from MD. The utilization of global IQ scores in some of the aforementioned studies reduces their generalizability, particularly in those instances where the confounding effects of motor speed and motor control are not considered. It is clear that further research will be necessary to determine whether and to what extent MD children actually suffer from specific cognitive deficits.

Leibowitz and Dubowitz (1981) have reported evidence of greater behavioral problems in younger than in older MD children. However, it is not at all clear whether and to what extent this finding reflects the influence of inappropriate child management techniques. For example, parental overprotectiveness may tend to foster manipulative behavior on the part of the child. In addition, improved attentional deployment is often reported in older MD children coincident with confinement to a wheelchair. In any case, there may well be a number of factors in the environment that contribute collectively to the behavioral difficulties that are often reported in younger MD children, as the following cases illustrate.

Case 4-1: Clifford

Clifford, a 9-year-old boy with MD, had spent two years in kindergarten, following which he was transferred to a special education program. Despite every effort to teach him, he had exhibited very little in the way of meaningful academic progress. Clifford's teacher reported that he seemed unwilling to put forth any effort when presented with academic tasks. She had formed the impression, on the basis of observations during Clifford's interactions with other children in nonacademic situations, that he was much more capable than his academic performance seemed to indicate.

She was reluctant to "frustrate" him by making unrealistic demands, but at the same time she felt that he was capable of much better performance than he had heretofore exhibited.

Clifford's parents were quite cooperative in providing information about him. However, they displayed a tendency to be very overprotective of the youngster. For example, he was not allowed to participate in playground activities or ride on the school bus. His teacher had also observed that Clifford was inclined to be very dependent upon others. For example, if an adult were present, he would not attempt to dress himself before leaving the classroom. However, if left to his own devices, she discovered that he was quite capable of putting on his coat, boots, and so forth.

Neuropsychological testing of Clifford proved to be rather difficult. While not openly antagonistic, he assumed a passive, noncompliant demeanor, putting forth very little effort on most of the tasks presented to him. It was interesting to note that in the presence of his mother he was quite dependent, having to be lifted in and out of his wheelchair. However, when alone with the examiner he spontaneously moved in and out of his chair without obvious difficulty. While he readily accepted whatever assistance was offered, he did not always specifically request help.

Because of the difficulties encountered when attempting to engage this boy in many of the test activities, we were unable to complete a full assessment. The test results that were obtained are presented in Figure 4-1. It is clear from inspection of these data that the majority of his performances were well below age-expectation. However, there were some exceptions. For example, on the Peabody Picture Vocabulary Test (PPVT) he obtained an IQ score of 105. Although the Matching Pictures Test is not typically administered to 9-year-olds, we did so in an effort to involve him in the testing; it is interesting to note that he obtained a score of 18 correct out of 19 items on this test. On the Verbal section of the Wechsler Intelligence Scale for Children (WISC) (all tests were administered except the Digit Span subtest) his responses were often quite silly. For example, in response to the question, "What is the thing to do if you lose one of your friend's balls?," he responded, "Get it back, kiss the ball, and sit on it." It was the examiner's impression that this sort of response was quite deliberate on his part. On the Spelling subtest of the Wide Range Achievement Test (WRAT) he was unable (or unwilling) to identify any letters of the alphabet, with the exception of the letter K. On the Arithmetic subtest, he identified correctly one- and two-digit numbers, and he responded correctly to items requiring the judgment of whether numbers were greater or less than each other. His performance on the Grooved Pegboard Test reflected motor control difficulties, and most of his graphomotor performances were much poorer than those typically observed in children of this age.

Figure 4-1. Neuropsychological test results—Case 4-1 (Clifford).

Age		9 yr, 3 mo	
WISC		*PPVT*	
Verbal IQ	66	IQ	105
Information	5	Mental Age	9–8
Comprehension	5	*WRAT*	
Arithmetic	2	Reading (grade equiv.)	n/a
Similarities	7	Spelling (grade equiv.)	1.1
Vocabulary	4	Arithmetic (grade equiv.)	K.1
Digit Span	n/a	Auditory Closure (*T* score)	24
Performance IQ	—	Sentence Memory (*T* score)	12
Picture Completion	8	Matching Pictures (*T* score)[a]	54
Picture Arrangement	5	Progressive Figures (*T* score)[a]	11
Block Design	n/a	Category Test (*T* score)[a]	30
Object Assembly	7	Pegs Right Hand (*T* score)	−5
Coding	n/a	Pegs Left Hand (*T* score)	−7

[a] *T* score based on normative data for 8-year-olds.

On the basis of such information it is, of course, very difficult to make meaningful statements with respect to the functional integrity of cerebral systems. However, it was our impression that Clifford was much more capable than many of his test performances indicated. It seemed rather likely that parental attitudes were playing some role in his noncompliant attitude.

In our brief interaction with the mother, it was clear that she had adopted a rather fatalistic attitude regarding her son, and she seemed quite content to refrain from making any demands of him. We felt that the parents would benefit from counseling designed (1) to develop more effective child-management techniques and (2) to assist them in helping Clifford to exploit the abilities that he possessed. In an attempt to elicit some support for this recommendation, we contacted the attending physician in order to discuss this plan. Unfortunately (at least from our point of view), the family physician was of the opinion that applying any special child management techniques would prove to be counterproductive. He stated that the best attitude on the part of the parents was one of "encouragement" without expecting very much in return. He expressed the view that some "well-meaning" counselor might "push" the parents in a manner that would imply criticism or would propose treatment which would prove to be of limited value. In view of this response, as well as the mother's attitude, it seemed that there was little that could be offered to this family, and no further contact was initiated.

In summary, the neuropsychological evaluation of Clifford did not yield a clear picture of his adaptive strengths and weaknesses. However, his responses to some tests, in addition to our observations of his behavior during the test session, did provide a basis for the inference that he was more competent intellectually than had been previously demonstrated. The test results pointed in a clear direction with respect to treatment, namely, counseling of the parents and consultation with school personnel aimed at developing a behavioral management program. While we were not successful in implementing this course of action, the case does illustrate how even minimal test results can assist in formulating a treatment plan. A somewhat more successful outcome is illustrated by the next case.

Case 4-2: John

Family dynamics also constituted an important element in our second case, that of John, a 6-year, 11-month-old boy who was seen for a neuropsychological evaluation during the course of treatment as an in-patient in a clinic for emotionally disturbed children. John was first seen for a speech and language evaluation when he was approximately 2½ years of age. On the basis of this assessment, he was recommended for therapy designed to increase appropriate verbal contact as well as to improve voice quality and inflection. This therapy was provided for the next 3 years. On termination, he was said to exhibit poor expressive and receptive language skills, thought to be due in large part to his impulsivity and distractibility. During this period of treatment, it also became evident that John was exhibiting increasingly bizarre and unacceptable behavior in the home. Inappropriate behaviors included yelling, grunting, screaming, punching himself in the head and genitals, fighting with other children, not listening to instructions from his parents, poor table manners, and poor sleeping habits. An attempt was made to assist the parents with these problems on an out-patient basis by means of family counseling and instruction in child-management techniques. This action proved to be largely unsuccessful.

In reviewing the medical history, it was learned that the mother had undergone a very difficult pregnancy, during which she experienced toxemia, resulting in several hospitalizations. John was delivered with the assistance of forceps and his mother was subsequently hospitalized for 12 days. During infancy, he exhibited frequent bouts of colic, colds, and diarrhea. He suffered from pneumonia on several occasions. In addition, he was hospitalized at 3 months of age for gastroenteritis and at 12 months of age for a urinary tract infection. His mother reported that John sat up unsupported at 6 or 7 months, walked alone at 12 months, spoke his first words at 8 months, and talked in sentences by approximately 2 years. He exhibited allergic reactions to several substances, including penicillin, gamma globulin, and ragweed. At approximately 6 years of age, he was tentatively diagnosed as having Duchenne muscular dystrophy. Subsequent electromyogram study and muscle biopsy confirmed the diagnosis.

At the age of 6 years, 9 months, John was admitted to a residential treatment center for emotionally disturbed children; it was clear that his behavior was deteriorating and that efforts to assist the family on an outpatient basis had been unsuccessful. Coincidentally, he was referred for a neuropsychological evaluation because his performance in school and his behavior on the ward had raised some questions regarding his cognitive skills.

John was evaluated in two test sessions; the testing time totaled approximately 7 hours. On both occasions, his behavior varied dramatically: At times he seemed very interested and involved in the task at hand; on other occasions he was inattentive, resistant, and difficult to control. In general, he seemed to experience difficulty in deploying his attention effectively for any prolonged period of time. He was extremely active, climbing over, under, and around the examining desk, sliding off his chair onto the floor, picking up objects on the examining desk, and so forth. His ambient levels of gross motor coordination and balance were poor. His articulation was also poor (e.g., said "tatewo" for "zero," "twing" for "spring," etc.). He frequently placed testing objects in his mouth and on at least one occasion he was observed sniffing the test equipment. For the most part, neuropsychological examination of this youngster was quite difficult.

Inspection of the test results (see Figure 4-2) suggests that John had a number of relatively well-developed adaptive skills. While there was a marked discrepancy between Verbal IQ and Performance IQ on the WISC (in favor of the latter), it is interesting to note that his performances on the Auditory Closure, Sentence Memory, and Verbal Fluency Tests were within acceptable limits for his age. Except for the Coding subtest, WISC Performance subtest scaled scores were quite good, ranging from 11 on the Picture Arrangement subtest to 14 on the Picture Completion subtest. He also performed fairly effectively on the Progressive Figures Test, suggesting that he was reasonably flexible in his thinking and able to shift set on the basis of task demands. Although he did exhibit clear difficulties on tests involving static and kinetic motor steadiness, his finger-tapping speeds were only slightly reduced, and he performed proficiently on the Grooved Pegboard Test.

In view of his untoward behavior throughout the examination, these test scores were surprisingly good. Indeed, one would be inclined to infer that if his behavior were more controlled, he would have responded much more effectively on many of these tasks. In view of the foregoing, it seemed rather unlikely that this child was experiencing any significant dysfunction at the level of the cerebral hemispheres.

In presenting our recommendations to clinic staff, we focused primarily upon ways and means of assisting John to develop greater self-control. His involvement in the residential program provided an opportunity to

Figure 4-2. Neuropsychological test results—
Case 4-2 (John).

Age	6 yr, 11 mo
WISC	
Verbal IQ	85
Information	6
Comprehension	9
Arithmetic	10
Similarities	6
Vocabulary	9
Digit Span	6
Performance IQ	110
Picture Completion	14
Picture Arrangement	11
Block Design	13
Object Assembly	13
Coding	6
Full Scale IQ	96
PPVT	
IQ	93
Mental Age	6–3
WRAT	
Reading (grade equiv.)	1.0
Spelling (grade equiv.)	1.2
Arithmetic (grade equiv.)	K.9

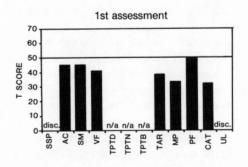

SENSORY-PERCEPTUAL ABILITIES
John was very uncooperative during the administration of the sensory-perceptual portion of the battery. He was inattentive, resistant, and difficult to manage. No valid results were obtained.

APHASIA SCREENING TEST
There was no evidence of dysnomia, right-left confusion, or disorientation for body parts. However, he misread all three of the reading items and he was unable to compute correctly the arithmetic items.

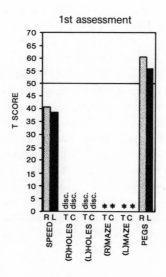

1st assessment

develop a behavior modification regimen designed to extinguish undesirable behavior. The following suggestions were offered as general guidelines in the development of such a program.

We indicated that he was likely to perform best in a relatively small, contained work area, in which potentially distracting elements could be kept to a minimum. We recommended that instructional material should be presented "one thing at a time"; for example, when one activity was completed, the material should be removed before introducing the next activity. Routinizing day-to-day activities was also seen as an important factor. We suggested in this context that potentially difficult academic tasks might be alternated with activities in which John expressed some pleasure or interest. (The point was to utilize the latter as a reinforcement for completion of the former.) In short, we were recommending a behavior modification program along the lines that are typically used for hyperactive or attentional disordered children. For more detailed presentation of this particular approach, the interested reader is referred to Barkley (1981).

In general, John responded well to the structured environment of the residential program. However, it was often noted that his behavior would deteriorate following weekend visits with his family. His progress in the program resulted in his discharge from the treatment center after a period of approximately 4 months, despite the fact that it was felt that there had been little improvement in his parents' consistency in their dealings with John in the home. During the next 4 years he was involved in various inpatient and out-patient services because of behavioral problems. John's home situation was extremely disorganized, with continual conflict between the parents surrounding their handling of the child. Efforts to assist the family proved to be unproductive, as the parents were either unable or unwilling to follow through on counseling recommendations.

At 12 years of age, John was admitted to hospital on an emergency basis because of damage secondary to self-abuse. Following this, he was readmitted to the residential treatment program. Again he responded positively to the consistent and firm guidelines provided within the program. Psychiatric evaluation at that time yielded a diagnosis of "adjustment disorder of childhood with depression."

At the time of his second admission, his physical condition had deteriorated considerably, and it was becoming increasingly difficult for him to walk. It was estimated that within approximately 6 months he would be confined to a wheelchair, and that his life expectancy was judged to be no more than 8 years. In discussions with the mother, it became clear that she did not want John's therapist to discuss the subject of death with her son. She seemed to be completely overwhelmed regarding his progressive deterioration and approaching death. She was quite incapable of providing him with the consistent and supportive guidance necessary to manage his fears regarding his physical deterioration.

Individual and joint therapy sessions with family members were continued in an effort to assist the parents to deal with their feelings about John's condition. In our most recent contacts with them, it was evident that the mother had become much more able to discuss her feelings regarding John's impending death and her problems in managing his behavior. In addition, John had begun to question his mother regarding his condition, and there was evidence that she was beginning to answer his questions in a much more direct and honest fashion. John's father, on the other hand, was quite unable to discuss his feelings regarding his son's illness. He seemed aware that he should be spending more productive time with John, but he was inclined to develop rationalizations (e.g., demands of his profession) about why he was unable to do so.

Case 4-3: Alec

Alec, a 6-year, 9-month-old boy, was referred for a neuropsychological evaluation because of learning and attentional difficulties. Two months prior to his referral, muscle biopsy had yielded a diagnosis of Duchenne muscular dystrophy. In the 9-month period prior to the rendering of this diagnosis, he had been examined by a number of physicians and other health care professionals who performed an extensive range of tests and investigations, including the following: hearing, vision, body X-ray (e.g., pelvis, chest), brain scan, EEG, EKG, and EMG. After all of these investigations, a number of unanswered questions remained regarding (1) the nature, seriousness, and extent of his learning difficulties, and (2) appropriate behavioral management and educational intervention strategies that would be best suited for him.

Alec's developmental history included delayed motor milestones, marked diminution of muscular power, and progressive problems with muscle cramping. Nevertheless, until his fifth year he seemed to his parents to be in most ways a "normal" child. He was the eldest of two children in a strong, supportive family setting.

In the testing situation, Alec seemed to tire rather quickly and he was inclined to give up easily on some tasks. Consequently, a good deal of encouragement from the examiner was necessary to ensure that he put forth maximal effort. He appeared to be mildly distractible, although his motor activity level was not excessive. Generally speaking, it was felt that the results obtained constituted a fairly reliable and valid reflection of his ability structure.

An examination of the neuropsychological test results (see Figure 4-3) yielded a number of findings that proved to be quite helpful in consulta-

Figure 4-3. Neuropsychological test results—
Case 4-3 (Alec).

Age	6 yr, 9 mo
WISC	
Verbal IQ	114
Information	12
Comprehension	11
Arithmetic	8
Similarities	15
Vocabulary	16
Digit Span	11
Performance IQ	103
Picture Completion	10
Picture Arrangement	14
Block Design	11
Object Assembly	8
Coding	9
Full Scale IQ	109
PPVT	
IQ	112
Mental Age	8–3
WRAT	
Reading (grade equiv.)	1.9
Spelling (grade equiv.)	1.9
Arithmetic (grade equiv.)	1.7

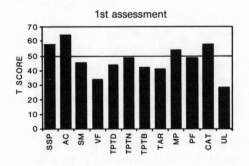

SENSORY-PERCEPTUAL ABILITIES

For the most part, the sensory-perceptual portion of the examination was negative. A Sweep Hearing Test yielded results consistent with normal acuity for pure tones with both ears. He was able to detect simple auditory stimulation delivered under conditions of unilateral and simultaneous bilateral presentation. There was no evidence of tactile imperception and suppression, finger agnosia, or astereognosis for forms. However, he did exhibit marginal difficulty bilaterally on a test requiring him to discriminate X's and O's written on his fingertips. There was no evidence of visual field defects.

APHASIA SCREENING TEST

Alec's performance on this test was unremarkable.

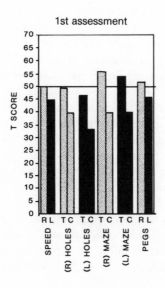

tion regarding his current educational and general adaptive difficulties. In the motor and psychomotor realms, some very mild difficulties were noted with respect to motor steadiness in both the kinetic and static dispositions bilaterally, and he exhibited a very obvious lack of muscle power as measured by grip strength. On the positive side, simple motor speed with the upper extremities and complex eye–hand coordination under timed conditions were found to be normally developed. Alec exhibited clear information-processing strengths within the psycholinguistic and language-related realm. For example, he obtained outstanding scores on the WISC Similarities and Vocabulary subtests (scaled scores of 15 and 16, respectively). Furthermore, there was no evidence of deficiencies in immediate and short-term auditory–verbal memory, and he performed very efficiently on the Speech-Sounds Perception and Auditory Closure Tests. In addition to average scores obtained on the Performance section of the WISC, his excellent Category Test performance and fairly normal Tactual Performance Test performance suggested that his visual–spatial, visual-constructional, and nonverbal problem-solving abilities were roughly age-appropriate. Some minor difficulties were noted with respect to visual "parts-to-whole" reasoning abilities (Object Assembly subtest) and in retaining and reproducing visual–spatial sequences (Target Test). Other test findings were generally unremarkable.

The pattern of neuropsychological test results exhibited by Alec largely contraindicated any significant dysfunction at the level of the cerebral hemispheres. There was some evidence of mild difficulties in motor steadiness, problems in deploying his attention effectively, and a tendency to fatigue. However, for the most part, he exhibited a broad range of adequately developed adaptive skills.

In a subsequent interview with Alec's mother (the father was unable to attend this interview), she made it abundantly clear that both she and her husband wanted their son to live his life to the fullest extent possible. This being the case, we formulated a program of instruction for him that was based almost exclusively on his particular configuration of neuropsychological abilities.

We recommended that Alec be placed in a "contained" classroom in which there would be much emphasis upon structure and organization, and where his activities could be closely monitored. In view of his excellent language skills, we suggested that he should be taught to use these abilities in order to monitor and guide his behavior (especially in situations that required passive attention) through the utilization of teaching methods along the lines suggested by Meichenbaum (1979). For example, it seemed likely that Alec would encounter problems in accurately copying material from the chalkboard, and that he might miss details in his written work because of failure to deploy attention and concentration skills effectively. Indeed, in a subsequent conference with school personnel, his teacher did report problems in these areas. We recommended that he be trained to read aloud material to be copied, and to label verbally the graphic symbols when, for example, completing mechanical arithmetic questions.

Concern was also expressed regarding the quality of Alec's printing and associated problems with letter and number reversals. With respect to the latter, such "educational" symptoms are not uncommon in children of this age. We would expect that, with additional experience, this sort of difficulty would disappear. However, since Alec's motor skills would deteriorate over time in conjunction with development of muscular dystrophy symptoms, we offered to provide more detailed evaluation of his fine motor abilities in order to assist in monitoring these skills. The problem of deteriorating motor skill would have to be dealt with as a practical issue by deemphasizing speeded graphomotor requirements in classroom activities and by utilizing compensatory "crutches" (e.g., using a tape recorder, providing copies of notes, etc.).

In summary, it was felt that Alec had the ability to deal effectively with the normal academic demands of an elementary school curriculum. In addition to aiding in the formulation of practical suggestions designed to deal with Alec's attentional and motor difficulties, the test results served to reassure his parents and his teachers that he had adequate cognitive and adaptive skills to deal effectively with the academic and social demands of an elementary school program.

The clinical cases described above illustrate several important points with respect to the neuropsychological assessment of children afflicted with Duchenne muscular dystrophy.

First of all, there would seem to be very little evidence to suggest that children with MD are any more or less prone than are other children to exhibit information-processing deficits that are likely to lead to the retardation of cognitive/intellectual and academic skills. In other words, there is good reason to believe that dysfunction at the level of the cerebral hemispheres is not a necessary component of this disorder. The results of a recent investigation of the neuropsychological status of MD patients by Sollee, Latham, Kindlon, and Bresnan (1985) would seem to support this inference. In addition, these investigators found that younger (ages 6 to 10 years) children with MD were inferior to older (ages 11 to 16 years) MD children on some tasks requiring language and attentional–organizational skills. In this connection, it should be pointed out that attentional difficulties were a prominent feature of all three of the MD cases presented above.

It is well known that serum creatinine phosphokinase (as well as other enzymes) are especially elevated during the early stages of neuromuscular disease. In the case of Duchenne muscular dystrophy, excess elevation is frequently noted in the second or third year of the disease, followed by a gradual decline to normal levels as the child reaches puberty. It has been suggested that excessive elevation of such enzymes in the blood may affect adversely the development of regulatory brain functions (Rosman & Kakulas, 1966). However, in the absence of more definitive support, one would be inclined to question the validity of this hypothesis. Furthermore, it is clear that any number of psychological factors are particularly salient in the evolution of attentional problems in children afflicted with MD. In addition, as the case of Alec illustrates, children with MD usually respond positively to well-structured, consistent environments that are designed to enhance their attentional skills. At the same time, as was seen in the cases of both Clifford and John, parental attitudes can be primary elements in less than desirable outcomes.

In all of this, the potential value of negative neuropsychological findings should not be underestimated. Children such as those described above often exhibit academic underachievement, and it is tempting for those working directly with them to attribute poor academic performance to limitations or deficits in abilities that are associated with, or even caused by, MD. If it can be demonstrated via a neuropsychological assessment that a particular child has an adequate range of adaptive strengths and weaknesses, it is much more likely that academic remediational and other treatment efforts will be directed in an apropriate and productive fashion. This is not to suggest that children afflicted with MD cannot also suffer from a learning disability. However, it is very important that the latter condition, if present, be differentiated in such a way that parents, teachers, and others working with the child do not assume that it is a necessary manifestation of MD.

Turner's syndrome (ovarian dysgenesis)

Turner's syndrome is a disorder of females that can be diagnosed through chromosomal analysis, known as karyotyping, and classified according to the karyotypic characteristics that are revealed. Instead of possessing the normal complement of 46 chromosomes, Turner's syndrome females have 45 chromosomes, with only one X and no other X or Y chromosome present. Approximately half of these patients exhibit what is known as mosaicism, a condition in which some cells contain XO and other XX chromosome material. Shortness of stature, infertility, and failure of secondary sexual characteristics to develop are the most outstanding physical and biological features of this syndrome. There is some variability in the incidence and degree of expression of other typical physical and biological characteristics associated with Turner's syndrome (e.g., those persons who have mosaicism tend to exhibit the fewest number of physical characteristics associated with the condition). Some of the common characteristics represented and their estimated percentages among persons with Turner's syndrome are as follows: atypical fingernails (43%), webbed neck (41%), low hairline (54%), shield chest (55%), atypical (low-set) ears (48%), heart murmur (43%), chronic otitis media (43%), and skeletal abnormalities (40%) (Charney & Smillie, 1983). It is these sorts of physical and other biological characteristics that have traditionally attracted the concern and attention of medical practitioners, the parents of children with Turner's syndrome, and the patients themselves.

More recently, the cognitive impairments that may be associated with this condition have become an increasingly important subject for study. While there is a wide range of individual variation in the cognitive strengths and weaknesses of Turner's syndrome patients, many such individuals have been found to exhibit particular weaknesses in the nonverbal information-processing realm (Money & Alexander, 1966; Watson & Money, 1975). The following case illustrates how a comprehensive understanding of the neuropsychological ability structure of a person with Turner's syndrome was helpful in the designing of a program of intervention for her.

Case 4-4: Carol

Carol was referred for a neuropsychological assessment when she was 12 years, 6 months of age. She had been referred primarily because of academic underachievement, with particular difficulty noted in reading comprehension, in mechanical arithmetic, and in following directions on her own without verbal clarification. Carol's teacher reported that, in those situations where she was merely required to memorize material (such as a list of spelling words), she tended to perform quite well. Indeed, her spelling to dictation was estimated to be at the Grade 6 level. However, her written output in other contexts (e.g., creative writing) did not always reflect such a high level of spelling ability. Her written compositions tended to be rather simple and concrete, and she typically did not utilize language commensurate with her ability to spell. She was able to carry out simple multiplication (she had memorized the multiplication tables), but she was unable to compute simple addition and subtraction problems in a consistently correct fashion. Described as "immature for a 12-year-old," she seemed to get along well with peers, although her teacher noted some tendency for other children to "indulge" her. Her medical history included a diagnosis of Turner's syndrome and essential hypertension. The latter condition was being treated with medication (Inderal).

In the testing situation, Carol was pleasant, friendly, and cooperative; rapport was easily obtained with her. She was attentive, seemed to comprehend task instructions readily, and put forth good effort during the tasks presented to her. Despite wearing a dental appliance designed to correct the alignment of her teeth, she was very articulate and the quality of her speech was excellent. In light of the foregoing, the results obtained were thought to constitute a reliable and valid reflection of her adaptive ability structure.

The general configuration of test results (see Figure 4-4) reveals a number of difficulties on tasks involving complex visual–spatial organizational skills within the context of somewhat better performances on activities involving some overlearned verbal and auditory–perceptual abilities. For example, her WISC scores were characterized by a marked discrepancy between Verbal IQ (85) and Performance IQ (69), in favor of the former. Except for the Coding subtest (scaled score 9), Performance subtest scaled scores were uniformly deficient. In contrast, there was considerable variability among the Verbal subtest scaled scores. Her drawing of a complex key was quite primitive for her age, and her renderings of simple geometric forms were mildly distorted from a visual–spatial standpoint. On both the Target Test and the Trail Making Test, Part A, she performed very efficiently. Although it is difficult to say for certain, it would seem likely that she was able to utilize some sort of verbal coding strategy when performing these tests. There was evidence of poor psychomotor control, particularly on more complex psychomotor tasks (e.g., Maze Test, Grooved Pegboard Test). The utilization of tactile–kinesthetic information also appeared to be somewhat problematic for Carol. It is noteworthy that she encountered considerable difficulty in discriminating numbers written on her fingertips, especially on trials with her left hand, and she exhibited a very slow performance on all three trials of the Tactual Performance Test. With respect to the latter test it is important to note, however, that she did exhibit a positive practice effect, suggesting that she was deriving some benefit from experience with the task.

In evaluating her verbal skills, it is immediately apparent that she was sensitive to the phonological structure of spoken words as reflected by her performances on the Auditory Closure and Speech-Sounds Perception Tests. Furthermore, the quality of her reading and spelling performances indicated clearly that Carol had an age-appropriate understanding of sound–symbol relationships. In this context we would expect (as reported by school authorities) that her reading comprehension would be somewhat less well developed than was her skill in word recognition. It is also noteworthy that she performed rather poorly on the Sentence Memory Test, suggesting that she was not particularly adept at utilizing contextual cues and meaning as aids for the recall of connected discourse. In general, it seemed likely that Carol would perform poorly in any situation that required higher-order problem-solving skills and the appreciation of the contextual dimensions of even minimally novel situations.

In this particular case, one would have to raise some questions regarding the functional integrity of those abilities normally thought to be subserved primarily by right hemispheral structures and systems. Marked kinetic tremor and other eye–hand coordination deficiencies are sometimes seen in children with impaired right hemispheral systems. However, it is also clear that these psychomotor deficiencies would suggest that neocerebellar and/or some other form of subcortical involvement cannot be entirely ruled out.

In a subsequent interview with Carol's mother, it became apparent that she was not fully aware of the possible consequences and manifestations of Turner's syndrome. Although she was aware that Carol's secondary sexual characteristics might not develop in a normal fashion, she had not been apprised of the possible cognitive or intellectual deficits that might accompany this malady. Over the years, she had become rather suspicious of the latter, since Carol was experiencing such obvious difficulty with school work. She had also noted that Carol was inclined to associate with somewhat younger children, and she recognized quite clearly that her daughter was socially immature as compared to her peers. The mother also made it clear that she wanted us to communicate our findings to school personnel, since she felt quite certain that Carol's teachers were not fully aware of the cognitive deficiencies that her daughter was experiencing. In order to do this, we arranged for an educational conference with the appropriate school personnel.

In this conference, Carol's teachers reported that she was very well behaved and that they felt that she had adapted (socially) quite well to the program provided for her. However, they did raise serious questions as to whether or not they could provide an appropriate program to meet Carol's very special learning needs. For this reason, it was decided that she should be considered for a special day-care treatment program. The goals of this program were specified as follows: (1) specific remediation in mathematical skills, including the use of a calculator and/or implementation of specific verbal problem-solving strategies to serve as aids in developing these skills; (2) the development of practical life (activities of daily living) skills, particularly those which required an understanding of cause–effect relationships (e.g., the use of money); (3) preparation for a suitable secondary school program; and (4) counseling with the family and Carol that would focus on the implications of her atypical secondary sexual development.

With respect to (4), it is typically the case that individuals afflicted with Turner's syndrome fail to develop breasts, to menstruate, or to exhibit other secondary sexual characteristics in conjunction with the onset of puberty. This condition is a result of failure to produce sufficient sex hormones and can be treated with estrogen therapy. We therefore

Figure 4-4. Neuropsychological test results—Case 4-4 (Carol).

Age	12 yr, 6 mo	14 yr, 6 mo
WISC		
Verbal IQ	85	81
Information	7	6
Comprehension	4	9
Arithmetic	6	4
Similarities	12	9
Vocabulary	9	8
Digit Span	7	6
Performance IQ	69	65
Picture Completion	5	5
Picture Arrangement	6	6
Block Design	4	3
Object Assembly	4	4
Coding	9	7
Full Scale IQ	75	71
PPVT		
IQ	77	86
Mental Age	9–5	11–9
WRAT		
Reading (grade equiv.)	5.6	6.0
Spelling (grade equiv.)	4.6	5.7
Arithmetic (grade equiv.)	3.9	4.3

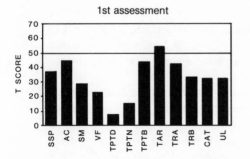

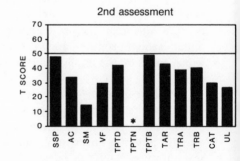

140

SENSORY-PERCEPTUAL ABILITIES

On the first examination, a Sweep Hearing Test yielded evidence of mild hearing loss (25–40 db) at lower frequencies (250–1,000 Hz) with both ears. However, Carol performed without error when required to discriminate auditory clicks delivered under conditions of unilateral and simultaneous bilateral presentation. There was no compelling evidence of visual field defects. There was no evidence of simple tactile imperception. However, on 2 occasions (out of 12 trials) she suppressed such stimulation delivered to the left hand—once when the right hand was simultaneously stimulated and once when the right face was simultaneously stimulated. There was no evidence of finger agnosia. However, she experienced difficulty, especially with her left hand, when required to (1) identify numbers written on her fingertips and (2) discriminate between coins of various denominations exclusively on the basis of tactile analysis. Reassessment yielded very similar results.

APHASIA SCREENING TEST

On the initial examination, Carol experienced no problems with the reading, naming, or auditory–verbal agnosia items of this test. However, she misspelled the word "square," and she failed to compute correctly one arithmetic problem. Her drawings of simple shapes and a complex key were somewhat distorted from a visual–spatial standpoint. She also exhibited very mild enunciatory dyspraxia. Except for mild distortions in her drawings and minor difficulty in the enunciation of several complex multisyllabic words, Carol's performance was unremarkable in the second assessment.

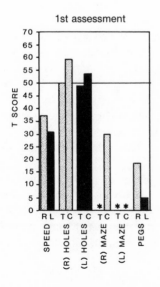

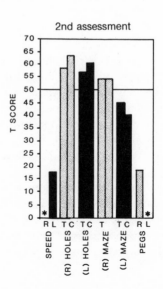

recommended that counseling be conducted in conjunction with consultation from the attending physician.

Several months following the neuropsychological assessment, we arranged to meet with Carol in order to conduct further testing designed to investigate other aspects of her deficient problem-solving skills, namely, "conservation" and "class inclusion" abilities. With respect to conservation, we utilized procedures suggested by Goldschmidt and Bentler (1968). The results indicated that Carol was able to conserve two-dimensional space and number. However, conservation of substance, weight, area, and length were not achieved. Administration of class inclusion problems (derived from the work of Hatano & Kahara, 1971) revealed that "some and all" and "pictorial class inclusion" problems were not clearly understood by her.

In terms of the theoretical formulations of Piaget (Flavell, 1963), Carol was functioning at the level of concrete operational thought, a stage of development that is thought to emerge during middle childhood (approximately 7–11 years of age). The results illustrated clearly that Carol's higher-order cognitive skills were poorly developed for her chronological age. One might anticipate that Carol would encounter increased difficulty within the academic realm coincident with the demands for abstraction, mathematical and verbal reasoning, and independent thinking that characterize senior elementary and secondary school programs.

Carol was subsequently seen for neuropsychological reevaluation when she was 14 years, 6 months of age. Although the general configuration of test results did not reveal any dramatic change in her adaptive ability structure over this 2-year period, some comments regarding specific test performances are warranted. With respect to her motor skills, some results suggested that her absolute levels of performance had actually deteriorated since our first assessment of her. These included tests for motor speed with the upper extremities and speeded eye–hand coordination with her left hand. Conversely, her kinetic motor steadiness abilities appeared to have improved significantly with both hands. Her performances on both the Auditory Closure and Sentence Memory Tests were somewhat poorer than those noted in our initial assessment. Indeed, one might have expected some improvements in these areas simply on the basis of normal maturation. In any case, it certainly appeared as though this child's neuropsychological development was proceeding in a somewhat uneven, atypical fashion.

Our recommendations regarding approaches to treatment were not fundamentally different from those proposed following our initial evaluation of her. In addition, we recommended that educational remediation focus upon exercises specifically designed to enhance her understanding and comprehension of reading material. We also emphasized the need to

provide Carol with verbal explanations and directives when it was anticipated that she might face any change in routine or otherwise have to deal
with a novel or complex situation.

We learned that the attending physician had not yet begun hormonal
therapy. Apparently, skeletal X-rays had revealed some potential for bone
growth. It was judged unwise to initiate such therapy, since it might
produce uneven bone growth and consequently some distortion of Carol's
appearance. Her status in this regard was being closely monitored.

We arranged for the family to contact a Turner's syndrome support
program that had recently been established in our area. This support
group was specifically designed to provide counseling, educational information, and related services to adolescents, adults, and parents of individuals with Turner's syndrome.

In summary, we would maintain that the general and specific adjustmental difficulties faced by Turner's syndrome patients, whether they be
children, adolescents, or adults, cannot be fully appreciated until the
neuropsychological characteristics of the individual have been taken into
account. For example, the nonverbal information-processing deficiencies
that are typically associated with this syndrome are often found in conjunction with peer interactional difficulties (Strang & Rourke, 1985). The
recommended treatment for such disorders in older children involves,
among other things, teaching them how to use their verbal strengths to
proper advantage. Sometimes this includes teaching the children "how,"
"when," and "what" to say in different sorts of clearly identifiable social
situations. It has been our experience that teaching children such verbal
strategies can assist them to automatize complex procedures. (See Chapter 6 for an extensive discussion of therapy for such children.)

In Carol's case, the neuropsychological test results revealed specific
deficits with respect to conceptualization, nonverbal problem solving, and
tactile–kinesthetic and psychomotor skills in the context of relatively well
developed "automatic" language abilities. Reevaluation served to demonstrate that such skills were developing at a somewhat uneven pace. In light
of this information, it was possible to develop and, where appropriate,
modify treatment plans that were consistent with her ability structure and
the demands of her environment.

Renal dysfunction

Renal disease represents one of a number of medical disorders for
which there may be cerebral consequences (Adams, Sawyer, & Kvale,
1980; Ratner, Adams, Levin, & Rourke, 1983). Behavioral decrements
thought to be associated with the disruption in sodium–potassium transfer

in the CNS have been observed in nephrecotomized rats and primates (Fishman & Raskin, 1967; Sharp & Murphy, 1964). A number of investigators have demonstrated cognitive deficits suggestive of cerebral dysfunction in end-stage renal disease patients (Abrams, 1969; Greenberg, Davis, & Massey, 1973) as well as in hemodialysis patients (Murawski, Spector, & Tollette, 1973; Ratner et al., 1983). The precise nature of the cognitive, sensory–perceptual, and psychomotor deficits in such patients is not entirely clear from the literature, although it does appear that peripheral neuropathy associated with dialysis may interfere with the efficient performance of psychomotor and proprioceptive tasks (Ratner et al., 1983). In any case, the majority of studies in this area have dealt primarily with adults and little is currently known regarding possible effects of renal dysfunction on the developing nervous system. The following case offers some information along these lines.

Case 4-5: Aaron

Aaron, an 11-year-old boy, was referred for a neuropsychological evaluation primarily because of school-related difficulties. He was enrolled in a Grade 5 program where his teacher reported problems with spelling, sentence structure, and written output. He had received some remedial assistance with reading and vocabulary development. His fine motor coordination was described as very poor. He was said to be well liked by other children, but he did not appear to have any close friends in his classroom, usually preferring solitary play activities. Aaron's teacher described him as a gentle, polite youngster who was always cooperative, respectful, and helpful.

Investigation of his clinical history revealed that Aaron suffered from a moderate degree of chronic renal failure due to vesicoureteric reflux and reflux nephropathy. Surgical treatment to correct this condition when he was an infant had been only partially successful. He was also treated surgically for bilateral, undescended testes when he was 7 years of age. At the time of assessment, he was on a low-protein, low-phosphorus diet in an attempt to delay the progression of his renal disease. While Aaron was viewed as generally healthy by the attending nephrologist, it was felt that the ultimate prognosis was not especially favorable. It was thought that renal failure would likely progress, leading eventually to dialysis and (possibly) the need for transplantation. His parents had been advised that he should avoid contact sports, such as hockey and football, since such patients frequently exhibit metabolic bone disease. Otherwise no restrictions were placed on his physical activities. He was evaluated every 6 months in order to monitor his nephrological status.

Aaron presented as a rather frail, somewhat undersized youngster who appeared to be physically younger than his stated chronological age.

Throughout the examination he was very pleasant, friendly, and cooperative; rapport was easily obtained. He was attentive and seemed to comprehend instructions readily. Informal observation did not suggest any difficulties with balance, gait, or gross motor skills. However, it was noticed
that his left hand was occasionally tremulous, particularly when he was
involved in fine motor tasks. Overall, testing proceeded very efficiently,
and the results obtained seemed to constitute a fairly reliable and valid
reflection of his adaptive skills.

An examination of his test results (see Figure 4-5) revealed a number
of well-developed adaptive skills. There was no compelling evidence that
he was experiencing any particular difficulties with respect to the processing of information presented via the visual or auditory modalities. He
seemed to be able to formulate and maintain fairly effective plans of action
on tasks of a problem-solving nature (e.g., Category Test, Tactual Performance Test). However, he did exhibit reduced motor speed with the upper
extremities and a test for speeded eye–hand coordination (Grooved Pegboard Test) proved to be moderately difficult for him. Qualitative evaluation of his cursive letter formations and his drawings of simple geometric
forms suggested a mild degree of graphomotor discoordination. He also
exhibited fairly marked finger agnosia, finger dysgraphesthesia, and astereognosis for coins bilaterally. In summary, it appeared that Aaron's
major adaptive difficulties centered around tasks involving motor and
graphomotor output as well as difficulties with some aspects of tactile
perception.

We recommended that those working with Aaron seek ways to modify demands for graphomotor output. We suggested that he might be able
to utilize a tape recorder to his advantage in some situations. For example,
if he were required to produce a written project, he could dictate into the
tape recorder and then arrange to transcribe the content. We suggested
that written tests be supplemented with oral assist, multiple-choice, and
fill-in-the-blank types of evaluations. We also recommended that he be
referred for an occupational therapy evaluation in order to determine
whether he would benefit from remedial programming for his sensory–
motor skills. The results of this evaluation indicated that Aaron's fine and
gross motor abilities were underdeveloped for his age. While many of his
sensory–perceptual skills and movement patterns were thought to be
intact, his problems in maintaining fine motor stability were serving to
reduce his manual dexterity skill development. The occupational therapist
arranged to visit his classroom teacher and provided a list of techniques to
aid in the development of his motor steadiness skills. The teacher agreed to
incorporate these procedures in classroom situations that required Aaron
to carry out complex graphomotor tasks.

In order to monitor the development of his adaptive skills, Aaron was
reevaluated when he was 12 years, 7 months of age. In a pretest interview

Figure 4-5. Neuropsychological test results—Case 4-5 (Aaron).

Age	11 yr, 0 mo	12 yr, 7 mo
WISC		
Verbal IQ	109	95
Information	8	9
Comprehension	10	7
Arithmetic	8	10
Similarities	15	10
Vocabulary	12	12
Digit Span	9	7
Performance IQ	113	103
Picture Completion	16	12
Picture Arrangement	13	14
Block Design	11	10
Object Assembly	11	10
Coding	8	6
Full Scale IQ	112	99
PPVT		
IQ	125	109
Mental Age	15–5	15–3
WRAT		
Reading (grade equiv.)	4.4	4.5
Spelling (grade equiv.)	3.5	4.8
Arithmetic (grade equiv.)	4.3	4.3

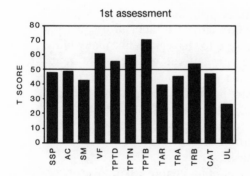

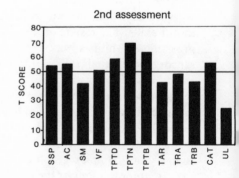

146

SENSORY-PERCEPTUAL ABILITIES

In the initial assessment, Aaron exhibited evidence of fairly prominent finger agnosia and finger dysgraphesthesia bilaterally. Also, he suppressed tactile stimulation delivered to his right hand on one occasion (out of four trials) when his left hand was simultaneously stimulated. There was marginal evidence of astereognosis for coins with his right hand. The remainder of the sensory-perceptual tests were negative. In the second assessment, Aaron continued to exhibit bilateral finger agnosia, finger dysgraphesthesia, and astereognosis for coins. Otherwise, his performance was unremarkable.

APHASIA SCREENING TEST

In the first assessment, Aaron failed to spell correctly several relatively simple words (three oral; one written). There was also evidence of very mind enunciatory dyspraxia. The remaining items of this test were performed competently. Reevaluation yielded virtually identical results.

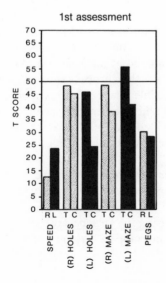

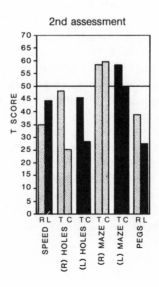

his mother reported that during the previous 18 months Aaron had seemed to be much stronger and that he was much more resistant to viral infections, colds, and so forth than had been the case during earlier stages of development. In the academic situation, he continued to encounter some minor difficulties with reading and spelling, although his mother was of the opinion that his writing had improved greatly since his last evaluation.

As we had observed previously, Aaron was very cooperative, pleasant, and friendly in the test situation. He seemed to put forth good effort, and testing proceeded in a very efficient manner. Inspection of the test results (see Figure 4-5) indicated that the overall configuration of scores had not changed in any dramatic way since our initial evaluation of him. There was no compelling indication of deterioration in his general level of adaptive skills and, relative to his previous scores, actual improvements were noted with respect to grip strength, simple motor speed, and kinetic motor steadiness.

Despite these generally positive results, Aaron appeared to have made little academic progress. In this second testing, he obtained grade-equivalent scores on the Reading (word recognition), Spelling, and Arithmetic subtests of the WRAT approximately 2½ to 3 years below chronological age expectancy. His reading centile score had actually declined from 23 to 7; in Arithmetic, from 14 to 6. However, his relative standing in spelling was essentially unchanged.

Several possibilities, not mutually exclusive, can be considered in our effort to account for his failure to make academic progress. First, it should be noted that his performances on the Digit Span and Coding subtests of the WISC were somewhat poor in the second assessment as compared to the first assessment. Whether or not these particular findings constituted significant changes in his skill levels is difficult to say. However, one might raise the possibility that there had been deterioration in his immediate memory skills. If in fact this were the case, one would expect some negative impact with respect to the development of his academic skills. It therefore seemed reasonable to recommend that he be examined on a regular basis in order to monitor any possible changes in this regard. It should also be noted that he continued to exhibit finger agnosia and finger dysgraphesthesia. There was also some evidence of mild deterioration in his static steadiness skills. All of this suggests that the possibility of some CNS dysfunction cannot be entirely ruled out.

A second factor that might account in part for his academic difficulties emerged from our discussions with school personnel. Contrary to what Aaron's mother had reported, we learned that he had been absent from school for considerable periods of time during the year because of illness. We recommended that school personnel attempt to arrange for supplementary home instruction to be provided during periods of time when Aaron's physical status did not allow attendance at school. It was suggested that this sort of program should be maintained as long as necessary, and in this regard the school system was most cooperative.

In summary, it seems rather unlikely that Aaron was experiencing significant cognitive impairment as a direct result of his medical condition. However, the neuropsychological test results did raise the possibility that very subtle deterioration in his adaptive skills was playing some role in his presenting academic problems. On the basis of such data, careful monitoring of his development seemed to be warranted. The test results also assisted school personnel to identify and develop appropriate compensatory strategies for him.

With respect to the relationship between renal disease and development of the CNS, it is difficult to draw any definitive conclusions on the basis of this particular case. At the same time, it is possible that the tactile–perceptual and psychomotor difficulties which Aaron exhibited were related to peripheral neuropathy. This inference would certainly be consistent with the results of investigations of adult patients. Having now obtained baseline data, we were in a good position to determine whether or not this youngster would experience any significant degree of adaptive deficit as a result of further development of renal disease.

Cardiovascular disease

The cardiovascular system is, among other things, responsible for maintaining adequate cerebral blood flow in order to deliver oxygen, glucose, and other nutrients, and to remove carbon dioxide and metabolic by-products. That maintenance of cerebral blood flow is crucial to CNS functioning is reflected in the fact that the brain, while accounting for only 2% of body weight, receives approximately 17% of normal cardiac output and 20% of the entire body's oxygen consumption (Brust, 1982). Interruption in cerebral blood flow for even a few minutes is likely to have significant consequences for subsequent brain functioning.

Cerebral vascular disease is most frequently observed in the elderly and is usually not considered a common event in children. However, according to Gold, Hammill, and Carter (1974), cerebral vascular diseases account for 5% of admissions to pediatric neurology departments and 10% of pediatric pathology referrals. The following case is an example of a neuropsychological investigation of a child with congenital heart disease. The case is also interesting because the evaluation constituted a test of possible neuropsychological sequelae arising from the use of an experimental medication.

Case 4-6: Peter

At the time of referral, Peter was 10 years, 7 months of age. Review of his clinical history revealed that he had been diagnosed as suffering from a form of congenital heart disease that involves transposition of the great arteries. At 5 months of age he underwent a so-called "Mustard" operation (a type of repair procedure). This operation was successful and Peter was well until approximately 4 years of age, when he developed difficulties with heart rhythm. Efforts to control this symptom utilizing traditional medication were unsuccessful, and when Peter was 7 years of age, it was decided to utilize a procedure involving an experimental drug (Amiodarone). Unfortunately, this procedure resulted in cardiac arrest. However, Peter was quickly resuscitated, and at that time there was no obvious evidence of significant neurological impairment. Subsequently, this agent and Digoxin therapy were continued for the next 3 years.

Peter's parents and teachers expressed concern regarding unusual memory problems. Apparently on occasion he would exhibit a total unfamiliarity with subject material which had been discussed or taught very recently. Although Amiodarone was known to cause some side effects, including (extremely rarely) peripheral myopathy, the attending pediatric cardiologist reported that to his knowledge problems with mentation in the use of this drug had never been reported. Nevertheless, he felt that a neuropsychological evaluation would be of benefit with respect to determining whether and to what extent there was any possible "organic" basis for the child's presenting symptomatology. In addition, it was thought that such information would assist in the development of appropriate treatment, if such were required.

From the outset, it was clear that Peter was upset with the prospect of a day-long examination session. Upon entering the testing room he began to cry, and efforts on the part of his parents and clinic staff were only partially successful in reassuring him that nothing untoward would happen. Although he was clearly reluctant to leave his mother, he was eventually coaxed to attempt some of the tests. For the remainder of the test session he was somewhat anxious and ill at ease. Although he was rather sullen and exhibited little in the way of animated behavior throughout the rest of the day, he did not offer any active resistance to complying with task demands. Indeed, he seemed to be attentive and he appeared to comprehend task instructions without difficulty. His balance, gait, and motor coordination appeared to be normal. His speech was clear. All in all, it appeared that the results obtained constituted a fairly reliable and valid reflection of his adaptive ability structure.

Peter's test results (see Figure 4-6) reflect a fairly broad range of adequately developed adaptive skills. The only exceptions to this otherwise "clean" profile were some evidence of bilateral finger agnosia and finger dysgraphesthesia, relatively slow performance on the initial trial (involving his right hand) on the Tactual Performance Test, and some suggestion of a mild to moderate bilateral static tremor. In addition, his performance on the Underlining Test, while accurate, was a good deal slower than is typically observed in children of this age.

To the extent that it can be determined from this battery of tests, there was no evidence of memory deficiencies. His immediate auditory–verbal memory appeared to be intact. For example, he was able to recall a series of six digits in forward order and four digits in reverse order (a normal level of performance for a child of this age), and he encountered no particular difficulty on the Sentence Memory Test. His incidental recall of the shapes and spatial locations of the blocks used on the Tactual Performance Test (as reflected in a freehand drawing of the formboard) yielded results within normal limits. He obtained an average score on the Target Test. The final subtest of the Category Test (designed as a review of previously correct solutions) also yielded an average score.

In short, there was no compelling evidence of any significant deficiencies in Peter's information-processing abilities. In our opinion, there was little in this profile to suggest that this youngster was experiencing significant functional impairment at the level of the cerebral hemispheres. All things being equal, one would expect Peter to perform adequately in the classroom as well as in other realms of day-to-day functioning. For the most part this seemed to be the case, although we did note that his performance on the WRAT Spelling subtest was somewhat poorer than expected (grade-equivalent score of 4.8; centile score of 37), as was his Arithmetic performance (grade-equivalent score of 3.9; centile score of 18). It is difficult to determine whether this constituted a significant finding, although progress in these academic skill areas did seem to bear monitoring.

We met with Peter's parents in order to apprise them of the test results. Utilizing practical language, we explained that we had found little compelling evidence of any signficant memory difficulties, and the positive nature of his ability structure was described in some detail. At the same time, it was pointed out that the mild tactile–kinesthetic and static steadiness difficulties which we observed might be the side effects of his medication, although further investigation and monitoring would be necessary in order to make such a determination. Peter's anxious behavior during our examination suggested that he had become somewhat sensitized to hospitals and other situations which he perceived as being related to medical matters. In view of his long history of frequent hospitalizations, this behavior was not surprising. We offered to consult regarding desensitization procedures if his parents felt it was necessary at some time in the

Figure 4-6. Neuropsychological test results—
Case 4-6 (Peter).

Age	10 yr, 7 mo
WISC	
Verbal IQ	99
Information	8
Comprehension	8
Arithmetic	12
Similarities	10
Vocabulary	10
Digit Span	11
Performance IQ	114
Picture Completion	10
Picture Arrangement	13
Block Design	11
Object Assembly	10
Coding	16
Full Scale IQ	107
PPVT	
IQ	98
Mental Age	10–10
WRAT	
Reading (grade equiv.)	6.4
Spelling (grade equiv.)	4.8
Arithmetic (grade equiv.)	3.9

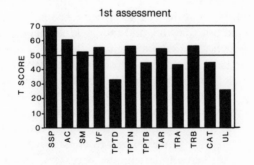

SENSORY-PERCEPTUAL ABILITIES
Peter exhibited mild to moderate difficulty with both hands on tests for finger agnosia, finger dysgraphesthesia, and astereognosis for coins. The remainder of the sensory-perceptual tests were performed in a competent manner.

APHASIA SCREENING TEST
Peter encountered no difficulty with the reading, naming, or right-left orientation items. However, he failed to spell correctly the words "square" and "triangle" ("squear"; "triagle"); he was unable to compute correctly two simple arithmetic problems (one oral; one written); he exhibited very minor difficulty in the enunciation of complex multisyllabic words.

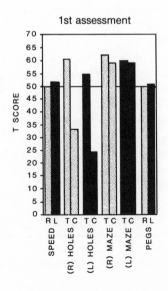

1st assessment

future. We also recommended that any further reports of episodic memory loss would constitute cause for neuromedical monitoring. As a precautionary measure, we suggested that his neuropsychological status be monitored in yearly examinations.

Summary and conclusions

In this chapter, we have examined the neuropsychological test results of six children suffering from various disorders that for the most part could be considered to be nonneurological in nature. The presentation of these cases constitutes a recognition that diseases in or damage to other organs and systems of the body can impinge directly upon CNS functioning.

As has been illustrated by the cases in this chapter, the neuropsychological assessment can serve to evaluate whether and to what extent information-processing deficiencies (presumably as a result of cerebral dysfunction) are an accompanying feature of a particular disease process. For example, in the cases of Clifford, John, and Alec, in whom muscular dystrophy was the presenting diagnosis, it appeared that neuropsychological deficits were not a significant factor. As a consequence, we did not have to deal with this dimension in the formulation of treatment recommendations. In other cases, such as that of Carol, a neuropsychological evaluation yielded evidence of significant impairment in adaptive skills. This finding proved to be a very important element in the formulation of treatment and rehabilitation plans for her.

The neuropsychological assessment also serves to provide baseline data against which subsequent monitoring can be compared in order to determine any neuropsychological effects that might coincide with the progression of the disease process. This was a very important consideration in our examination of both Aaron and Peter. Viewing this matter from a broader perspective, such clinical investigations can also serve to elucidate possible relationships between other functional systems in the body and the CNS.

To repeat, the CNS does not function in a vacuum, and damage to other systems may thus have very specific and definable consequences with respect to behavior and cognition. We would strongly agree with Adams *et al.* (1980), who advocate the need for clinical neuropsychology to focus on conditions that produce brain impairment as a secondary elaboration of primary disease in another physical system. An obvious example of this is the complications that can arise with cardiovascular disorders. According to Brust (1982), diseases of the blood vessels rank third as the cause of death in the adult American population and, more important in this context, probably first as a cause of functional incapacity. There is a vast and extensive literature regarding the various mechanisms of occlusive disease, hemorrhage, and other conditions that lead to vascular insufficiency. However, the long-term effects on behavior of reduced oxygenation have only recently begun to be investigated in any systematic fashion. For example, Delaney, Wallace, and Egelko (1980) have demonstrated that transient ischemic attacks (TIA) can result in significant impairment on measures of higher cortical functioning, including complex memory, abstract concept formation, perceptual–motor integration, and verbal fluency. These results clearly challenge the view that TIA, by definition, is not accompanied by irreversible infarction of affected brain substance (Walton, 1977).

In the context of development, much less is known regarding the neuropsychological sequelae of, for example, cyanotic congenital heart and rheumatic valvar disease, which is thought to lead to cerebral emboli in children. We expect that neuropsychological investigation of children suffering from hepatic, renal, nutritional, muscular, and skeletal disease will yield important information regarding the relationship between the CNS and other systems of the body. Finally, from a clinical point of view, it would seem to be entirely appropriate to consider for neuropsychological assessment any child suffering from a disease for which there is a known or suspected relationship to adaptive and cognitive functioning.

References

Abrams, H. S. (1969). The psychiatrist, the treatment of chronic renal failure, and the prolongation of life. *American Journal of Psychiatry, 126,* 157–167.

Adams, K. M., Sawyer, J. D., & Kvale, P. A. (1980). Cerebral oxygenation and neuropsychological adaptation. *Journal of Clinical Neuropsychology, 2,* 189–208.

Barkley, R. A. (1981). *Hyperactive children: A handbook for diagnosis and treatment.* New York: Guilford.

Black, F. W. (1973). Intellectual ability as related to age and stage of disease in muscular dystrophy: A brief note. *Journal of Psychology, 84,* 333–334.

Brust, J. C. M. (1982). Stroke: Diagnostic, anatomical, and physiological considerations. In E. R. Kandel & J. H. Schwartz (Eds.), *Principles of neural science* (pp. 667–679). New York: Elsevier/North-Holland.

Charney, S., & Smillie, A. (1983). *The X's and O's of Turner's syndrome.* Downsview, Ontario: York University.

Delaney, C. R., Wallace, J. D., & Egelko, S. (1980). Transient cerebral eschemic attacks and neuropsychological deficits. *Journal of Clinical Neuropsychology, 2,* 107–114.

Dubowitz, V. (1979). Involvement of the nervous system in muscular dystrophies in man. *Annals of the New York Academy of Science,* 431–439.

Fishman, R., & Raskin, N. (1967). Experimental uremic encephalopathy. *Archives of Neurology, 17,* 10–21.

Flavell, J. H. (1963). *The developmental psychology of Jean Piaget.* New York: D. Van Nostrand.

Gold, A. P., Hammill, J. F., & Carter, S. (1974). Cerebrovascular diseases. In S. Carter &

A. P. Gold (Eds.), *Neurology of infancy and childhood* (pp. 112–118). New York: Appleton-Century-Crofts.

Goldschmidt, M. L., & Bentler, P. M. (1968). *Concept assessment kit—Conservation.* San Diego: Educational and Industrial Testing Service.

Greenberg, R. P., Davis, D., & Massey, R. (1973). The psychological evaluation of patients for a kidney transplant and hemodialysis program. *American Journal of Psychiatry, 130,* 274–277.

Hatano, G., & Kahara, K. (1971). Training on class inclusion problems. *Japanese Psychological Research, 14,* 61–69.

Karagan, N. J. (1979). Intellectual functioning in Duchenne muscular dystrophy: A review. *Psychological Bulletin, 86,* 250–259.

Karagan, N. J., & Zellwager, H. U. (1978). Early verbal disabilities in children with Duchenne muscular dystrophy. *Developmental Medicine and Child Neurology, 20,* 435–441.

Knights, R. M., Hinton, G. G., & Drader, D. (1973). *Changes in intellectual ability with Duchenne muscular dystrophy* (Research Bulletin No. 8). Ottawa, Canada: Carleton University.

Leibowitz, D., & Dubowitz, V. (1981). Intellect and behavior in Duchenne muscular dystrophy. *Developmental Medicine and Child Neurology, 23,* 577–590.

Meichenbaum, D. (1979). Teaching children self-control. In B. Lahey & A. Kazdin (Eds.), *Advances in child clinical psychology* (Vol. 2, pp. 1–33). New York: Plenum.

Money, J., & Alexander, D. (1966). Turner's syndrome: Further demonstrations of the presence of specific cognitive deficiencies. *Journal of Medical Genetics, 3,* 47–48.

Murawski, B. J., Spector, E. L., & Tollette, W. (1973). Elucidation of the toxic nature of uremia. In *Proceedings of the Sixth Annual Contractors Conference,* DHEW Pub. (N.I.M.) 74–248, Bethesda, MD.

Ratner, D. P., Adams, K. M., Levin, N. W., & Rourke, B. P. (1983). Effects of hemodialysis on the cognitive and sensory–motor functioning of the adult chronic hemodialysis patient. *Journal of Behavioral Medicine, 6,* 291–311.

Rosman, N. P., & Kakulas, B. A. (1966). Mental deficiency associated with muscular dystrophy: A neurological study. *Brain, 89,* 769–787.

Sharp, J., & Murphy, C. (1964). Conditioned avoidance behavior in primates during various experimental uremic states. *Nephron, 1,* 172–179.

Sollee, N. D., Latham, E. E., Kindlon, D. J., & Bresnan, M. J. (1985). Neuropsychological impairment in Duchenne Muscular Dystrophy. *Journal of Clinical and Experimental Neuropsychology, 7,* 486–496.

Strang, J. D., & Rourke, B. P. (1985). Adaptive behavior in children who exhibit specific arithmetic disabilities and associated neuropsychological abilities and deficits. In B. P. Rourke (Ed.), *Neuropsychology of learning disabilities: Essentials of subtype analysis* (pp. 302–328). New York: Guilford.

Walton, J. N. (1977). *Brain's diseases of the nervous system.* New York: Oxford.

Watson, M. A., & Money, J. (1975). Behavior cytogenetics and Turner's syndrome: A new principle in counselling and psychotherapy. *American Journal of Psychotherapy, 2,* 166–177.

Worden, D. K., & Vignos, P. J. (1962). Intellectual function in chlidhood progressive muscular dystrophy. *Pediatrics, 29,* 968–977.

5. Special problems in academic remediation

Introduction

Many children are referred for neuropsychological assessment because they are doing very poorly in school, and it is thought that they are either "slow learners" or "learning disabled." The referral question may be phrased in a variety of ways, but the principal concerns of the educators in question (who are most likely to be the primary referral sources) is the type of educational milieu or program that would be of maximal benefit to the child. Ordinarily, it is assumed that a "slow learner" (i.e., a child who is of "borderline" intelligence or classified as "mildly retarded") will benefit most from an academic setting that is not qualitatively distinct from that to which "normal" students are exposed, but that has the potential for offering roughly the same types of material at much slower rates and with much more time for repetition, drill, and concrete applications. On the other hand, it is usually assumed that the "learning-disabled" child would benefit most from a program of instruction that is geared to the amelioration of his/her specific weaknesses in information processing, and that once these particular deficiencies are alleviated, a "normal" program of instruction would be most beneficial.

The material in this chapter is designed to deal specifically with some of these very common academic concerns as they relate to the process and result of neuropsychological assessment. While doing so, we trust it will become apparent that almost always the information-processing and other capacities and deficiencies of the child with outstanding academic difficulties call for rather more subtle and finer-grained habilitational and rehabilitational programs than are likely to result from the simple determination of the presence or absence of "slow learning" or "learning disability." Indeed, were this not a probable result of a comprehensive neuropsychological assessment, there would be no clinically relevant reason for conducting one.

Although our case examples in this chapter deal with rather special problems in academic remediation, it would be well to view these cases and their attendant issues within the general context of contemporary research in the area of learning disabilities. Recent neuropsychological investigations in this area have been rather unique in their emphasis on the determination of subtypes within this heterogeneous population.

Subtypes of learning-disabled children

The systematic differentiation of subtypes of learning disabled children began in earnest in the mid-1970s. Precursors of this empirically based effort included the very important clinical observations of Johnson and Myklebust (1967) and the preliminary investigations of particular aspects of spelling–reading patterns that these inspired (Boder, 1973). Other clinical efforts that were of considerable heuristic import include the widely cited observations of Mattis, French, and Rapin (1975). With these clinical observations and essentially post-hoc clinical studies as background, a series of investigations began appearing from a number of laboratories that attempted to arrive at a determination of reliable and valid learning disability typologies through the use of multivariate models and methods. An up-to-date summary of most of these efforts is contained in Rourke (1985). Rather than review these studies in detail, we will mention only some of the more salient parameters of their results that are of interest within the present context.

It is clear that reliable typologies of learning disabled youngsters can be generated on the basis of reading-related variables (Doehring, 1985), neuropsychological measures (Fisk & Rourke, 1979; Morris, Blashfield, & Satz, 1981; Petrauskas & Rourke, 1979), and a combination of these (Lyon, 1985). Patterns of academic achievement can also form the basis for a typology (e.g., Rourke & Finlayson, 1978; Rourke & Strang, 1978; Strang & Rourke, 1983), and that the subtypes generated thereby can be replicated and shown to have external validity in different laboratories (e.g., Fletcher, 1985). Further, these subtypes, although based exclusively on patterns of academic achievement, have been shown to have relevance for the prediction of personality disturbances (Strang & Rourke, 1985a), dimensions of social sensitivity (Ozols & Rourke, 1985), and patterns of adaptive behavior in adulthood (Rourke, Young, Strang, & Russell, 1986).

Investigations of the qualitative differences evident in the misspellings of disabled spellers have highlighted the vastly different patterns of neuropsychological abilities and deficits that so-called phonetically accurate and phonetically inaccurate disabled spellers exhibit (Sweeney & Rourke, 1978, 1985). These differences in turn suggest that quite different forms of academic intervention may be appropriate for these two subtypes of disabled spellers. By the same token, investigations that have demonstrated the extraordinary differences evident among subtypes of children who display arithmetic disability have fairly obvious educational ramifications (Strang & Rourke, 1985b). However, in these and other cases where subtypes of academically disabled children have been identified and hypotheses regarding beneficial habilitative–rehabilitative have been generated (e.g., Rourke & Strang, 1983), it remains necessary to submit such hypotheses to rigorous empirical test. It is for this reason that the educational validation studies conducted by Lyon (1985) are so crucial. In the absence of hard evidence along these lines for most of the learning disability typologies that have been generated, we will have to content ourselves in the pages that follow with suggestions for intervention that we have found to be efficacious in the individual case. At the same time, it will be necessary to suggest some preliminary—and admittedly hypothetical—guidelines for intervention that the clinician may use and, hopefully, test in his/her own practice with similar subtypes of learning disabled children.

It should be emphasized that this brief summary of the contemporary literature in this area is anything but exhaustive, and that it is meant to provide nothing more than a flavor of the investigative efforts that are continuing in this area. The interested reader should consult Rourke (1985) for a more thoroughgoing analysis of the neuropsychological models, measures, methods or analysis, representative results, and clinical implications of these studies.

For our present purposes, we begin with a discussion of the role of neuropsychological assessment in the academic remediation enterprise. In what follows, we should point out once again that we are particularly interested in demonstrating the implications of the interactions between central processing abilities and deficits, brain impairment, and adaptive skill development.

Neuropsychological assessment and intervention

From a somewhat simplified and pragmatic perspective, one might conceive of three outstanding tasks that should be addressed before an efficacious program of academic remediation is implemented for the brain-impaired child. The first task involves obtaining a comprehensive, reliable, and valid assessment of the child's neuropsychological ability structure (Step 1 in our model). The second task involves translating the assessment information into a realistic remedial educational plan (Steps 2 through 6). The third task involves communicating information concerning the nature and significance of the child's pattern of neuropsychological strengths and weaknesses as well as specific remedial educational recommendations for him/her in a clear and succinct manner to the child's parents, teachers, and other caretakers. These assessment, remedial planning, and consulting tasks will be discussed in detail within the context of case presentations that were selected to illustrate special problems in academic remediation. Before presenting in detail issues relating to the translation of a child's neuropsychological test results into a realistic remedial educational plan, some of the prominent limitations of common forms of "psychoeducational" assessment will be considered.

Limitations of "standard" psychoeducational assessment

In our clinical and consulting experience, we have found that the types of tests used to assess children's learning handicaps that are in vogue within the educational setting may pass into and out of fashion for any number of reasons. Unfortunately, these reasons are seldom related to the reliability, validity, or demonstrated clinical utility of the tests and measures that are retained, discarded, or adopted. Psychoeducational test batteries, for the most part, do not adequately cover the range of abilities that we feel needs to be assessed if one is to obtain an accurate picture of the nature and degree of a child's ability-related strengths and weaknesses for the purposes of specific remedial educational planning. Furthermore, the personnel administering the tests may vary considerably with respect to their professional training and psychometric sophistication. For example, teachers, special educational consultants, speech and language pathologists, as well as school psychologists may administer psychological tests in the 11 school systems with which we consult. Obviously, this diversity of personnel may have a negative impact on at least the reliability of the obtained test results. Of additional concern is the fact that psychoeducational test results are often interpreted primarily (or exclusively) from a level-of-performance perspective, in a seemingly atheoretical manner, and with far too much emphasis on the face validity of the tests administered. In addition, often scant attention is paid to the child's capacities to adapt to (1) informal learning situations (e.g., play), (2) social relationship requirements (within the family and with age-mates), and (3) long-term learning and social developmental demands (see Step 2, Chapter 1). Instead, almost exclusive focus on the immediate demands of the academic milieu is the rule. With these comments as background, a case study is presented that should serve to illustrate some of these shortcomings and a set of possible solutions for them.

Case 5-1: Douglas

Douglas, an 11-year-old boy, was referred for neuropsychological assessment by a special educational consultant at his school board. School personnel, including this boy's teachers, were somewhat perplexed by the nature and extent of his educational difficulties. They noted that he was inattentive, and they attributed the difficulties that he exhibited in following directions and his relatively low level of productivity in the classroom situation to this. Many standard and special educational approaches had been used to help him circumvent and deal with these problems, but none had a lasting impact on him. At the time of neuropsychological assessment he was enrolled in a regular Grade 6 program, and was faring quite poorly in it. His grades on a recent report card ranged from a high of C (60–69%) to lows of D (50–59%); there was an even split between the C's and D's on his report card.

Douglas had undergone psychoeducational assessment before the referral was made to our department. He had been given a battery of tests that constituted the current psychoeducational assessment utilized by the special services department at his school board. This psychoeducational battery included the following: the Wechsler Intelligence Scale for Children—Revised (WISC-R; Wechsler, 1974); the Wide Range Achievement Test (WRAT; Jastak & Jastak, 1965); the Sentence Memory Test (Benton, 1965); the Spache Diagnostic Reading Tests (Spache, 1981); the Slosson Drawing Coordination Test (Slosson, 1967); and the Visual–Aural Digit Span (Koppitz, 1977). These tests had been administered and (at different times) interpreted by two special education consultants.

The psychoeducational reports rendered on this child suggested strongly that the tests were interpreted primarily from a level-of-performance standpoint. These school board officials concluded that Douglas had an average level of intelligence, that he processed information somewhat better when the input was aural rather than visual, that he had problems in "tracking," and that there were evident difficulties with fine motor control. No conclusions were drawn with respect to the nature or degree of his information processing deficiencies. In fact, the referring party asked of us whether and to what extent this boy exhibited legitimate learning difficulties. Douglas's neuropsychological test results are presented in Figure 5-1.

Within the context of a fairly wide range of well-developed neuropsychological strengths, this boy exhibited some rather circumscribed and apparently interrelated deficiencies that were thought to underlie his problems with handwriting, mechanical arithmetic, and his so-called attentional and productivity weaknesses.

These neuropsychological test results revealed a clearly lateralized pattern of sensory–perceptual and psychomotor deficiencies. For example, he performed in an impaired and relatively inferior manner with his right hand as compared to his left hand on many of these tests, even though he wrote with his right hand and was found to be exclusively right-handed on tests for lateral dominance. His pattern of lateralized sensory–perceptual and psychomotor deficiencies was of critical importance in determining the nature and significance of this boy's information-processing limitations.

Figure 5-1. Neuropsychological test results—
Case 5-1 (Douglas).

Age	11 yr, 3 mo
WISC	
Verbal IQ	111
Information	10
Comprehension	12
Arithmetic	12
Similarities	16
Vocabulary	12
Digit Span	9
Performance IQ	110
Picture Completion	14
Picture Arrangement	9
Block Design	8
Object Assembly	11
Coding	15
Full Scale IQ	112
PPVT	
IQ	106
Mental Age	12–3
WRAT	
Reading (grade equiv.)	8.4
Spelling (grade equiv.)	6.8
Arithmetic (grade equiv.)	4.5

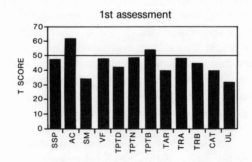

SENSORY-PERCEPTUAL ABILITIES
Douglas performed in a normal manner on the Sweep Hearing Test. There was some evidence of tactile suppression on the right side of his body. Tests for finger agnosia were performed somewhat poorly, particularly with his right hand. There was some evidence of fingertip dysgraphesthesia with his right hand. In addition, there was evidence of astereognosis for coins bilaterally.

APHASIA SCREENING TEST
Douglas was unable to fashion a graphic reproduction of a Greek cross in an age-appropriate manner. There was one arithmetic calculation error as well. All other findings were negative on this test.

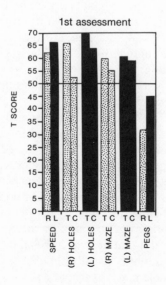

Douglas exhibited problems in visual–spatial orientation (including left–right discrimination) within the context of basically well-developed visual–motor–constructional skills. His visual–spatial orientation and directionality weaknesses were evident in his drawings on the Aphasia Screening Test, in his WISC Block Design performance, and in his Target Test performance. His handwriting was very large, although his letters were reasonably well formed and quite legible under these special testing conditions. (It should be noted that the amount of handwriting that he was required to produce was limited and that there were no time limits imposed on him during this exercise.)

Although these neuropsychological findings are not diagnostic of any neuropathological condition, they were thought to reflect a developmental deficiency that might be associated with impaired functional integrity of the posterior parietal and adjacent cortical regions of the left cerebral hemisphere. Furthermore, this boy exhibited a rarely found pattern of deficiencies, the developmental Gerstmann syndrome, that has been described by Kinsbourne and Warrington (1963) and Benson and Geschwind (1970). In addition, these findings would fit with the theoretical explanation of the brain–behavior relationships typically thought to underlie this syndrome. That is, there was evidence of finger agnosia, dysgraphesthesia, dyscalculia, and problems in left–right (including general directional) orientation. Furthermore, this boy's sensory–perceptual and psychomotor deficiencies were lateralized to the right side of the body. This would fit with the hypothesis that the developmental Gerstmann syndrome indicates a disturbance of functions primarily within the parietal lobe of the left cerebral hemisphere. However, as we have described in detail in some of our other works (e.g., Rourke & Strang, 1978; Strang & Rourke, 1983), the vast majority of children who exhibit specific and outstanding difficulties on the WRAT Arithmetic subtest, and who perform in an at least age-appropriate manner on the WRAT Reading and Spelling subtests, exhibit a pattern of sensory–perceptual (including finger agnosia) and psychomotor (including handwriting) deficiencies that are usually more pronounced on the left side of the body and that tend to implicate right hemispheral systems as being dysfunctional.

In Douglas's case, his teachers and parents found it somewhat reassuring that his pattern of neuropsychological strengths and weaknesses could "explain" the nature and degree of his educational difficulties, although this new perspective created some cognitive dissonance for them. In our communications with his parents and teachers, we emphasized that Douglas had sufficient information-processing strengths to compensate for his educational difficulties, so long as he was well motivated and was given special consideration and training in the academic situation. For example, it was pointed out that he would probably exhibit some difficulty in operating on material that is visually detailed (e.g., copying notes from the board). For this problem, it was recommended that he take advantage of his well-developed reading skills and read to himself any work to be copied before taking pen in hand. Moreover, we were confident that he could easily be taught strategies for editing his written work.

Further investigation of his difficulties in a Remedial Educational Conference confirmed our expectation that his attentional problems were quite selective rather than generalized. As we have found with children who exhibit this particular pattern of neuropsychological strengths and weaknesses, Douglas tended to become confused and/or disorganized in his approach to information processing when he was given large amounts of novel information. With this finding in mind, it was pointed out to his teachers and other educational officials that he probably would learn best if new information were delivered to him in a highly structured, verbal manner whenever possible. In addition, we suggested that he should be taught to ask his teachers direct questions whenever he felt confused with respect to the task requirements or the concept being presented. Again, with his relatively well-developed problem-solving skills in mind, it was suggested (1) that he should benefit from being taught directly the strategies needed to organize and assimilate his new work, and (2) that he should always be encouraged to seek a conceptual relationship between the new information presented to him and information that he had already learned.

Rather than having him continue with those exercises to improve his handwriting speed and neatness that had been prescribed on the basis of the psychoeducational assessment, we suggested that he should be taught to type as one mode of preparation for secondary school. We suggested that, when necessary, he should be given extra time to complete written tests, and that his teachers set a standard for his handwriting that was commensurate with his demonstrated capabilities and limitations in this area.

Task analysis of his arithmetic errors in the context of his pattern of neuropsychological strengths and weaknesses indicated that he would benefit from being taught directly the verbal rules that would help him to remember the steps involved in new arithmetic operations, and that he should be encouraged to commit these verbal rules and procedures to memory. Furthermore, it was suggested that he should be encouraged to use a hand calculator to check the accuracy of his work; this recommendation was presented in the context of the many different types of "editing" procedures that we had suggested for him.

Finally, it was suggested that his special "remedial withdrawal" program should emphasize the direct teaching of ways to organize his notes for the express purpose of studying for examinations. In this connection we recommended that he be taught directly how to study for each of the common types of educational examination formats that he would likely face at the present time and in the future (e.g., multiple-choice format, essay-type format).

When these remedial recommendations were discussed with his

teachers and his parents at the Remedial Education Conference, there was some difficulty in completely reframing the nature of Douglas's educational difficulties. Indeed, we encountered a somewhat dogged persistence in the view that poor motivation explained, in large part, his academic limitations. Nevertheless, there was good reason to anticipate that his school caretakers would follow through with our specific remedial educational recommendations for him if they would simply try out some of the suggestions that we had formulated. One reason for this confidence was that we were quite certain that his academic performances would show dramatic positive changes, with consequent positive impact on any motivational problems that he may have had. This type of change usually encourages teachers and others in the academic setting who are involved with "special children" to continue to apply the successful formula, and to do so with increased enthusiasm.

In this case, and in many others that we have seen, the psychoeducational assessment did not lead to a well-defined explanation of the nature or degree of the youngster's information-processing deficiencies. Some of Douglas's prominent behavioral symptoms were identified by the educational specialists (e.g., tracking problems, fine motor control difficulties), as was his information processing style (he tended to process aural information better than visual information). Unfortunately, these findings did not serve to explain the nature or significance of Douglas's information-processing difficulties, nor did they lead to effective treatment recommendations for him. Consequently, we were not surprised that Douglas was not well understood by his teachers or his parents.

We found that the lateralized pattern of psychomotor and sensory-perceptual findings, viewed within the context of his general configuration of neuropsychological strengths and weaknesses, was particularly helpful in identifying the nature and degree of his information-processing deficiencies. In this regard, the levels of performance and the configuration of his neuropsychological test results were considered to be consistent with the presence of a brain-related deficiency that would serve to explain the presence of his academic difficulties. Moreover, consideration of the type and degree of Douglas's neuropsychological impairments and strengths, in conjunction with his immediate and most probable future academic difficulties, led directly to the formulation of a remedial educational program that was tailored to meet his needs.

Teaching a learning-disabled blind child to read

Next we examine a case that should serve to illustrate further how neuropsychological and other relevant information can be translated into a realistic remedial plan for the academically retarded brain-impaired child. This particular case example was selected because the child's level and pattern of neuropsychological test results indicated clearly how one might best address the specific referral questions asked. Furthermore, since this patient has been (legally) blind since birth, we feel that our findings serve to illustrate the power and range of the neuropsychological assessment when employed for the purpose of designing appropriate remedial–habilitational interventions.

Case 5-2: Larry

Larry came to our attention when we were consulting at his school regarding another child who was experiencing academic difficulties. The educational consultant involved in this case mentioned in passing that she was concerned about a 9-year-old boy who was legally blind, yet who could see details in pictures. His attending physicians also felt that Larry had sufficient visual acuity to learn how to read. Nevertheless, Larry was educationally retarded to the point that he was unable to name the letters of the alphabet through oral recitation or when their graphic characteristics were presented to him visually. The educational consultant was particularly concerned about Larry's lack of progress because of his relatively advanced age. In addition, there had already been a great deal of time, effort, and resources expended on remedial educational interventions for him.

Before presenting the details of Larry's neuropsychological assessment, it would be instructive to examine other aspects of his developmental and educational histories. This boy had three older siblings, all of whom were performing reasonably well at school. He resided with his family, including his mother and step-father, at the time of the assessment. Although presenting as a reasonably resourceful, well-intentioned family, it was clear that financial exigencies had from time to time eventuated in some strain within the family unit. The parents indicated to us that they wanted Larry to develop his full potential. They pointed out that they had actively encouraged him to participate in activities in the home environment that were typical of sighted children (e.g., bike riding within a restricted area) as a way of doing their part in facilitating his growth and development. They also stated their strong preference for having him remain at home (rather than in a special school setting where he would have to board away from home) during the remainder of his childhood and adolescence.

Larry was born with what his ophthalmologist described as probable optic hypoplasia (small underdeveloped optic nerves resulting in reduced vision) in conjunction with ocular nystagmus. In addition, repeated ophthalmological examinations had revealed that there might be blind spots located centrally in his visual fields or scattered throughout the visual fields. At 7 years of age, ophthalmological evaluation revealed that his visual acuity was accurate for a projection of light in his right eye and for finger counting at 3 feet with his left eye. There was a constant horizontal nystagmus described in these medical reports and, apparently because of the nystagmus, accurate visual field details could not be obtained. Both fundi revealed the characteristic appearance of optic nerve hypoplasia, with the maldevelopment of the optic nerve being more pronounced in the left eye.

Larry had a long and varied educational history. He entered a school for developmentally handicapped children at 2 years of age. When he was 4 years old, he attended a "regular" preschool before entering kindergarten in a "regular" elementary school. He performed poorly during his kindergarten program, and because of this was transferred to another regular Grade 1 class which was thought to be better equipped to provide him with special educational assistance. Even with this assistance, he made very little progress during his Grade 1 year. Therefore, a decision was made to transfer him to a specialized School for the Blind during his Grade 2 school year. This school placement was approximately 200 miles from his home, and consequently it was necessary for him to reside there. He did not perform well in this specialized school setting, even though it was the opinion of his teachers that he had adequate vision to enable him to learn to read. His vision and related ocular problems continued to be tested regularly by ophthalmologists and other specialists who were responsible for providing services for the blind. This led to a fairly wide range of alternative instructional methods being prescribed for him, including Braille. None of these interventions eventuated in substantial progress in any form of reading.

Because of his lack of progress in the School for the Blind and his parents' deep affection for him, they requested that he return home. He was then enrolled in a regular community school where he was placed in a class for trainable mentally retarded children for the remainder of his Grade 3 school year. It was during his second year in this classroom (equivalent to an age-appropriate Grade 4 school year) that he was brought to our attention.

It should be pointed out that, just prior to his neuropsychological assessment (which was conducted several days following his tenth birthday), fairly extensive educational and vision-related assessment had confirmed that he could match phonemes with their visual counterparts within a workbook format. However, he was still unable to identify the graphic counterparts of alphabetical letters that were named for him and/or name the letters of the alphabet upon visual presentation. Furthermore, it should be stressed that a wide range of educational techniques and interventions had been employed with him to this point. At the time of the neuropsychological assessment, he was having alphabetical letters magnified considerably for him during regular sessions in his academic regimen, although this did not seem to have any efficacious impact on his reading proficiency. With this information as background, the referral questions posed to us included the following: (1) Is this boy able to learn how to read? and if so, (2) What approach(es) should be used in teaching him to read?

For the most part, this youngster was assessed in the usual routine manner by technicians who had undergone extensive, systematic training in the administration of our neuropsychological test batteries. Larry was examined by one psychometrist during the morning session and another during the afternoon session. It took Larry somewhat longer to complete the test battery than is typical of most other 10-year-olds; this was primarily due to his visual limitations. In any case, he was administered all of the measures in our standard neuropsychological test battery for older (9- to 15-year-old) children, except for the Speech-Sounds Perception Test and the Miles ABC Test for Ocular Dominance.

When presented with detailed visual information during the examination, Larry scanned such material with his head virtually on the page. During such exercises, there was a great deal of head movement, suggesting the presence of multiple visual field defects. There was a rotary type of nystagmus in evidence bilaterally, although this would subside at times. He had a tendency to say "I can't see it" when in fact he was simply having difficulty with other (information-processing) aspects of the task requirements. For example, on the Aphasia Screening Test he said "I can't see it" when presented with the sentence, "SEE THE BLACK DOG." Nevertheless, he was able to copy the word, "SQUARE," with reasonable accuracy, even though the printed letters were exactly the same size as those in "SEE THE BLACK DOG." Thus, it was quite difficult for the examiner to determine exactly what Larry could and could not see. Obviously, it was necessary to bear such factors in mind when interpreting his neuropsychological test results.

At this juncture, it should be noted that Larry's test results were interpreted "blindly" by the neuropsychologist. In this case, the neuropsychologist knew only that the child had failed to make gains in reading, despite extensive remedial educational efforts, that he was legally blind, and that there were some difficulties involved in testing him as reflected by the psychometrist's comments. Some of these neuropsychological test results are presented in Figure 5-2.

To illustrate the method involved in constructing a reasonable and realistic remedial intervention plan designed to address this boy's reading impairments and to highlight important aspects of his neuropsychological test results, the initial six steps of our developmental neuropsychological remediation–habilitation model are discussed in detail as they relate to this case.

STEP 1: NEUROPSYCHOLOGICAL ABILITY STRUCTURE

First, it was determined that Larry's general capacity for adaptation (including his ability to think and form concepts) was somewhat limited. It

Figure 5-2. Neuropsychological test results—
Case 5-2 (Larry).

Age	10 yr, 0 mo
WISC	
Verbal IQ	90
Information	8
Comprehension	10
Arithmetic	4
Similarities	9
Vocabulary	11
Digit Span	8
Performance IQ	68
Picture Completion	10
Picture Arrangement	4
Block Design	8
Object Assembly	4
Coding	1
Full Scale IQ	77
PPVT	
IQ	76
Mental Age	6–10
WRAT	
Reading (grade equiv.)	K.1
Spelling (grade equiv.)	K.2
Arithmetic (grade equiv.)	1.9

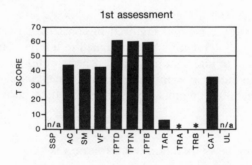

SENSORY–PERCEPTUAL ABILITIES

Performance on a Sweep Hearing Test was negative. Tests for simple visual imperception and suppression were not completed due to Larry's ocular and visual limitations. There was evidence of bilateral finger dysgraphesthesia and astereognosis for coins.

APHASIA SCREENING TEST

Larry exhibited considerable difficulties on this test. Reading, spelling, and arithmetic errors were in evidence. He was unable to repeat correctly any of the complex multisyllabic words. There was some evidence of dysnomia and auditory–verbal agnosia. He was able to reproduce graphically a triangle, a square, and (with some practice) a Greek cross.

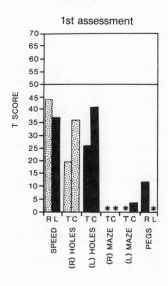

1st assessment

would seem probable that Larry's inability to benefit from the many different sorts of remedial interventions that had already been prescribed for him was in part a reflection of his somewhat limited higher-order cognitive capacities. With this information in mind, we thought that he would require a systematic, straightforward remedial reading program that would include direct instruction designed to take best advantage of his neuropsychological strengths, and that would also include exercises that should help him to generalize newly learned information and skills.

Larry's general configuration of neuropsychological test results included the following: somewhat poor motor and psychomotor abilities; impaired primary visual, visual–spatial, and visual–motor abilities; below-average concept-formation and related problem-solving skills; at least age-appropriate tactile–kinesthetic abilities when nonsymbolic information was involved; basically adequate verbal expressive and auditory–perceptual skills. In part because of the number and types of systems–capacities that were compromised, Larry's general configuration of neuropsychological impairments was considered to be consistent with the presence of mild to moderate, somewhat generalized neurological dysfunction.

Larry's neuropsychological strengths were at best average (from a level of performance standpoint) as compared to age expectations. Nevertheless, in consideration of the specific nature of his information processing strengths (auditory–perceptual, verbal expressive, and tactile–kinesthetic abilities) and his current most salient environmental demands (learning to read), it was suggested that, with appropriate training, some degree of success in reading should be forthcoming. At the same time, it was clear that we could not rely on his fund of stored engrams (e.g., his knowledge of sound–symbol relationships) as a source of strength to serve as a foundation for his remedial reading program. Rather, it was felt necessary to design a remedial reading program that would start at "square one." As an example of the necessity for adopting the latter tack, it was found that he obtained only a 50% success rate in naming letters that were presented randomly to him on the WRAT.

All of the neuropsychological and other evidence (e.g., medical) that we obtained suggested that Larry's suspected brain impairment was of the chronic variety. There was no evidence of any (other) sort of neurological disease process or of any seizure disorder. Furthermore, his ophthalmologists reported that his visual condition was stable and was not likely to deteriorate. In fact, they agreed that Larry would probably improve his functional vision-related capabilities with experience and practice.

STEP 2: ENVIRONMENTAL DEMANDS

Larry's formal (environmental) demands were quite circumscribed at this time. His teachers, educational consultant, and parents wanted him to learn to read, if this were possible. Outside of the school situation he functioned reasonably well, although he was unable to compete with the other youngsters in complex psychomotor activities (e.g., soccer games). Nevertheless, he was liked by other children and he participated actively with them in many of their neighbourhood play activities.

It was obvious that learning to read would considerably enhance Larry's educational and vocational opportunities. At the same time, it had to be borne in mind that his educational and vocational prospects were already somewhat restricted because of his primary visual, psychomotor, and general cognitive limitations. Also taken into account when planning his remedial reading program was the likelihood that he would manifest secondary socioemotional disturbances in the future if he were not (1) taught to take advantage of his better developed neuropsychological strengths and (2) given the opportunity for regular success experiences during his preadulthood years.

STEP 3: BEHAVIORAL OUTCOME PREDICTIONS

In light of the results of Larry's neuropsychological examination and his educational history (which included a lack of responsiveness to the wide range of special educational reading techniques that had been prescribed for him), our initial prediction was that he would not make gains in reading without a specific program that would take advantage of his neuropsychological strengths while minimizing the impact of his primary sensory handicap. We also felt that he would make substantial gains in learning how to read if he remained well motivated and if he were involved in a systematic instructional method that would emphasize his relatively well developed auditory–perceptual and verbal abilities. It was thought that Larry would be at considerable risk for the development of significant socioemotional difficulties if he were to fail to make any further progress in the educational milieu, the current focus of which was reading instruction.

STEPS 4, 5, AND 6: IDEAL REMEDIAL PLAN; AVAILABILITY OF REMEDIAL RESOURCES; REALISTIC REMEDIAL PLAN

For Larry, the "ideal" short-term intervention plan did not have to be modified significantly before it was implemented. His family was very cooperative and supportive of any sort of remedial intervention that was thought to be required within the school and (to some extent) home settings. His parents and teachers agreed that his educational program should focus on teaching him to read. He attended a school within a Board of Education that had an excellent track record in treating reading-impaired children, in part due to their fine staff of highly skilled educational consultants and special education teachers. Furthermore, the administrative structure within this School Board was such that a remedial educational program designed outside of the immediate school setting could be implemented directly if the educational consultant thought that the program would be beneficial for the child. In addition, Larry's teacher was willing to try anything that would help him learn to read.

At the same time, it was clear that the long history of failure to teach Larry to read had the net effect of casting this particular remedial plan as a kind of last resort. Indeed, the position taken by the school authorities was that, if a program built around our remedial recommendations failed with Larry, they would initiate a "talking books" program with him.

With this information as background, we decided that a modification of established educational programs and procedures would be necessary to communicate this boy's treatment needs to this teacher and to help her facilitate the actual treatment program. In Larry's case, it was clear that a carefully structured program involving systematic approximations of preestablished goals was indicated. With these treatment principles in mind, the remedial reading program that follows was designed for application to this youngster.

THE READING PROGRAM

1. Choose a highly phonetic reading series and then select the first reader in that series.

2. Select the first four letters–consonants in the initial reader and then have Larry engage in oral rehearsal of their phonemic equivalents in a prespecified order (note in this connection that his forward digit span on the WISC was found to be five). Have him rehearse this phonemic series until it has been overlearned/automatized by him. To provide a reasonable estimate of his rate of learning of this task, count the number of trials needed for him to rehearse this phonemic series without error. Use this time estimate as an approximation of the time needed to repeat this step in his program.

3. Print in ¼-inch bold capital letters the graphic equivalents of the four consonant sounds that he has overlearned (automatized), in the sequence in which he has learned them. (Note that we had found that he could see well the bold ¼-inch lettering on the Aphasia Screening Test card items.)

4. Then have him produce the phonemic counterpart of each printed consonant while pointing at it until this has been automatized for him. Again, make note of the number of trials to acquisition.

5. Randomize two, then three, then all of the letters in the sequence until Larry is able to produce the phonemic equivalent of each grapheme

without error, regardless of the order in which they appear in the sequence. Count the number of trials to acquisition.

6. If necessary, have him trace the graphemes with his fingers (obviously they have to be larger than ¼-inch) while having him produce their phonemic equivalents if this is needed to help him to automatize the sound–symbol relationship. (As it turned out, this step was required in the actual remedial program.)

7. Go through this same process with two more consonants (from the beginning stages of his reader) and the first two short vowel sounds.

8. Continue to add to his repertoire all the new consonants and vowels found in the early stages of his reader. When he has overlearned the sound–symbol relationships for eight consonants and two vowels, introduce him to the first words in his reader; these should be printed in ¼-inch bold type on separate cards.

9. Have him sound out or decode each of these words while employing a phonics-based strategy.

His teacher was asked to work with Larry on this remedial reading program for 30 minutes in the morning and 30 minutes in the afternoon, 5 days per week. She was able to give him her individual attention for both of these sessions, while her assistant took the rest of the class. We asked Larry's mother to carry out the same program with him at home for 30 minutes each night (Monday through Thursday). She did this for about 5 weeks, and then found it difficult to follow through when the weather got warmer and he wanted to play with the other children in the neighborhood during daylight hours.

Our first follow-up was conducted 10 weeks after the remedial reading program had commenced. Larry had already begun to exhibit remarkable success, especially in view of his academic history. With 10 weeks' training, he was able to identify consistently 18 sound–symbol combinations (small letters), including consonant and short vowel sounds. He could also identify without error the sound–symbol combinations for five capital letters. His teacher reported that he was consolidating new sound–symbol relationships at a rate of 1 per school day at the 10-week mark of this remedial intervention.

When putting into play his newly learned skills, Larry was able to decode novel, phonetically accurate words that were up to four letters in length, provided that these included the sound–symbol relationships that had already been consolidated by him (e.g., the word "raft"). It was found that the type employed in a "primary school" typewriter was sufficient to meet his visual needs. Therefore, his teacher began to retype his reader, as he was already able to read whole paragraphs without error.

Approximately 1 year later, Larry was reading comfortably at the Grade 2 level. His oral reading was slow, but he maintained excellent comprehension for the material that he had read. He was expected by his teachers and by us to continue to make substantial gains in the reading area and eventually reach a "functional" (say, Grade 5 or Grade 6) reading level. His parents and teachers were exceptionally pleased with his progress. He was now at a point in remediation where he required considerably less individual attention, and consequently he was integrated into a self-contained class for children with learning disabilities that was available in his home school.

Other educational problems surfaced for Larry during the 1-year period following our initial assessment of him. For example, he had difficulty in printing between the lines on his page. In the 1-year follow-up meeting, we made some further remedial recommendations (e.g., suggesting that he work on raised lined paper until he developed a kinesthetic appreciation for writing between the lines on his page). It was clear that at this point his teachers felt quite confident in their ability to help Larry to deal effectively with these new educational challenges. This may have been a reflection of their recent successes with him and their more complete understanding of how his neuropsychological strengths and weaknesses and primary sensory input difficulties were interacting with his educational needs.

In summary, Larry's primary sensory handicap (legal blindness) served to complicate the clinical picture that his teachers and other professionals had generated of him. Confusion surrounding this clinical picture spilled over into academic remedial planning for him. This is not an atypical set of affairs in that the learning and information-processing handicaps of children who suffer from pervasive physical handicaps are not easily understood by most of their teachers or other caretakers. In this case neuropsychological examination provided the opportunity to generate inferences relating to Larry's level and pattern of neuropsychological strengths and weaknesses; this information led directly to the formation of a realistic and successful remedial reading program for him. The remedial issues in this case were quite clear, thus providing an opportunity to illustrate in a straightforward fashion how the neuropsychologist might go about constructing a remedial educational program that is tailored to meet some of the child's presenting and future adaptational needs.

The fact that Larry, his parents, and his teachers were particularly cooperative and well motivated is one reason for the positive intervention results. Nevertheless, there were many other critical aspects of his remedial reading program (e.g., the size of type used for his letters and words; the systematic "auditory presentation" approach employed when teaching him sound–symbol relationships; tying his remedial program in with an available reader series that was familiar to his teacher), any one of which, if omitted, may have led to failure in his program. These and other critical aspects of his remedial program were determined with his neuropsycho-logical test data and our remedial/habilitational model in mind.

Identifying and treating a psychogenic learning disorder

In the first case presented in this chapter (Douglas), the child was referred by school authorities for validation and clarification of his learning difficulties. In the second case (Larry), school personnel wanted to know if the child could learn to read, and if so how best to teach him. It is important to note that in both instances the neuropsychological examination led to substantial changes in the child's remedial educational program. The same is true for this next case (Stephen). School authorities referred this boy for clarification regarding the nature of his "learning disability," and for information regarding ways and means of enhancing their remedial efforts with him. As was the case for Douglas and Larry, extensive time, effort, and expense had been provided for Stephen (with little in the way of positive results) prior to our examination of him. In fact, at the time of his neuropsychological assessment, Stephen's educational progress was thought to be at a standstill.

Case 5-3: Stephen

At the age of 11½ years, Stephen was referred for neuropsychological assessment by a special educational consultant at his School Board because of a history of long-standing academic difficulties. Despite what appeared to be an adequately developed ability structure, he had failed to respond to the wide variety of remedial education formats that had been provided for him. At the time that Stephen was referred, his teacher reported that he tended to be disorganized, that he did not complete the work assigned to him, and that he had made little progress over the past 3 academic years.

Included in his early medical history were periodic hearing difficulties (apparently associated with middle-ear infections) that had gone largely untreated until about the kindergarten level. At that time he underwent surgery (myringotomy) that involved the placement of tubes into his ears. In addition, he suffered from allergies for which he had received ongoing treatment (medication) since his preschool years.

Stephen's academic difficulties were first noticed at the Grade 2 level. At that time, he was described as somewhat passive and difficult to motivate. His mother had referred him for psychoeducational assessment while he was in Grade 2; this referral led to an ongoing series of special educational interventions for him. It was necessary for him to repeat

Grade 3 because of academic underachievement and since that time he had received remedial withdrawal assistance, initially for work in phonics and word-attack skills (20 minutes per day, 5 days per week). Just prior to assessment, his remedial withdrawal educational program had expanded to approximately 150 to 200 minutes per week and was considered to be a "general assistance" program, since he was exhibiting difficulties in many academic areas.

School personnel had noted that he seemed to lack the capacity for long-term retention of his school work: Stephen was able to comprehend lessons at the time that they were delivered to him, but was unable to recall the same material later on in the week. While at school, he seemed to be somewhat introverted and shy, even with his peers. Generally, he was found to be only passively involved in peer-group activities. It was noted that his behavior was worsening in the home situation and that he was becoming physically abusive with his two younger siblings (he was the eldest of three children). Stephen's mother reported that he was becoming increasingly noncompliant.

During the neuropsychological examination, Stephen was coopera-tive and rapport was easily obtained with him. He conversed in an average fashion, and his general level of physical activity was age-appropriate. He was attentive throughout the examination and his motivation to do well was never in doubt. He exhibited a friendly and confident demeanor, and he seemed to enjoy the testing session.

In general, Stephen's neuropsychological test results (Figure 5-3) were reflective of a well-developed and balanced ability structure. There was no evidence of any significant form of neuropsychological impairment. Never-theless, he exhibited considerable difficulty when required to take a pencil in hand. For example, on the Underlining Test he performed in a clearly below-average manner on 12 of the 13 critical subtests; also, his handwrit-ing (and to a lesser extent drawings and WISC Coding performances) was tremulous in appearance. These performances stood in marked contrast to his superior performances with each hand on tests of static and kinetic motor steadiness and speeded eye–hand coordination (Grooved Pegboard Test).

The Personality Inventory for Children form completed by his mother reflected her concern about Stephen's general level of socioemo-tional adjustment. She saw him as being somewhat anxious, disruptive, and inappropriate. This was consistent with the impression gained from her pattern of responses on the Behavior Problem Checklist (Quay & Peterson, 1979).

It was hypothesized that this boy's early (periodic) hearing difficulties, in combination with his allergies, may have predisposed him to academic difficulties during the initial stages of his educational career. (We have often noted slow progress in psycholinguistic skill development and academic learning in children with this combination of problems.) It should be mentioned at this juncture that he showed no evidence of hearing deficiencies on the Sweep Hearing Test when we examined him. In the Remedial Educational Conference, which took place following the assessment, it was learned that Stephen's parents had been greatly concerned about his early educational difficulties, and as was noted earlier in our discussion of this case, they had responded by insisting on special educational intervention for him as early as the Grade 2 level. Furthermore, it was learned that Stephen's father had a history of learning difficulties and had not wanted his son to be confronted with limited vocational options (his self-perception) because of a lack of education.

Stephen, being the eldest son of a reading-disabled father, most likely had special pressure placed on him in an effort to prevent him from incurring the same type and degree of academic difficulties that his father had experienced (see Lenkowsky & Serposnek, 1978). These sorts of misunderstandings had led to the establishment of regular stringent homework drills for Stephen, which were typically combined with the parents' verbal urgings that he could always perform better. In addition, there was some disagreement between his parents regarding how best to intervene with Stephen. For instance, his mother would allow him to spell orally when practising for spelling dictation because of his difficulties with handwriting. His father, on the other hand, insisted that Stephen write his words out, even though it made him terribly anxious and appeared to be correlated with burgeoning behavioral problems.

It was our opinion that this boy's educational difficulties resulted primarily from socioemotional factors, including his considerable anxiety when confronted with academic tasks. His anxiety was reflected most obviously in the quality of his handwriting, despite his having adequate abilities in all of the component skills necessary for this activity. As often happens in such cases, considerable time, effort, and misguided attention had been applied to this child's adaptive (educational) difficulties. At the time that we assessed him, Stephen's difficulties were worsening rather than responding favorably to the remedial interventions that had been designed and implemented for him.

The remedial recommendations in this case were twofold: (1) that special educational interventions at school and on the home front should be withdrawn completely; and (2) that he should be gradually desensitized to academic school work, particularly pen-and-paper tasks, and systematically reinforced in a positive manner for any and all modest advances in academic work. It was suggested that his parents encourage him to play with his peers; more generally, we wanted them to encourage the development of Stephen's prosocial behavior through their facilitation of positive peer and family activities. Both school personnel and Stephen's parents were encouraged to communicate openly regarding his progress. At the

Figure 5-3. Neuropsychological test results—
Case 5-3 (Stephen).

Age	11 yr, 5 mo
WISC	
Verbal IQ	103
Information	8
Comprehension	10
Arithmetic	10
Similarities	11
Vocabulary	11
Digit Span	12
Performance IQ	118
Picture Completion	12
Picture Arrangement	14
Block Design	11
Object Assembly	15
Coding	11
Full Scale IQ	111
PPVT	
IQ	101
Mental Age	12–1
WRAT	
Reading (grade equiv.)	4.9
Spelling (grade equiv.)	4.5
Arithmetic (grade equiv.)	4.1

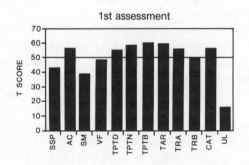

SENSORY-PERCEPTUAL ABILITIES

Stephen's performance on a Sweep Hearing Test was normal. There was some evidence of finger agnosia (left hand) and astereognosis for coins with both hands. He performed very well on tests for fingertip dysgraphesthesia.

APHASIA SCREENING TEST

Spelling difficulties and problems in arithmetic calculation were evident. He was unable to enunciate correctly any of the complex multisyllabic words. There were no indications of problems in naming, reading, or following simple directions on this test.

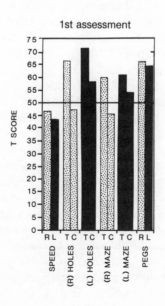

1st assessment

same time, it was pointed out that continued sensitization of Stephen to the academic situation would be counterproductive.

In summary, educational authorities were unable to establish the primary reason for Stephen's academic learning difficulties, although they had tested him through the employment of a psychoeducational test battery. On the basis of the results of the psychoeducational assessment, it was concluded that Stephen had well-developed abilities and that he should respond to additional instruction in his weak academic areas. Subsequently, his academic progress was reviewed by his teachers, and his phonics skills were identified as being particularly underdeveloped. A remedial withdrawal program that focused on phonics skills training was undertaken with him, beginning at the Grade 2 level. Having continued with this treatment approach for a number of years and reaping little in the way of benefits, neuropsychological assessment was then requested to delineate more precisely the nature of Stephen's learning disability and give suggestions about how to treat it.

In our clinic setting, as many as 10% of the children who are referred because of academic underachievement and suspected learning disabilities *do not* exhibit evidence of neuropsychological impairment. Such cases pose particular difficulty for educators because the children do not exhibit blatant behavioral disturbance (and therefore cannot be classified as having a behavioral or emotional disorder for the purposes of special class placement). At the same time, there is insufficient evidence to "rule in" or "rule out" the possibility of a learning disability. When such a child's parents undertake to make certain that special educational assistance is provided for him/her, the matter often proves to be most costly and emotionally draining for all concerned. As in Stephen's case, once the possibility of a significant central processing deficiency has been ruled out (in this case, on the basis of a neuropsychological examination), the child's teachers and other educational authorities are most often quite relieved, especially when the direction for further interventions is clear.

At this point in our discussion of this case, it should be noted that Stephen's parents would probably benefit from a course of goal-oriented psychotherapeutic intervention aimed at enhancing their communication skills with each other and with their children, especially Stephen. Within the context of such a goal-oriented family intervention, Stephen's learning difficulties could be put into the sort of meaningful perspective that would help his parents to gain a better understanding of his needs in conjunction with their own needs. It is difficult for some parents to deal with this sort of recommendation and the conflicts which its implementation are perceived to involve. In cases where such family intervention is unavailable or is refused, encouraging the child's parents to adopt specific roles (as we did in those aspects of Stephen's remedial programs that involved the encouragement of prosocial behavior and the carrying out of homework assignments) may in itself prove to be particularly helpful.

Later-emerging learning disabilities: Assessment and consultation

The next case presented in this chapter was selected to illustrate two special problems in academic remediation. The first is the proper identification and concomitant treatment of children who, after having fared reasonably well during the early grades, exhibit significant academic difficulties (and often some degree of behavioral disturbance) during the later elementary school grades. We have found that children who present with this academic–behavioral history are often misidentified and/or treated ineffectively by educators and other professionals (including psychologists) associated with the educational process. The second problem to be discussed in this section relates to the manner in which the neuropsychologist might consult effectively with the child's teachers and other caretakers. This is especially important when the understanding that these caretakers have of the child is quite different from that derived from the neuropsychological assessment data and a developmental neuropsychological perspective.

There are at least three subtypes of learning disabled children whose academic learning difficulties are not usually outstanding until the children reach the Grade 4 to 5 level. Unfortunately, it is often assumed that such children have motivational or behavioral difficulties, and that these are the causes of their emerging academic and other adaptive problems. We have found that, when such an attitude is held by the child's teachers and/or his parents, it often serves to exacerbate the presenting problems and promote the development of secondary disturbances of emotion and conduct.

One later-emerging learning disability subtype exhibits outstanding problems that are associated primarily with deficits in the nonverbal behavioral realm. We have discussed in considerable detail the adaptive behavioral (including educational) difficulties of such children in other places (see Strang & Rourke, 1985a, 1985b), and some of these issues are dealt with in Chapter 6 of this volume. A second subtype of later-emerging learning disability has long been identified, although the educational and other needs of such children would not appear to be well understood by most professionals. These children typically exhibit difficulty in tasks that involve higher-order verbal sequential reasoning, organizing and/or retrieving multiple verbal cues, and related difficulties in verbal output (including oral and written verbal expression). When such deficiencies are operative within the context of age-appropriate nonverbal reasoning, visual–spatial, tactile–perceptual, psychomotor, and auditory–verbal receptive skills, they may well be effectively masked during the early school years. However, such children typically exhibit increasing academic difficulty as the degree of complexity of the input, storage, organization, and retrieval requirements of the academic work load increase significantly.

Again, in our (Canadian) school systems, it is at about the Grade 4 to 5 level that such children face significant academic difficulty, and school failures at the Grade 6 level are not uncommon.

The subject of this section is yet another subtype of later-emerging learning disability. Among the neuropsychological characteristics that represent the hallmarks of this learning disability are the following: poorly developed concept-formation and problem-solving skills, difficulty in generating and modifying appropriate plans of action, and other associated higher-order cognitive disabilities. In some cases, these problem-solving deficiencies may be fairly generalized (i.e., the children perform poorly on all problem-solving tasks and/or on more complex components of other types of information processing tasks, such as the planning component of the Grooved Pegboard Test). In other cases the child's pattern of neuropsychological deficiencies may be associated primarily with the presence of underdeveloped nonverbal reasoning abilities. One might argue that these differentiations may represent further subtype distinctions that should be made. Nevertheless, the clinical ramifications for children who fit this general category of later-emerging learning disability would appear to be quite similar, even when taking into account the neuropsychological diagnostic distinctions that most often can be made. The following case example should serve to illustrate the educational and general adaptive ramifications of deficiencies in higher-order problem solving, planning, and other closely associated capabilities.

Case 5-4: Ted

Ted's three assessments covered the years from early childhood to middle adolescence. The span of years between his first and last assessments as well as the similarity in test measures employed with him should serve to illustrate how his underlying pattern of neuropsychological strengths and deficiencies remained remarkably consistent throughout his middle childhood and early adolescence. However, it is also clear that some aspects of his pattern of test results underwent significant change. The latter findings are typical of this subtype of learning-disabled child as well as many others (Fisk & Rourke, 1979). In accordance with the findings at each age at which he was tested, changes and adaptations in Ted's prescribed remedial program and other intervention formats were made and are described here. In these respects, Steps 5, 6, and 7 in our remedial–habilitational model are highlighted during the course of this case presentation.

Ted was first referred for neuropsychological assessment at 5 years, 8 months of age by a clinical psychologist; he was tested shortly following his sixth birthday. The primary reasons for referral at that time centered around his behavioral difficulties. He was said to be uncontrollable, destructive, and aggressive towards neighborhood children. It was reported that he engaged in such behavior as breaking windows, throwing his mother's jewelry into the furnace, and pouring paint across the front of his house. His mother had been recently divorced and was remarried. Even within Ted's reconstituted family, poor parental management skills were identified by the referring party as being one factor that was serving to promote his behavioral difficulties. It should also be noted that Ted's parents had refused assistance from the clinical psychologist who had originally assessed Ted to help them develop more effective child-management skills.

Ted did not exhibit any outstanding behavioral difficulties while at school. His teachers reported that he had some friends in his class, although he was not very outgoing and seemed to be lacking in confidence. In our testing situation he was cooperative and well behaved. It was noted that while being tested he was inattentive at times, and he exhibited considerable difficulty in understanding test instructions. Special efforts were made to make certain that his instructional needs were met before a new task was undertaken.

The results of this boy's neuropsychological assessments are presented in Figure 5-4. A quick perusal of these data reveals that a number of measures that are typically administered to children within the 5- to 8-year age range were not completed by Ted during his initial assessment. This was in part due to his attentional difficulties and other problems that he had in complying with the complexities of some task requirements. These factors were taken into consideration when evaluating his neuropsychological test results. The following tentative generalizations were formulated on the basis of the results obtained.

1. Ted exhibited difficulty in dealing effectively with nonredundant information introduced via the visual and auditory modalities.

2. Measures that involved planning, problem solving, and/or abstract reasoning were performed poorly by him.

3. His visual–perceptual–organizational skills were found to be mildly underdeveloped.

4. Ted's level of performance on measures of auditory–perceptual and verbal abilities fluctuated somewhat. Nevertheless, these ability areas were viewed as being relative strengths for him.

5. Due to this boy's test-taking disposition, it was difficult to generate confident inferences regarding the integrity of his cerebral hemispheres at the time that this examination was conducted. Nevertheless, we now would hypothesize that this pattern of neuropsychological strengths and weaknesses is consistent with the presence of mild impairment in the abilities associated primarily with the functional integrity of prefrontal brain regions, more so within the right cerebral hemisphere.

Based on the results of Ted's first neuropsychological assessment and

Figure 5-4. Neuropsychological test results—Case 5-4 (Ted).

Age	6 yr, 0 mo	7 yr, 0 mo	13 yr, 5 mo
WISC			
Verbal IQ	101	100	77
Information	12	9	6
Comprehension	12	12	5
Arithmetic	8	8	6
Similarities	9	13	8
Vocabulary	13	13	8
Digit Span	7	5	5
Performance IQ	86	96	89
Picture Completion	11	8	7
Picture Arrangement	9	8	8
Block Design	7	7	7
Object Assembly	9	12	11
Coding	4	12	9
Full Scale IQ	93	98	81
PPVT			
IQ	89	108	97
Mental Age	5–1	7–10	12–7
WRAT			
Reading (grade equiv.)	K.3	1.5	5.4
Spelling (grade equiv.)	K.8	1.3	4.1
Arithmetic (grade equiv.)	K.6	1.8	3.3

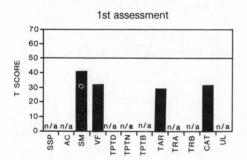

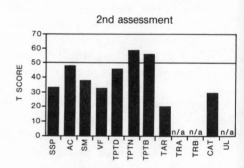

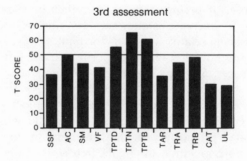

SENSORY-PERCEPTUAL ABILITIES

There was no sign of hearing acuity problems on the Sweep Hearing Test. During Ted's first examination, there was some marginal evidence of finger agnosia, more so on the left side. Tests for dysgraphesthesia were discontinued because of his attentional difficulties. His second examination did not reveal any serious sensory-perceptual deficiencies. Nevertheless, his inattention may have led to some errors during tests for visual imperception and suppression. On his third testing there was some marginal evidence of finger agnosia (left hand) and astereognosis for coins (right hand). Overall, he was not thought to exhibit any significant sensory-perceptual deficiencies.

APHASIA SCREENING TEST

Ted's results on the Aphasia Screening Test were somewhat inconsistent in the first two examinations. For example, he responded correctly to items involving right-left discrimination during the first examination and erroneously to both of these items during the second examination that was conducted one year later. On the other hand, he made improvements on those test items involving reading (naming numbers and letters and identifying simple words). On both occasions he was unable to produce a reasonable facsimile of a Greek cross, and there were some perseverative tendencies evident in his drawings. His printing was much improved during his second examination, and he computed correctly all three mechanical arithmetic calculations that he had failed during his first testing. There were no naming errors on the Aphasia Screening Test in either of his first two testing sessions. In the third testing session, there were oral and written spelling errors in evidence. He performed both arithmetic calculations incorrectly, and he was unable to repeat exactly any of the complex multisyllabic words.

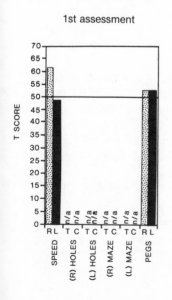

1st assessment

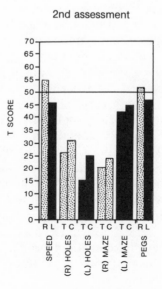

2nd assessment

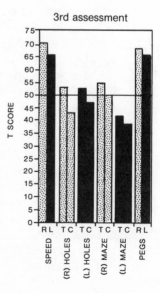

3rd assessment

187

the other factors associated with our remediational–habilitational model, the following remedial recommendations were made to this boy's parents and his teachers. First, we emphasized the need for Ted's parents to undergo training in systematic behavior management techniques. The parenting program that was being offered in our Center at the time (Directive Parental Counseling; Holland, 1983) was thought to be especially suitable for Ted's behavior management needs. The remedial academic recommendations included (1) direct training in visual–motor and visual–spatial skills, in conjunction with (2) exercises designed to shape and increase his attentional skills. Finally, it was recommended that Ted be reassessed 1 year later to obtain a more precise picture of his neuropsychological ability structure and to update our remedial recommendations for him.

During the interval between Ted's first and second neuropsychological assessment, he underwent a clinical electroencephalographic examination. The EEG findings were interpreted by a neurosurgeon who was reasonably well versed in reading young children's EEG recordings. It was his opinion that Ted's EEG was "borderline" because of dysrhythmia arising from the frontal areas of the brain. This dysrhythmia was nonspecific in apearance, but suggested mild to moderate disturbance of brain functions in the anterior brain regions.

At the time of his second neuropsychological assessment, Ted's school report was reasonably favorable; he was described by his teacher at this time as being cheerful, courteous, and cooperative. There was, however, concern with respect to his seeming lack of confidence and apparent need for the teacher's approval of his work efforts. His written work, in particular, seemed on many occasions to be completed in a careless, disorganized manner. In addition, he exhibited some problems with number work and in beginning reading skills. It should be noted that there had been three school moves during the current school year; these changes no doubt had an adverse effect on his academic progress.

Ted was cooperative and appeared to put forth his best efforts during his second neuropsychological assessment. Nevertheless, he required close monitoring of his behavior by the examiner to help him maintain attention to the tasks at hand. Notwithstanding these observations, his test results were thought to be a reasonably reliable and valid reflection of his neuropsychological ability structure. The following are some generalizations derived from Ted's neuropsychological test results.

1. His general attentional difficulties were once again evident. However, they were most clearly associated with test situations that involved concept formation, problem solving, and generating appropriate plans of action.

2. In general, he exhibited considerable difficulty in problem-solving tasks, except for the Tactual Performance Test.

3. Some fluctuations were evident in his levels of performance on visual–perceptual and visual–spatial tasks; he exhibited both relative strengths and weaknesses in this realm.

4. His vocabulary was well developed, and he did not exhibit outstanding problems in auditory–verbal comprehension when information was presented in a meaningful context.

5. He exhibited marked difficulty on tests of motor steadiness in the static and kinetic dispositions.

6. His neuropsychological test results were thought to be consistent with the presence of mild, chronic dysfunction of the prefrontal and adjacent brain areas bilaterally; dysfunction within these regions of the right cerebral hemisphere was thought to be particularly probable.

At this juncture, it should be noted that many of Ted's initial presenting behavioral difficulties were no longer considered to be especially problematic. With this in mind, his presenting behavioral difficulties in the home and community settings were not thought to be related directly to his learning disability. Although a child who is hampered by Ted's type of learning disability may be less able to cope with stress in general (e.g., stresses within the family), because of his/her "masked" problem-solving, concept-formation, and associated higher-order cognitive deficiencies, we have observed that the majority of children who fit this subtype do not exhibit significant behavioral problems; for those children who do not exhibit behavioral difficulties, we have found that prudent manipulation of environmental contingencies (e.g., academic demands and expectations of the child) can often result in a remarkably quick "normalization" of the child's behavior. In those cases in which a behavior problem is present for a child with this pattern of abilities and deficits, we most often discover poor child management by his/her adult caretakers and/or negative reactions of the child to his/her inability to comply with other environmental (including school and community) demands. In Ted's case, both of these factors were operative.

The remedial recommendations included an emphasis on a phonics-based reading approach in conjunction with other techniques and methods (e.g., sight–word approaches) to help promote the development of Ted's reading skills. A highly structured classroom situation and routine were thought to be best suited for Ted's immediate formal learning needs. Direct training to improve his printing skills was recommended. Once again, the importance of systematic behavior management in the home and school environments was stressed.

Ted was referred for his third neuropsychological assessment at 13 years of age; academic problems represented the primary referring complaint. The special educational consultant who referred Ted to us noted that he had been assessed by us when he was much younger, and he felt that neuropsychological deficiencies might somehow be hampering his academic progress. At the same time, Ted's teachers and school principal held rather strong opinions regarding the nature (including the etiology) of his learning difficulties. Simply put, he was characterized by them as being "lazy." He was observed to "give up" when tasks became more complex, and this was felt to be direct evidence in support of their hypothesis of a motivational deficiency. These issues were dealt with directly at Ted's Remedial Educational Conference, which was attended by his teachers and special educational services personnel. However, before broaching this, a summary of the results of his third neuropsychological assessment is in order.

At 13½ years of age, Ted presented as a large, overweight, somewhat lethargic adolescent. Although he tended to respond very quickly to the task requirements of the assessment, he did not appear to be physically overactive (in contrast with his previous assessments). Although cooperative while he was being tested, he tended to speak only when spoken to; this made it somewhat difficult to assess his level of motivation. Testing was completed in a minimal amount of time.

Ted's neuropsychological test results (presented in Figure 5-4), when compared with those of his previous assessment, revealed a number of important findings, as follows:

1. His WISC Full Scale IQ dropped considerably as compared to those obtained in his previous assessments (12 to 17 points). This decline appeared to be related primarily to poorer performances on the Vocabulary, Comprehension, Information, and Similarities subtests. It could be argued that his motivation in the testing situation would account for these findings. However, it would seem far more likely, in view of his other neuropsychological limitations, that the increased complexity of these verbal tasks (including the associated storage, reasoning, and output requirements) posed particular difficulty for him. These findings are viewed as one manifestation of a developmental change in the expression of an underlying neuropsychological handicap.

2. Consistent with the above, he continued to perform in an impaired manner on the Category Test and on other tests (with the exception of the Tactual Performance Test) in which problem solving and/or concept formation constituted the primary requirements.

3. His pattern and level of test results on the Performance section of the WISC remained virtually the same as those exhibited in his second assessment. In addition, he continued to perform in a below-average manner on the Target Test, this being consistent with his previous test results.

4. Remarkable improvement was demonstrated by him in the motor, and especially the psychomotor, realms. In fact, complex eye–hand coordination was found to be exceptionally well developed. These findings are of interest for a number of reasons. First, his improvements in static and

kinetic motor steadiness were exhibited in conjunction with a distinct reduction in overt motor activity and restlessness. It might be speculated that the improvement in motor steadiness was a reflection of maturation of subcortical brain areas, which in turn had the effect of eliminating the driven quality of his behavior that was in evidence at 6 to 7 years of age. Second, Ted essentially caught up to his age-mates in the psychomotor areas, after having lagged substantially behind them when he was a young-ster. This may be viewed as support for some of the contentions of those theorists and clinicians who espouse the "developmental lag" hypothesis. However, it should be noted that while Ted's "lower-order" (in terms of an information-processing hierarchy) abilities developed considerably, he con-tinued to exhibit substantial deficits in the development of higher-order information-processing abilities. In fact, his complex reasoning deficien-cies were in many respects more limiting when he reached adolescence than they had been for him as a child. This was in part due to the increasingly complex nature of the formal and informal environmental (including learning) demands that he was encountering. The point here is that the most serious of Ted's information-processing deficiencies con-tinued to limit his capabilities when he was older. That is, he continued to perform poorly relative to his age-mates in some very basic adaptive ability areas, despite having made considerable gains (i.e., "caught up") in some skill areas.

5. Ted made progress in all academic areas, despite the fact that he attended a regular Grade 7 class and had received only part-time remedial educational assistance in the past. His pattern of performance on the WRAT was in keeping with his identified weaknesses in nonverbal reason-ing and in other forms of complex information processing. In this regard, he performed most poorly on the WRAT Arithmetic subtest. A task analysis of his WRAT Arithmetic performance revealed many different types of errors, including the following: misreading the mathematical sign and multiplying rather than adding two sets of numbers; omitting a step in a subtraction question; misaligning columns of numbers in a multiplica-tion question; and making an error in a simple addition problem. No doubt this type of production, in combination with his overtly complacent behavioral style, provided strong support for his teacher's contention that he was poorly motivated.

6. The results of Ted's neuropsychological assessment were thought to be consistent with the presence of cerebral dysfunction involving pri-marily the prefrontal regions of the brain, particularly those of the right cerebral hemisphere. In addition, questions were raised regarding the functional integrity of the parieto-occipital regions of the right cerebral hemisphere.

Following the assessment, we consulted with Ted's parents and teachers. A separate interview was held with his parents prior to the

Remedial Educational Conference. Essentially, their concerns were two-fold: (1) how best to prepare Ted (educationally) for adulthood; and (2) how to motivate him.

When speaking with Ted's parents, an attempt was made to determine the discrepancy between their understanding of him and the information and inferences that we had derived from Ted's repeated neuropsychological examinations. In this regard, it was clear that Ted's parents had observed his behavior closely and could predict accurately how he would be likely to behave in various situations. Nevertheless, they concluded that Ted's behavioral style, including his poor performance at school, was the result of a lack of motivation on his part. Through further discussion and probing comments, it was determined that Ted performed adequately when task requirements were clearly specified for him and/or he had available an overlearned routine for dealing with the task demands (e.g., cleaning up his room). On the other hand, he tended to perform very poorly when he was assigned a task that was not well structured and/or which required some degree of novel problem solving on his part. In his parents' words, he seemed to be "unable to do anything properly on his own."

While venting his feelings on this subject, his father provided an example of Ted's difficulties that was particularly instructive in the feedback situation. Ted had been asked to pile bricks that were strewn about in the yard following a building project; the complaint was that he had failed to complete the job. Questioning of the father revealed that Ted had actually spent considerable time and effort attempting to complete the task, but that he had become discouraged when the strategy that he was employing failed. With respect to the latter, Ted had piled the bricks in single piles rather than interlocking them for greater stability. When each brick pile was more than 8 or 10 bricks high, it inevitably collapsed; Ted's father recalled that he had observed him starting brick piles over again (in the same manner) once they had fallen down. At this point, an attempt was made to help Ted's parents to understand that it was precisely this type of task that had been in the past, and would continue to be in the future, the most difficult for Ted. It was explained to them that Ted's deficiencies in generating appropriate plans of action, especially in novel problem-solving situations, were especially problematic for him. After some further discussion of these and related issues, Ted's father was able to reflect on (and understand in a new light) other situations in which (1) he had provided his son with a strategy, and (2) this type of assistance had led to adequate results. For example, Ted was able to change a tire on his father's car "without any problem" after he had been shown a number of times how to do it and his initial attempts at the task had been supervised closely by his father. This discussion appeared to assist his parents to acquire a better understanding of their son and to see him in a more positive light. They stated that they felt better able to motivate him when necessary, and were quite satisfied with our recommendations to school personnel, which are discussed next.

When meeting with school personnel, we found that their concerns were much the same as were those held by Ted's parents. Ted's teacher in particular wanted to know how to motivate him in the classroom situation, while his school principal and special educational consultant were more concerned with long-term educational planning. Through some discussion and pointed questioning, it was determined that Ted performed best in the classroom situation on redundant tasks and when he had available an automatized strategy for dealing with task requirements. On the other hand, the teacher's comments revealed that Ted most often appeared to lose interest in a task or perform very poorly when some degree of independent problem solving was required.

Ted's neuropsychological test results were then presented within the context of the problems and concerns identified by his teachers, and the following comments and remedial educational recommendations were discussed and elaborated.

1. Ted should perform best within a highly structured learning format in which he is given ongoing feedback regarding the adequacy of his performance.

2. He should benefit from direct instruction in specific strategies that are tailored to help him deal with frequently occurring problematic situations.

3. It is likely that he will need additional time to complete successfully those tasks that require complex information processing.

4. Complex concepts and novel procedures should be introduced to him in parts that can be memorized. After he has memorized each part of the procedure or concept, it would be beneficial to help him gain a better understanding of the whole through direct experience rather than through cognitive abstraction.

5. Novel or otherwise complex information should be presented within a concrete meaningful context. This should help Ted to perceive, integrate, and remember the pertinent information.

6. Finally, it was pointed out that Ted would be able to learn routine skills of a mechanical nature if he were taught in a systematic manner. With this in mind, he seemed to be well suited for a number of programs that are typically offered in vocational secondary school settings. During his remaining year at the elementary school level, it was recommended that efforts be directed toward helping him to improve his basic academic skills (e.g., reading and arithmetic) so as to enhance his opportunity for success in his vocational school program.

The explanation of Ted's neuropsychological test results in conjunction with these comments and remedial recommendations were perceived as quite helpful by his teachers. They proceeded to design a remedial educational program for him that involved withdrawal from his home classroom for several hours per week; during these occasions, specific exercises and training in line with our recommendations were carried out. This program was deemed by all persons involved to be in keeping with Ted's immediate and long-term educational needs.

In summary, Case 5-4 represents an example of a later-emerging learning disability that is characterized by a deficiency in concept formation, problem solving, and generating appropriate plans of action. Initially, the nature and significance of his learning disability was not well understood by his parents or his teachers. Repeated neuropsychological assessments and consultation revealed a consistent clinical picture that included particular difficulties in novel, unstructured tasks.

At the time that Ted was first referred for neuropsychological assessment, his hyperactivity and externalized behavioral difficulties were of primary concern. In adolescence, he was no longer found to be hyperactive. Instead, the identified areas of concern included his level of motivation and academic difficulties. In keeping with his changing remedial needs and ongoing pattern of neuropsychological strengths and weaknesses, modifications were necessary in the direction and focus of our remedial reocmmendations for him.

Moderate to severe reading disability

The final case selected for inclusion in this chapter was designed to illustrate three special considerations in academic remediation: (1) the markedly debilitating effects of even rather subtle forms of neuropsychological impairment with respect to the acquisition of reading and related academic skills; (2) the stability of this reading-impaired person's neuropsychological characteristics throughout his middle childhood, adolescence, and early adulthood years; and (3) the importance of establishing and, where possible, implementing the ideal remedial plan. We have followed this young man for a period of 17 years, during the last 2 of which he has participated in an intensive remedial educational program that has led to significant gains in his reading and related academic skills. His clearly exceptional level of motivation, the availability of excellent remedial resources, the appropriateness of the demands in his environment, and the precise tailoring of his remedial educational program to take best advantage of his neuropsychological strengths represent the key ingredients in the success of this intervention program.

Case 5-5: Fred

Fred was first referred for neuropsychological assessment at the age of 9 years, 3 months because of reading and spelling difficulties. Despite his best efforts and those of his parents and his teachers, he was essentially unable to read.

He was referred to our center for neuropsychological assessment by an educational official in conjunction with his paternal grandfather, a pediatrician, who was especially sensitive to Fred's academic difficulties. Fred's grandfather volunteered that he had experienced reading difficulties as a youth and that he did not learn to read effectively until his later teens. Fred's father also had a history of reading difficulties; he too did not learn to read effectively until the later stages of adolescence. Consequently, Fred's father and his mother had been particularly sensitive to his difficulties in the reading area, and in fact expected that he may have had this type of problem. They were prepared to help their son in any way they could; at the same time, they were careful not to place undue pressure on Fred to achieve in the academic situation. In many respects, this was an ideal family situation for this young boy.

Fred underwent three neuropsychological assessments: The first two took place during middle childhood; the third was completed when he was a young adult. The results of these neuropsychological assessments are displayed in Figure 5-5. First, the initial two assessments are discussed briefly.

On the WISC he exhibited consistently low scores on the Arithmetic, Digit Span, and Coding subtests. These subtests have the common requirements of the mental manipulation of symbols and the necessity for immediate alertness and attention. For the most part, his other verbal skills as tapped by the WISC Verbal Scales were within normal limits. Especially during his second assessment, he performed very well on the other Performance subtests. He exhibited mildly deficient levels of performance on the Trail Making Test, Parts A and B; both of these tests require the mental manipulation of language symbols. His performance on the Speech-Sounds Perception Test was particularly poor, and he had difficulties on the Sentence Memory and Auditory Closure Tests. His Verbal Fluency Test performance was also mildly deficient from a level-of-performance standpoint.

On the positive side, there were no notable motor or psychomotor deficiencies in evidence, although he performed somewhat poorly with his right hand and with both hands together on the Tactual Performance Test during his first assessment. He performed in an age-appropriate manner on the Halstead Category Test during his first two assessments.

Relatively speaking, his WRAT Reading, Spelling, and Arithmetic performances were uniformly impaired, although arithmetic was not cited in the referral information as an area of academic concern for him.

Following his first neuropsychological assessment, he was enrolled in a special classroom setting for children with learning disabilities. At that point special intervention techniques were employed with him, including regular individual attention from his teacher. As can be seen by comparing

Figure 5-5. Neuropsychological test results—Case 5-5 (Fred).

Age	9 yr, 3 mo	10 yr, 9 mo		23 yr, 11 mo
WISC				*WAIS*
Verbal IQ	97	96		97
Information	10	11		9
Comprehension	10	11		12
Arithmetic	7	7		6
Similarities	13	13		13
Vocabulary	12	8		10
Digit Span	5	6		6
Performance IQ	101	121		114
Picture Completion	13	15		11
Picture Arrangement	11	13		12
Block Design	11	14		17
Object Assembly	8	16		13
Coding	8	7	(Digit Symbol)	8
Full Scale IQ	99	109		104
PPVT				
IQ	106	107		n/a
Mental Age	9–8	12–4		n/a
WRAT				
Reading (grade equiv.)	2.1	2.5		4.3
Spelling (grade equiv.)	2.3	2.5		3.0
Arithmetic (grade equiv.)	3.0	2.6		4.3

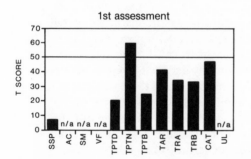

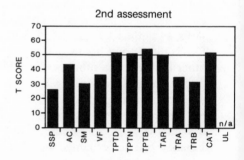

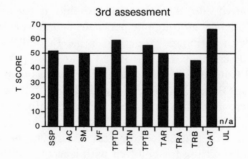

SENSORY-PERCEPTUAL ABILITIES

Fred exhibited mild to moderate difficulty (more so with his right hand) on tests for finger agnosia, finger dysgraphesthesia, and astereognosis for coins during his first two assessments. There was some evidence of finger agnosia with his right hand only revealed in his third assessment. He performed all other sensory-perceptual tests in an age-appropriate manner.

APHASIA SCREENING TEST

Fred exhibited marked problems in reading, spelling, and enunciation of complex multisyllabic words in each examination. On the other hand, his graphic reproductions of geometric forms were age-appropriate in all instances.

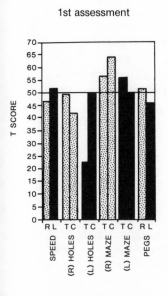

1st assessment

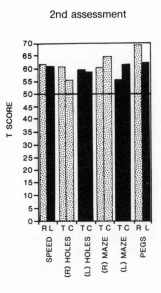

2nd assessment

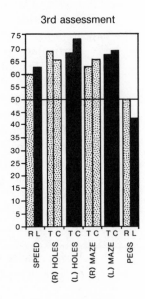

3rd assessment

197

his WRAT Achievement scores in his first two testings, Fred made few appreciable gains on these measures of reading, spelling, and arithmetic. Throughout this period he did not exhibit any behavior problems. Furthermore, he did not appear to have any sort of exceptional difficulty in mustering adequate motivation to put forth his best efforts while at school.

Fred next appeared in our clinic at the age of 23 years, 11 months. At this point, he referred himself for neuropsychological assessment to gain information that he hoped would help him to make improvements in reading and related educational skills. Although he had completed 4 years of secondary school (with special programming considerations), he did not ever achieve a functional reading level. He was unable to read the newspaper and never attempted reading unless it was absolutely necessary to do so. He was employed as a "large rig" truck driver, and he did not see any prospects for improving his vocational status unless he achieved further education. At the time of this assessment, he was enrolled in a community college program (a Canadian educational equivalent of a technical college that is open to students interested in obtaining primarily prevocational training in a wide range of semiskilled and skilled technical areas) in an effort to upgrade his reading and other educational skills.

The results of this third neuropsychological examination revealed a pattern of strengths and weaknesses that appeared to have persisted throughout the course of his development. He exhibited particularly poor scores on the Wechsler Adult Intelligence Scale (WAIS) Arithmetic, Digit Span, and Digit Symbol subtests, while performing in at least an age-appropriate manner on the other WAIS Verbal and Performance subtests. Trail Making Test, Part A (in particular) and Trail Making Test, Part B still proved to be somewhat problematic for him. His level of performance on the Auditory Closure Test had not improved relative to developmental expectations.

Particular strengths were noted in the visual–motor–organizational skill areas. He continued to exhibit well-developed motor and psychomotor abilities, with the exception of a low-average level of performance on the Grooved Pegboard Test with his left hand. Improvements were made by him on the Speech-Sounds Perception Test, most likely as a direct result of his intensive drill over the years in sound–symbol matching. He also improved his level of performance on the Sentence Memory Test. It would seem likely that he had learned to employ his well-developed visual–spatial and associated problem-solving skills to help him to remember verbal information better by relying on contextual cues. In this connection, it is noteworthy that his level of Halstead Category Test performance was well within the superior range during this third neuropsychological assessment. Nevertheless, it remained obvious that he could not read.

It was clear to us that Fred would need to be extremely well motivated and diligent in his pursuits of further education if he were to benefit from the "academic upgrading" program in which he was enrolled. We also felt that precise teaching techniques that were based on his neuropsychological strengths and weaknesses would be essential if he were to make any further substantial gains in reading and related academic skill areas. With these factors in mind, we arranged for him to engage the services of a highly qualified and equally well motivated special education teacher who was willing to provide him with a supplementary remedial education program designed to enhance his reading and related academic skill areas. This teacher had approximately 10 years of experience in teaching learning-disabled children. In addition, she had consulted regularly over the course of 1 year with other special educational teachers and educational officials on how best to implement in the classroom setting recommendations stemming from our neuropsychological assessments. Thus, she was quite well versed in the remedial educational significance of specific patterns of neuropsychological strengths and weaknesses for the learning-disabled child.

When consulting with Fred's tutor, we indicated that it was crucial that she teach him to make the best use of his well-developed visual–motor–constructional and related nonverbal problem-solving skills in his reading program. Essentially, it was suggested that, as much as possible, the learning-to-read process be fashioned as a visual–spatial task in which Jon would learn to benefit from spatial and other contextual cues when analyzing words. Two complementary remedial educational programs were selected with this information in mind: (1) Corrective Reading (Engelmann, Becker, Carmine, Meyers, Becker, & Johnson, 1973) to enhance his reading skills, and (2) Morphographic Spelling (Dixon & Engelmann, 1973) to enhance his spelling skills. Both of these programs emphasize the use of "word-chunking" techniques in which the student is taught systematically to look for "morphographs," or commonly occurring sections of words (e.g., "ter"), and to name rather than decode the word in a phonetic fashion. These programs fit well with his remedial needs, although it was necessary to modify and embellish some of the task requirements from time to time.

At the time of this writing, academic therapy with his tutor has been in progress for 25 months. Fred has participated in this program at least once per week, with each session lasting a minimum of 2 hours. Fred did not miss a single scheduled session during this period. Indeed, he completed his work through correspondence during a 17-week period when his tutor had taken a leave of absence.

From the beginning of this tutorial program, he was given homework assignments which took him a minimum of 1 hour each day to complete. For example, he was assigned 50 new words every week, which he was to practice for spelling from dictation the following week. The words were dictated by his instructor onto a tape, followed by the correct spelling of each word. He was to listen to the word and, in conjunction with the tape, spell the word; then, on review, take dictation from the tape and spell the words on his own. Finally, these new words were dictated to him by his instructor in the following week's session. In addition, he was instructed to look for morphographs in his natural environment. Since he continued to drive a truck when he was not attending school during the week, he would look for groups of letters on the licence plates of other cars and trucks that formed meaningful morphographs (e.g., "TRI"). One week he reported to his teacher, with some degree of amazement in his tone of voice, that the name of a local town was actually made up of two (already known to him) morphographs. He was beginning to learn to read, or at least to decode novel words.

An additional homework assignment involved learning to read the newspaper. He was assigned specific articles or sections in the newspaper and quizzed on their content during the following week's session. His reading comprehension improved very rapidly during this period.

A Neurological Impress teaching method was used to supplement his Corrective Reading and Morphographic Spelling programs. Utilizing this approach, his instructor read a paragraph along with him and then gradually stopped reading as, with practice, he was able to read the passage on his own.

It should be noted at this point that he was extremely anxious when he began these lessons. He mentioned at one point that he was very embarrassed about his reading disability, and that he found it difficult to return for sessions during the initial phases of his academic therapies. It was noted by his tutor that he became quite tense when he was reading: His face would redden and his knuckles would sometimes turn white from pressing his hands so hard against his desk. He sometimes complained of backaches after having completed a session. These overt signs of anxiety and frustration gradually disappeared as he made progress during his academic therapy sessions.

His academic upgrading program at the community college continued on a daily basis for 2 school years in conjunction with his special tutoring program. His reading program while in the formal curriculum of the community college consisted primarily of the SRA Reading programs (Shub, Friedman, Kaplan, Katien, & Scroggin, 1973). He had difficulty with these and sometimes found it necessary to repeat his reading labs. On the other hand, he excelled in the area of mathematics and performed more than adequately in the science areas. In fact, when he had earned his Grade 12 equivalency at the end of his 2-year school program, he achieved grades in the 90s in algebra and calculus and in the 70s in the sciences, including biology. He also obtained a grade of 70 in a computer literacy course, although he would have performed much better had he been able to punch in the words more quickly. On the other hand, his grades in the

English language courses were lower (in the low 60s), and he continued to exhibit considerable difficulty with grammar (e.g., paragraph construction and use of punctuation) and in general with written expression.

Fred completed the Morphographic Spelling and Corrective Reading programs after one year. In the second year of therapy, his sessions involved essentially an extension of the concepts and drills that had been part of these programs, in conjunction with the other remedial educational techniques that have already been mentioned.

He progressed from reading single newspaper articles for homework assignments to reading relatively complicated articles from a national magazine and answering questions the following week on the content of these articles. Special drills were designed to help him with other important academic skills such as test-taking. For example, when taking a short-answer type of test, he was taught to read each question four times to himself and then immediately jot down in rough form the main points that came to mind. It was suggested that he then rewrite his points in an organized paragraph form. Even after extensive tutoring in this specific area, he continues to have considerable difficulty with this task. In fact, even at the Grade 12 level, he found it difficult to complete written essay-type examinations within time limits. On the other hand, when he read the questions carefully, he tended to perform quite well on multiple-choice examinations.

At the present time, he is entering a preliminary year university program. His word-recognition skills are estimated to be at a Grade 6 level, and his reading comprehension skills are closer to a Grade 9 or Grade 10 level. His spelling is at about a Grade 5 or Grade 6 level.

It is clear that as a secondary benefit of his academic therapies he has developed a number of strategies, compensatory techniques, and supports that should help him with his next very challenging task. Some of the strategies and supports that he now employs are listed below.

1. He intends to take three courses rather than the usual five courses so that he will have additional time for study.

2. His parents, who are extremely supportive of his efforts, have offered to read all of his textbooks onto tapes for him.

3. He has sought expert direction regarding the courses which he will choose, and hopes to make arrangements with each of his new professors to help him to meet with the written demands of test-taking situations.

4. He will continue to receive academic support on a regular basis from his tutor; one of her tasks will be to edit his written essays before they are handed in for marking.

5. When taking notes, he has learned to sacrifice speed for accuracy; usually only he can read what he has written since he continues to misspell most words.

6. He has also developed another special strategy for note-taking; he

will strike up a relationship with a good note-taker in each class and then photocopy his/her notes following the class. Next, he goes home and compares his own notes with these and adds whatever he has missed or misunderstood.

7. He is now being taught by his tutor how to read textbooks to accentuate certain information (e.g., through color-coded highlighting).

At the present time, his prognosis in the academic situation continues to be guarded. Nevertheless, he has achieved a functional reading level, and even at this point in his development, his vocational options have been expanded. He remains highly motivated and in fact has sold his car to pay for his tutoring and for money toward his tuition. Even though his parents are in a financially comfortable and stable position, he will pay for the rest of his tuition through income earned in a part-time job as a truck driver while continuing to live at home.

SUMMARY

There would appear to be four key factors or variables that have led to relative success in this case. First, this young man is extremely well motivated and is willing to continue to make exceptional sacrifices to obtain a higher level of education. Second, he was able to learn to take advantage of his better developed visual–spatial and nonverbal problem-solving skills when learning to read through a highly prescriptive teaching method. In this regard, his tutor, who was equally well motivated and who has invested considerable effort in helping this young man to learn to read, has designed her programs specifically to take advantage of Fred's neuro-psychological strengths. Finally, his parents have been extremely support-ive of his efforts throughout the years and have never, to our knowledge, placed undue pressure on him to achieve in the academic setting. In every respect, then, this is an ideal therapy situation. It has produced exception-ally positive results for this reading-disabled man. Unfortunately, it is an outcome which we rarely see in clinical practice.

Summary

In this chapter we examined the neuropsychological profiles of five children (including one adult profile) who were of particular concern to their teachers and other school personnel because of the academic prob-lems that they were experiencing. Neuropsychological examination of these youngsters led to the formulation of remedial plans that in most cases differed substantially from the remedial educational programs in which they had been or were likely to be involved.

The cases presented are by no means characteristic of the usual types of learning disabled children who may be referred for neuropsychological assessment. For example, only one of the children (Fred, who was found to be exceptionally well motivated) exhibited a rather specific reading and spelling disability that could be attributed to the presence of a central processing deficiency. Nevertheless, the principal concerns of educators (i.e., type of educational milieu or program that would be of maximal benefit to the child) were addressed.

One of the principal aims of this chapter was to introduce the reader to special problems in academic remediation. In the first case presentation (Douglas), some of the limitations of the standard psychoeducational assessment were highlighted. The focus of the next case presentation was remediation. Based on the results of the neuropsychological assessment, a specific remedial reading program was designed and proved to be successful with a learning-disabled blind child. Stephen, the third case presented, is a child who was viewed by educational personnel as suffering from a fairly common type of learning disability, and he was seen to be highly resistant to the remedial efforts being expended on his behalf. On the basis of his neuropsychological assessment, however, it was determined that Stephen's academic learning difficulties were not the result of a central processing deficiency. These findings, when considered in conjunction with his academic and family histories, suggested that his learning difficulties were primarily of psychogenic origin. In this case, the neuropsychological assessment proved to be quite helpful in the differential diagnosis of Stephen's learning difficulties, and in encouraging his caretakers to focus on relevant dimensions of his remedial needs.

Next, test and retest neuropsychological data were presented on a youngster (Ted) with a later-emerging learning disability. This sort of learning disability is often misidentified by educators as being the result of a motivational deficiency. In consequence, inappropriate treatment is most often provided for such children. There were other points of interest in this case as well, especially when contrasted with the final case presentation (Fred). For example, serial testing on Ted revealed some significant changes in the level and configuration of his neuropsychological test results, while his underlying pattern of neuropsychological strengths and weaknesses remained largely unchanged. On the other hand, Fred's level and configuration of neuropsychological test results remained remarkably stable between the time of his first neuropsychological assessment and that which was carried out 14 years later. In accordance with these findings, our remedial educational recommendations for each were tailored to meet their identified needs. Finally, the findings from these long-term longitudinal follow-ups serve to underscore the need to consider the complex interaction(s) that may obtain between the child's developing pattern of neuropsychological abilities and the changing environmental demands that the child typically encounters with advancing chronological age.

References

Benson, D. F., & Geschwind, N. (1970). Developmental Gerstmann syndrome. *Neurology*, *20*, 293–298.

Benton, A. L. (1965). *Sentence Memory Test*. Iowa City, IA: Author.

Boder, E. (1973). Developmental dyslexia: A diagnostic approach based on three atypical reading–spelling patterns. *Developmental Medicine and Child Neurology*, *15*, 663–687.

Dixon, R., & Engelmann, S. (1973). *Corrective spelling through morphographs*. Chicago: Science Research Associates.

Doehring, D. G. (1985). Reading disability subtypes: Interaction of reading and nonreading deficits. In B. P. Rourke (Ed.), *Neuropsychology of learning disabilities: Essentials of subtype analysis* (pp. 133–146). New York: Guilford.

Engelmann, S., Becker, W., Carmine, L., Meyers, L., Becker, J., & Johnson, W. (1973). *Corrective reading program*. Chicago: Science Research Associates.

Fisk, J. L., & Rourke, B. P. (1979). Identification of subtypes of learning-disabled children at three age levels: A neuropsychological, multivariate approach. *Journal of Clinical Neuropsychology*, *1*, 289–310.

Fletcher, J. M. (1985). External validation of learning disability typologies. In B. P. Rourke (Ed.), *Neuropsychology of learning disabilities: Essentials of subtype analysis* (pp. 187–211). New York: Guilford.

Holland, C. J. (1983). *Directive Parental Counseling: The counselor's guide*. Bloomfield Hills, MI: Midwest Professional Publishing.

Jastak, J. J., & Jastak, S. R. (1965). *The Wide Range Achievement Test*. Wilmington, DE: Guidance Associates.

Johnson, D. J., & Myklebust, H. R. (1967). *Learning disabilities*. New York: Grune & Stratton.

Kinsbourne, M., & Warrington, E. K. (1963). The developmental Gerstmann syndrome. *Archives of Neurology*, *8*, 490–501.

Koppitz, E. (1977). *Visual–Aural Digit Span*. Los Angeles: Grune & Stratton.

Lenkowsky, L., & Serposnek, D. T. (1978). Family consequences of parental dyslexia. *Journal of Learning Disabilities*, *1*, 47–53.

Lyon, G. R. (1985). Educational validation studies of learning disability subtypes. In B. P. Rourke (Ed.), *Neuropsychology of learning disabilities: Essentials of subtype analysis* (pp. 228–253). New York: Guilford.

Mattis, S., French, J. H., & Rapin, I. (1975). Dyslexia in children and young adults: Three independent neuropsychological syndromes. *Developmental Medicine and Child Neurology*, *17*, 150–163.

Morris, R., Blashfield, R., & Satz, P. (1981). Neuropsychology and cluster analysis: Potentials and problems. *Journal of Clinical Neuropsychology*, *3*, 79–99.

Ozols, E. J., & Rourke, B. P. (1985). Dimensions of social sensitivity in two types of learning-disabled children. In B. P. Rourke (Ed.), *Neuropsychology of learning disabilities: Essentials of subtype analysis* (pp. 281–301). New York: Guilford.

Petrauskas, R. J., & Rourke, B. P. (1979). Identification of subtypes of retarded readers: A neuropsychological, multivariate approach. *Journal of Clinical Neuropsychology*, *1*, 17–37.

Quay, H. C., & Peterson, D. R. (1979). *Manual for the Behavior Problem Checklist*. (Available from author.)

Rourke, B. P. (Ed.). (1985). *Neuropsychology of learning disabilities: Essentials of subtype analysis*. New York: Guilford.

Rourke, B. P., & Finlayson, M. A. J. (1978). Neuropsychological significance of variations in patterns of academic performance: Verbal and visual–spatial abilities. *Journal of Abnormal Child Psychology, 6*, 121–133.

Rourke, B. P., & Strang, J. D. (1978). Neuropsychological significance of variations in patterns of academic performance: Motor, psychomotor, and tactile–perceptual abilities. *Journal of Pediatric Psychology, 3*, 62–66.

Rourke, B. P., & Strang, J. D. (1983). Subtypes of reading and arithmetical disabilities: A neuropsychological analysis. In M. Rutter (Ed.), *Developmental neuropsychiatry* (pp. 473–488). New York: Guilford.

Rourke, B. P., Young, G. C., Strang, J. D., & Russell, D. L. (1986). Adult outcomes of central processing deficiencies in childhood. In I. Grant & K. M. Adams (Eds.), *Neuropsychological assessment of neuropsychiatric disorders* (pp. 244–267). New York: Oxford.

Shub, A. N., Friedman, R. L., Kaplan, J. M., Katien, J. C., & Scroggin, J. C. (1973). *SRA: An instructional aid.* Chicago: Science Research Associates.

Slosson, R. L. (1967). *Slosson Drawing Coordination Test.* New York: Slosson Educational Publications.

Spache, G. D. (1981). *Spache Diagnostic Reading Tests.* New York: McGraw-Hill.

Strang, J. D., & Rourke, B. P. (1983). Concept-formation/nonverbal reasoning abilities of children who exhibit specific academic problems with arithmetic. *Journal of Clinical Child Psychology, 12*, 33–39.

Strang, J. D., & Rourke, B. P. (1985a). Adaptive behavior of children with specific arithmetic disabilities and associated neuropsychological abilities and deficits. In B. P. Rourke (Ed.), *Neuropsychology of learning disabilities: Essentials of subtype analysis* (pp. 302–328). New York: Guilford.

Strang, J. D., & Rourke, B. P. (1985b). Arithmetic disability subtypes: The neuropsychological significance of specific arithmetic impairment in childhood. In B. P. Rourke (Ed.), *Neuropsychology of learning disabilities: Essentials of subtype analysis* (pp. 167–183). New York: Guilford.

Sweeney, J. E., & Rourke, B. P. (1978). Neuropsychological significance of phonetically accurate and phonetically inaccurate spelling errors in younger and older retarded spellers. *Brain and Language, 6*, 212–225.

Sweeney, J. E., & Rourke, B. P. (1985). Spelling disability subtypes. In B. P. Rourke (Ed.), *Neuropsychology of learning disabilities: Essentials of subtype analysis* (pp. 147–166). New York: Guilford.

Wechsler, D. (1974). *Wechsler Intelligence Scale for Children—Revised.* New York: Psychological Corp.

6. Special problems in adaptive behavior

Introduction

One important perspective that has emerged from our ongoing research efforts (e.g., Rourke, 1975, 1978, 1982a, 1982b; Rourke & Fisk, 1981; Rourke & Strang, 1978, 1983; Strang & Rourke, 1985a, 1985b) is that children's problems in adaptation are often related to their patterns of neuropsychological abilities and deficiencies. Indeed, the vast majority of children whom we have seen for neuropsychological assessment exhibit some sort of identifiable adaptational deficiency that seems, at least to some degree, to be influenced by the child's particular pattern of neuropsychological strengths and weaknesses.

For the school-aged child, the three most critical realms for successful adaptation and adjustment include interactions which take place within the family unit, the community setting, and the school. In each of these settings, the child may exhibit inadequate receptive or expressive communicational skills, outstanding attentional difficulties, poor social perception skills, outstanding psychomotor deficiencies, and so on. Any of the aforementioned problems may be a direct reflection of the child's particular level and configuration of neuropsychological strengths and weaknesses.

In Chapter 5 we focused on the relationship between the child's particular pattern of neuropsychological strengths and weaknesses and his/her adaptive difficulties in school situations. In this chapter we have two principal aims: (1) to identify some of the practical difficulties in adaptation that may extend beyond the school situation for different types of neuropsychologically impaired children; and (2) to examine the relationship between the child's particular pattern of neuropsychological strengths and deficiencies, his/her adaptational problems, and personality adjustment. Cases of children who have specific and outstanding psychomotor deficiencies, attentional deficits, and nonverbal learning disabilities are presented in this chapter.

Outstanding motoric deficiencies

Case 6-1: Patricia

Patricia was referred for assessment by school authorities who had noted that she was exhibiting progressive slurring of speech and increasing graphomotor (including handwriting) problems. Because of these indications of deterioration in skilled performance, she was seen immediately for neuropsychological assessment. A simultaneous referral was directed to a pediatric neurologist for consultation. This particular neurologist had been reviewing her progress once per year since her rather stressful perinatal period. Specifically, during her delivery there had been signs of respiratory distress and some inferred degree of anoxia. Shortly after her birth, septicemia and seizures were identified and treated. There were no diagnosed ongoing seizures, although she did exhibit some motor difficulties in repeated neurological examinations.

Before proceeding with our neuropsychological assessment of Patricia, her mother was questioned regarding the behavioral concerns raised by educational authorities. The mother reported that she had not noticed any significant changes in her daughter's behavior, although she did want to have her assessed as soon as possible.

In the neuropsychological testing situation, Patricia was most cooperative and attentive. However, she was somewhat quiet and tended to speak only when spoken to. Her speech seemed to be slightly labored and monotonic. There was no clear evidence of slurring of words. She spoke in full sentences and appeared to have a well-developed vocabulary. In general, her gross motor coordination seemed to be somewhat poor. Her gait was awkward and there was evidence of toeing in, more so with her right foot. She tended to respond slowly to task demands during this assessment, especially when these involved even fairly minor degrees of motoric output requirements. Nevertheless, she appeared to be quite well motivated and eager to comply with the examination regimen. It is notable that she was able to complete this day-long assessment without becoming particularly fatigued, as is often observed in children who are experiencing progressive neurological deterioration. Patricia's neuropsychological results are presented in Figure 6-1a.

Patricia was exclusively right-handed (Harris Test for Lateral Dominance). Nevertheless, she exhibited markedly impaired performances with her right hand on 4 measures involving psychomotor skills: tests for motor steadiness in the static and kinetic dispositions, a test of fine motor dexterity, and the Tactual Performance Test. Her grip strength was marginally better developed with her left hand than with her right hand, although both scores were within the superior range for her age. Simple

Figure 6-1a. Neuropsychological test results—
Case 6-1 (Patricia).

Age	9 yr, 6 mo
WISC	
Verbal IQ	114
Information	12
Comprehension	9
Arithmetic	14
Similarities	14
Vocabulary	14
Digit Span	10
Performance IQ	113
Picture Completion	12
Picture Arrangement	17
Block Design	11
Object Assembly	8
Coding	11
Full Scale IQ	115
PPVT	
IQ	112
Mental Age	11–4
WRAT	
Reading (grade equiv.)	6.2
Spelling (grade equiv.)	5.7
Arithmetic (grade equiv.)	3.9

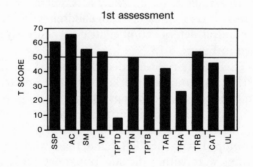

SENSORY–PERCEPTUAL ABILITIES

There was no evidence of simple tactile imperception. However, under conditions of bilateral simultaneous stimulation, Patricia reported the stimulus delivered to her right hand on only two of four occasions and to her left hand in only one of four instances. There was evidence of finger agnosia, particularly with her right hand. Her performance was age-appropriate on tests for dysgraphesthesia. There was some evidence of astereognosis for coins with each hand. There was no evidence of simple visual or auditory imperception or suppression. Her performance on a Sweep Hearing Test was normal.

APHASIA SCREENING TEST

Her drawings were quite tremulous in appearance, although they represented reasonable approximations of the models from which they were copied. There were two oral spelling errors and one "mental" arithmetic error in evidence. There were no clear aphasic signs in evidence.

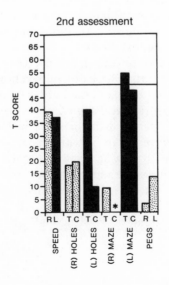

2nd assessment

motor speed with the lower extremities was well below average with each foot; her right and left finger-tapping speeds more closely approximated the average range.

Patricia's vocabulary was quite well developed. Although her speech was somewhat slow and labored, she articulated well and was able to repeat correctly several complex multisyllabic words. There were no syntactical difficulties in evidence and no notable problems with respect to auditory–perceptual and verbal expressive functions.

Selected aspects of visual–motor integration proved to be somewhat problematic for her. In this regard, it was found that, the more extensive the motor component of a task, the more obvious were her difficulties with it. At the same time, her visual–perceptual and visual–spatial functions appeared for the most part to be quite adequately developed.

She performed in an age-appropriate manner on tests involving verbal and nonverbal problem solving (Children's Word-Finding Test and Category Test). Her Wide Range Achievement Test (WRAT) Reading and Spelling scores were quite good, but she exhibited relative difficulty on the WRAT Arithmetic subtest.

Patricia's neuropsychological test results were thought to be contraindicative of dysfunction at the level of the cerebral cortex. However, her pattern of relatively lateralized motor and psychomotor deficiencies strongly suggested the presence of long-standing dysfunction within sub-cortical brain structures, including tracts involving the right cerebellar hemisphere.

The neurological examination completed at this time revealed no deterioration as compared to previous examinations. (It should be noted that at the time of Patricia's neuropsychological assessment, we were not aware that her condition was being monitored regularly by a pediatric neurologist.) The positive neurological findings included the following: intention tremor with both upper extremities, but good rapid alternating movements; impaired repetitive fine finger movements bilaterally; spastic lower extremities, more so on the right side; walking with toes in and difficulty in walking on her right heel; difficulty in hopping on her left foot; and increased deep tendon reflexes in both lower extremities, more so on the right side. In the neurological report, it was noted that, four years earlier, a CT scan had suggested the presence of lucencies in the lateral geniculate bodies that were felt to be within normal limits.

With this information now in hand, the question arose as to why there had been such concern for immediate action in this case. An extensive clinical interview with Patricia's parents and meetings with her teachers provided some information germane to this question. First, however, the nature and extent of Patricia's adaptive deficiencies will be discussed.

As the eldest of three children in a hard-working "ethnic" family, Patricia had been assigned regular chores in the household since she was very young. Although she was somewhat slow at completing tasks (according to her parents), she was able to make her bed, keep her room tidy, care for family pets, and play cooperatively with her younger sisters and cousins. On the other hand, tasks involving some degree of complex eye–hand or fine motor coordination had always proved to be problematic for her. For example, at 9½ years of age, it was not uncommon for her to spill milk while pouring it and to have difficulty buttoning her dresses, tying her shoes, setting the table (under time constraints), or manually operating a record player. The primary complaint of her parents was that she was slow in completing these sorts of tasks.

In the community, she did not participate actively in games involving psychomotor skills. This became increasingly apparent as she grew older. Her teachers reported that she would most often stand at the school wall during recess rather than participate in games and other activities with her age-mates. She was unable to kick or catch a ball properly and did not enjoy such activities. In general, she avoided any game or task involving strength, speed, or dexterity.

In the school situation, she was extremely slow in completing her written work. For example, it took her approximately 15 minutes to complete a four-sentence, eight-line paragraph for us. As the written requirements of the classroom situation increased, her motoric disabilities interfered more and more with her school work. In fact, her teachers noted that she was no longer considered to be the "top" student in the class, which had been her standing since Grade 1.

When her teachers were questioned further regarding their report of her slurred speech, it was revealed that this was noted only periodically, and was most often apparent when she was experiencing difficulty with some aspects of her school work. Furthermore, the reported increase in her psychomotor incoordination was related solely and directly to the neatness of her handwriting. In this regard, her teachers indicated that her written work had typically been quite neat in the past and was now sometimes completed in a rather "careless" manner. These observations and findings had led her teachers to describe a clinical picture that could be consistent with active neuropathological deterioration.

In the clinical interview that was conducted with Patricia's parents, it became apparent that they did not see eye to eye regarding the nature of her behavioral symptomatology: Her mother (who had the better command of the English language, English being the parents' second language) indicated that she felt that Patricia's condition had remained much the same throughout her childhood and that there were no notable increases in her motor or speech difficulties, whereas her father felt that she was "getting worse." Further questioning of Patricia's father revealed that the concept of "getting worse" appeared to be synonymous with "not trying hard enough." It was clear that there was very little communication between these parents during this lengthy interview session.

Patricia's mother expressed some concern and guilt regarding the condition of her daughter since her birth. She had hoped that Patricia would outgrow her motoric difficulties, but she was becoming increasingly convinced that her difficulties would be long-standing. With this in mind, she had expected that her daughter would excel at school to compensate for her insufficiencies in other areas. In fact, Patricia was required to spend long hours doing homework and was encouraged strenuously to be the top student in her class. Unfortunately, because of the increasing writing requirements of the Grade 4 situation, Patricia was unable to match her mother's expectations.

On the other hand, Patricia's father blatantly refused to accept the nature, extent, or importance of his daughter's condition. He felt that she simply needed to work harder at psychomotor activities and that with practice she would be "normal." He proudly informed us of "motor training" exercises and activities that he had arranged for his daughter, such as bike riding after dinner. Apparently Patricia and her father would go for bike rides around the neighborhood (they lived in a rural setting), and he would set a pace that he expected her to match. As an example of his attitude toward this exercise, he reported that Patricia had fallen off her bike a few nights before the interview took place, and that he had simply waited for her to pick herself up even though she was crying. He sincerely felt that this was in her best interests.

Patricia's parents saw little benefit in her playing with other children. Furthermore, they pointed out that, since they lived in a rural setting, there were not many children in the immediate area with whom she could play. Moreover, they preferred that she play with children (preferably her cousins) who spoke their native language. For the most part Patricia was expected to spend her time working to cure her disability or learning to excel in another area (especially her school work) to compensate for being disabled. Although these parents were well aware of Patricia's limitations from a negative standpoint (i.e., what she could not do), they were unable to take into consideration her disability and its effects in conjunction with their demands of her.

Further contact with her teachers and her parents revealed that Patricia had begun to exhibit some personality changes. She was becoming increasingly withdrawn from others and her work habits were slipping. There had been bouts of crying reported in the classroom situation because of her frustration with copying and/or writing. Where she had once readily offered answers to questions asked of the class by her teacher, she was becoming increasingly reluctant to raise her hand in class, even when it was apparent that she knew the answer. She wanted to remain in the classroom during recess and help the teacher clean the boards rather than play with the other children. Although she was well liked by other children, they too were noticing a difference in her. She increasingly avoided situations in which there was any sort of competitive atmosphere, even if these situations did not involve complex motoric output.

The Personality Inventory for Children (PIC) (depicted in Figure 6-1b) revealed a pattern which we have come to associate with the emergence of internalized psychopathology. Among the clinical scales, the Somatic Concern, Depression, Withdrawal, Anxiety, Psychosis, and Social Skill scales were most prominently elevated. The somewhat lower than expected F scale suggested that there may have been a tendency on her mother's part (the respondent) to underplay the extent of her daughter's personality adjustment difficulties. This would certainly be in keeping with her guarded responses in the clinical interview situation.

Patricia's parents were interviewed in two follow-up sessions, the last of which was attended only by her mother. While she was quite willing to take into account and probably utilize practical suggestions regarding ways in which Patricia might learn to compensate for her handwriting difficulties, the mother was very reluctant even to consider changing her expectations of methods of interacting with Patricia. Although other services were available to the parents, including family therapy intervention, they abruptly terminated their involvement with us after three encounters.

After meeting with the parents, a Remedial Educational Conference was held. A number of practical suggestions were made at this meeting, which was attended by Patricia's teacher and her mother. Included in these suggestions were the following: (1) teach her a systematic method in the use of common and other abbreviations that could be used for taking notes; (2) teach her how to take her notes in point form; (3) replace, where possible, essay-type examinations with oral examinations, multiple-choice tests, or those with a fill-in-the-blanks format; (4) avoid the imposition of time limits on her written work; (5) facilitate her involvement with other children on the playground; (6) allow her to practice with a word processor that has typewriter guards (raised borders around each key) to prepare her for the homework and essay requirements of secondary school. In addition, we recommended that she be enrolled in a club at school (such as the Library Club) in which her motoric difficulties would be unlikely to hamper her performance. Furthermore, we pointed out that some form of drama or acting (e.g., participating in the school Drama Club) may be quite therapeutic for her.

Her teachers were quite receptive and willing to help her in any way possible. Although they were somewhat surprised at the extent of her motoric difficulties (as compared with other children her age), they were

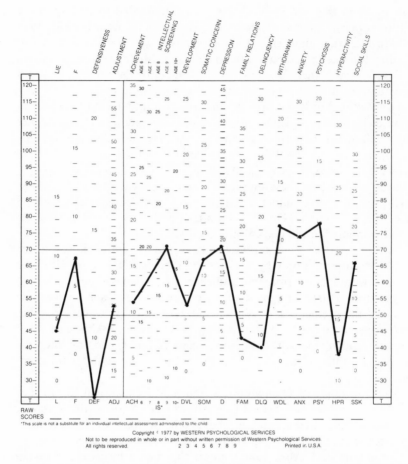

Figure 6-1b. Personality Inventory for Children profile—Case 6-1 (Patricia).

quite willing to accept our formulation regarding her and to give her special consideration when needed. On the other hand, her mother was somewhat reluctant to have all of these special suggestions carried out at school. In this regard, Patricia's mother was still not convinced that she needed all of this special attention, nor did the mother entirely accept the need for Patricia to involve herself actively with others in any sort of nonacademic pursuit. In this connection, it appeared to us that a secondary benefit of this Remedial Educational Conference was that school authorities gained an understanding of the pressures and expectations to which Patricia was subjected at home. They indicated to us that they would actively pursue with her mother Patricia's need for special interventions.

The practical adaptive limitations that are a direct result of Patricia's neuropsychological deficiencies were found to be quite predictable and are often seen in such cases. At the same time, her pattern of neuropsychological strengths and weaknesses suggested the possibility that she could develop a wide variety of compensatory strategies that would help to minimize her deficiencies. Moreover, the range of her neuropsychological strengths was sufficient to prepare her well for the cognitive demands of her educational situation and for adequate adult adjustment.

Nevertheless, Patricia was hampered by personality adjustment difficulties that were beginning to manifest themselves in a rather obvious manner. She lacked confidence in her social interactions, and her work habits at school were beginning to deteriorate. She was beginning to lose motivation, as she could no longer keep pace with the demands and expectations of her parents. This was having the secondary effect of lowering her self-esteem and contributing to a negative self-image.

In these respects, her pattern of neuropsychological strengths and deficiencies did not lead directly to personality adjustment difficulties. At the same time, her psychomotor deficiencies and their effect on the development of Patricia's adaptive abilities would appear to have occasioned a reaction in the parents that led them to make inordinate demands of her. It was the type, degree, and intransigence of the demands placed on Patricia (see Step 2 in our model), in light of her pattern of neuropsychological strengths and weaknesses, that led us to predict (Step 3 in our model) that the long-term behavioral outcomes were not particularly favorable in this case.

In the next case presented, we discuss the neuropsychological test results, adaptive limitations, and personality adjustment of a child who exhibited a similar pattern of neuropsychological strengths and weaknesses, but with somewhat different types of socioemotional problems.

Case 6-2: Morrie

Morrie was referred for neuropsychological assessment by an orthopedic surgeon because of what was reported to be "intrinsic weakness of the hands." This physician questioned the possibility of a neuromuscular disorder.

Morrie had been adopted at 10 days of age. The information available to the mother indicated that there had been some "complications" at Morrie's birth, but she was not privy to the details of these. He walked independently at 15 months, and he was able to put two to three words together at 16 months; this suggested a relative delay in walking. Morrie was the eldest of four children; two younger sisters and a brother were born to his (adoptive) parents after he had been adopted.

Morrie's referral to our department was accompanied by a somewhat urgent phone call from his mother who indicated that his motor skills seemed to be deteriorating; apparently this was reflected in his written work at school. She added that he had been promoted to Grade 6 on condition that his written work improve. This state of affairs was most distressing for her, particularly since he had been a top student during the early elementary school grades. Morrie's mother indicated further that his athletic abilities were poor and that he was losing status in his peer group.

Discussion with his mother indicated that Morrie had begun to exhibit behavioral difficulties at about 9½ years of age. She reported that he had become erratic in his written work at school, performing much better at some times than at others. He was increasingly argumentative at home, and outbursts of temper had been observed more frequently than in the past. His mother added that she had tried to give him emotional support and that she and her husband had continued to encourage him to participate actively in sports.

In the testing situation, Morrie was cooperative and appeared to be confident from the outset. Although somewhat shy at first, a good working rapport was quickly established with him. It was noted that he was very awkward when using his right hand, as he appeared to be unable to grasp properly with the third, fourth, and fifth fingers of this hand. Furthermore, he tended to avoid using his right hand on tasks that are typically completed bimanually (e.g., Wechsler Intelligence Scale for Children [WISC] Block Design and Object Assembly subtests). In addition, it was observed that his left eye drifted laterally (outward) on a number of occasions during this day-long assessment. His mother revealed that, 2 years prior to this assessment, he had undergone surgery performed by an ophthalmologist in an effort to tighten his eye muscles and prevent his left eye from drifting laterally. Morrie's mother added that his left eye now tended to drift only when he seemed to be nervous.

Morrie's neuropsychological test results are represented in Figure 6-2a. The most outstanding features of these results include the following:

1. Morrie exhibited a clearly lateralized pattern of motor and psychomotor deficiencies involving the right side of his body. Simple motor speed with the upper and lower extremities, grip strength, and in particular his Grooved Pegboard Test performance were found to be notably impaired. With respect to the latter, he dropped pegs on 17 occasions and required almost 5 minutes to complete this task with his right hand. By way of contrast, motor steadiness skills in the static and kinetic dispositions were found to be unimpaired bilaterally, and he performed normally with his left hand on other tests of motor and psychomotor abilities.

2. His handwriting was poor in quality, although not illegible. In general, he tended to perform somewhat poorly on paper-and-pencil tests (e.g., Underlining Test).

3. He performed in a superior manner on most other tests of information processing. In this regard, he exhibited strengths in verbal receptive and expressive abilities, visual–spatial abilities, and verbal and nonverbal problem-solving skills.

This boy's pattern of neuropsychological strengths and weaknesses is contraindicative of dysfunction at the level of the cerebral cortex. In view of his adequately developed motor steadiness and tactile–perceptual abilities, the limiting lesion in this case was thought to be below the level of the basal ganglia. There were no indications of an acute or progressive neurological condition.

Neurological examination and CT scan were completed shortly after our assessment. A report from the attending pediatric neurologist indicated that Morrie's CT scan was negative; his right-sided motoric weakness and external strabismus (left eye) were noted during the neurological examination. The pediatric neurologist concurred that the condition was chronic, and most likely involved an upper brain stem anomaly that had been present since birth.

The clinical interview that was conducted with this boy's parents was somewhat strained. They wanted to find *the* answer to his problems. This was difficult, since they tended to focus their questions and attention on matters relating to the status of their son's lateralized psychomotor deficiencies while inadvertently complaining about his behavior. When Morrie's reported behavioral difficulties were raised, his mother blamed them on the manner in which he had been treated at school, including his teacher's overconcern about his handwriting performances.

Through careful questioning, it was revealed that Morrie's behavior was becoming increasingly problematic in the home and in the community. He argued with his brother and sisters and often refused to do what his parents asked of him. He was more frequently becoming involved in fights with other children outside the home setting. Although his parents perceived that he was reasonably well liked by other children of his age, his group of friends had changed recently and he was now associating with children who exhibited delinquent tendencies.

Further discussion revealed that Morrie's father was athletic and had coached local baseball and basketball teams. He jogged regularly to condition himself, and explained that Morrie would not try to keep up with him. His father was disappointed by this, as he felt that participation in sports was good for any child. On the other hand, the father and mother did not openly demand that Morrie participate in any specific activity. In fact, there were few clearly stated demands directed to Morrie in his home environment. He had a few chores (including taking out the garbage and occasionally washing the dishes), none of which proved to be difficult for him. In fact, there were few activities that his parents thought were particularly problematic for him, other than handwriting and generally poor athletic ability.

It is notable that these parents did not discuss openly what appeared to be Morrie's principal presenting problems. Although Morrie was exhibiting increased behavioral difficulties in the home, community, and school settings that were often associated with aggressive behavior on his part, his

Figure 6-2a. Neuropsychological test results—
Case 6-2 (Morrie).

Age	11 yr, 8 mo
WISC	
Verbal IQ	116
Information	10
Comprehension	15
Arithmetic	12
Similarities	16
Vocabulary	13
Digit Span	10
Performance IQ	114
Picture Completion	14
Picture Arrangement	12
Block Design	11
Object Assembly	13
Coding	10
Full Scale IQ	117
PPVT	
IQ	124
Mental Age	15–9
WRAT	
Reading (grade equiv.)	8.7
Spelling (grade equiv.)	6.6
Arithmetic (grade equiv.)	6.0

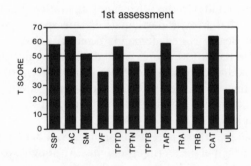

SENSORY–PERCEPTUAL ABILITIES

Morrie's performance on a Sweep Hearing Test was normal. There was no evidence of simple auditory or visual imperception or suppression. However, there was some evidence of tactile suppression with his left hand. In addition, there was some evidence of astereognosis for coins with each hand.

APHASIA SCREENING TEST

Although reasonably accurate from a visual–spatial standpoint, his drawings were slightly tremulous in appearance. He was unable to repeat correctly the word "Massachusetts"; otherwise, his performance on this test was without error.

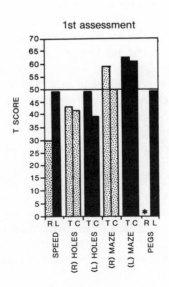

1st assessment

parents continued to focus their concerns on his motor problems. Furthermore, they accepted little in the way of responsibility for his behavior. In fact, they indicated that the cause of his behavior problem was "out there"; that is, his teachers were simply being too hard on him and they did not recognize that he had a handwriting problem. Finally, their household rules and parenting style tended to be lax and their expectations of this child and feelings toward him were not often clearly communicated. For instance, his father was especially disappointed by Morrie's poor athletic abilities. Morrie's mother was disappointed that he was no longer considered to be one of the top students in his class. Given the status of his well-developed problem-solving and other information-processing abilities, it would appear quite likely that Morrie perceived, at some level of consciousness, these unvoiced expectations and feelings about him.

Several sessions were held with Morrie's mother following the completion of his neuropsychological assessment. His father did not attend these sessions, asserting that he had received the information that he needed during the initial feedback session. Morrie's mother appeared on the surface to be quite well motivated during these meetings. However, she preferred to focus her concerns on possible concrete short-term solutions to alleviating Morrie's motoric difficulties rather than on attempts to gain a better understanding of his problems in adaptation from a larger perspective (i.e., taking into consideration his emerging personality difficulties). Because she continued to identify Morrie's teachers as the primary agents in his behavioral difficulties, a Remedial Educational Conference was convened for the purpose of consulting with them.

During this conference, the information provided by Morrie's teachers suggested that the difficulties he was exhibiting in the school setting were somewhat complicated. Although his teachers were aware of his considerable problems in copying from the board and completing his notes, and that the quality of his handwriting fluctuated considerably, they were most concerned about his behavioral difficulties. Morrie was described by them as a child who "was looking for someone to provoke him." At times, he was uncommunicative; at other times, he would bait children in the classroom, especially those who were having more difficulty than he in understanding the concepts and information presented in the classroom.

According to Morrie's teachers, he liked sports and other athletic activities, and had participated actively in them in the past. However, he was now avoiding them since he was not capable of the same competitive level as were most of his peers. In this regard, it was clear that his motoric handicaps impaired his performances in activities requiring bimanual coordination, speed, and/or physical strength.

As was the case for Patricia (Case 6-1), Morrie's teachers were somewhat surprised by the extent of his motoric deficiencies when they were presented in terms of his levels and patterns of performance. At the same time, they were most willing to modify their demands of him, and in fact had already made some modifications in his academic regimen. For example, he was allowed to copy from a book rather than required to copy from the board, since this was easier for him. Our remedial academic recommendations were much the same as they had been for Patricia. We added that his teachers might simply ask him to write a sentence on a blank card and then use this handwriting sample as a criterion from which they might judge his other handwriting performances. At the same time, they were encouraged to take into consideration time limitations and the general level of difficulty of the material when evaluating his written work. Other suggestions included involving him in a school club in which the focus was on nonacademic pursuits. Fortunately, there was a newspaper club in Morrie's school; this seemed to be reasonably well suited to him since he was an excellent reader, liked to read, and could be quite expressive under some conditions.

The PIC, which was completed by this boy's mother, provided additional information regarding the nature of his personality adjustment difficulties. These findings (Figure 6-2b) included significant elevations on the Adjustment and Delinquency scales and moderate elevations on the Hyperactivity and Social Skills scales. We have come to associate this pattern with children who manifest a primarily externalized form of psychopathology: They are likely to break common societal rules, and are at risk for becoming juvenile offenders. Morrie's reported aggressive behavior and recent tendency to associate with a delinquent subgroup provided some external validation for the PIC findings.

As was true in the previous case (Patricia), the behavioral adjustment and associated personality difficulties were seen as being more debilitating than the neuropsychological deficiencies exhibited by the child. In Morrie's case, reports indicated that he experienced less in the way of general adaptive deficiencies than did Patricia. Nevertheless, the demands placed on him in the home and school environments, including his parents' inability to come to terms with his motor problems and their general insensitivity to his developmental needs, no doubt contributed directly to his personality difficulties.

There are a number of similarities and differences between the two cases of specific psychomotor deficiency presented. In both cases, there was some degree of denial by the parents of the extent of the child's motoric difficulties and/or their possible effects on the child's self-esteem. In both instances, the father promoted the strategy of attacking the child's deficiencies directly. Patricia and Morrie exhibited increasing academic difficulty, which became evident at the Grade 4 level. It was the written requirements of tasks that proved to be especially problematic for them. In both cases there had been communication problems between the parents and the child's teachers. Furthermore, the child's teachers, particularly in

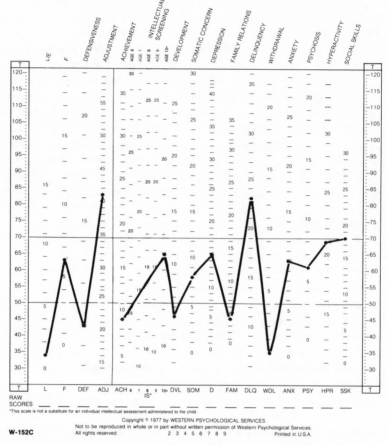

Figure 6-2b. Personality Inventory for Children profile—Case 6-2 (Morrie).

Patricia's case, did not appreciate fully the nature, extent, and significance of the child's motoric limitations. Both were the eldest children in achievement-oriented families, and in both instances there seemed to be at least some degree of communication difficulties between the child's parents.

Although Morrie and Patricia exhibited social adjustment and, more generally speaking, personality adjustment difficulties, there were some marked differences between them in the manifestations of these problems. Patricia tended to internalize her frustration and anxiety, whereas Morrie, for the most part, tended to act out. In this regard, it may have been the case that sex differences and sex-role expectations played some part. However, it should be noted that Morrie's mother felt that his problems were the result of teachers expecting too much of him, while Patricia's parents implied that Patricia herself was the principal problem. In a sense, then, the children appeared to act on and extend the defensive styles of their parents.

In Patricia's family there was a very strict, authoritarian child-rearing style; Morrie's parents were somewhat lax in their behavioral expectations and did not set many rigid rules for him. For example, even though Morrie's parents indicated that he was now starting to associate with a delinquent subgroup, they had not actively intervened to change this state of affairs. Finally, although both of the children's families had adequate income to meet their needs, Patricia's parents seemed to be more conscious and concerned about what others thought of them. It would seem probable that the ethnic background of Patricia's parents played some role in their feeling that they were "outsiders" in their neighborhood.

With the above similarities and differences in parental expectations and child-rearing styles in mind, the following conclusions seem to be warranted.

1. In both cases, the child's psychomotor impairments led directly to adaptive deficiencies that unquestionably hampered his/her ability to compete with peers within and outside of the school situation.

2. Both children were more vulnerable to the development of maladaptive behavioral tendencies because of the way in which their psychomotor limitations were perceived and treated by their parents.

3. Communication difficulties within the households and between the home and school led to the promotion of unrealistic demands on the children without any significant positive intervention on the part of the parents.

4. Many factors—including, possibly, sex-role expectation differences, differences in parenting styles, and the type and availability of peer groups—led to different manifestations in the child's personality difficulties.

In the next cases presented, we describe patterns of neuropsychological strengths and deficiencies that would appear to influence directly the nature and type of personality adjustment difficulties exhibited by the child.

Attentional deficit disorder with hyperactivity

The manifestations of attentional deficits in children are pervasive and multifaceted, and the quality of attentional deployment deficiencies may change very markedly with advances in developmental stage. The latter may be a function not only of changes in developmental task demands, but also of changes in hormonal balance and other factors relating to the developing child's general physiological (especially neurophysiological) maturity.

Another factor to consider in this complex interaction is the relationship of hyperactivity to attentional deficit disorder. Clearly, it is possible to delineate these two symptom complexes, at least insofar as it is possible to specify reliably children who have attentional problems with hyperactivity as opposed to those with attentional deficit who have no associated problems in motoric overactivity. Be that as it may, most clinicians would maintain that particularly serious problems are manifested by children who have both attentional deployment difficulties *and* problems in controlling their level of physical activity. Adaptational deficits in such cases tend to manifest themselves in home, school, and community settings. This being the case, the absence of any surcease for the child from his/her potential for interactional difficulties increases the likelihood that associated psychopathological and academic learning problems will emerge. Thus, the child so afflicted may have to carry the burden of school failure; peer, parent, and teacher negative evaluations; and any number of other stigmata that the home, school, and general community may perceive to be part and parcel of the child.

Neuropsychological assessments of children with this combination of disorders may be particularly illuminating because the nature and extent of the child's information-processing abilities and deficits may not be immediately apparent to teachers, parents, and others who are, quite naturally, overwhelmed with the manifestations of hyperactivity, impulsivity, and attentional-deployment difficulties of the child. Indeed, it is quite likely that treatment considerations will be directed entirely toward the manifestations of problems in attentional deployment, impulse control, and hyperactivity, without regard to any potential information-processing, linguistic, sensory–perceptual, or even basic motoric deficiencies that may also be complicating the child's attempts at adaptation. In addition, it is often the case that even those children who exhibit extreme difficulties in attentional deployment can be shown to demonstrate adequate attentional skills under some conditions. If this be the case, it is not difficult to see the potential therapeutic and educational benefit of attempting to replicate such conditions in the child's everyday life situation, both at home and at school. Furthermore, the need for specific forms of communication with the child for both social and academic information may be overlooked if proper attention is not given to the child's levels and patterns of information-processing abilities and deficits as well as any other specific or idiosyncratic deficiencies in abilities that he/she may exhibit.

Because of the variegated manifestations of this combination of disorders, it is not possible to convey in a single case all of the considerations that should obtain for the initiation of habilitational and rehabilitational intervention programmes for the child so afflicted. However, the case that follows does illustrate a number of significant aspects of this dual problem. In addition, we wish to highlight a pattern of information-processing capacities that often comes as a surprise to the child's primary caretakers because of their overbearing concern with the sociobehavioral implications of the child's manifest problems. This case also illustrates how important it is for such children to have a continuity of care that is integrated and well articulated, especially during the early and middle school years.

Case 6-3: Hector

At the time of his first referral for neuropsychological assessment, Hector was involved in a residential treatment program that was primarily geared to the care of children with outstanding socioemotional difficulties. It was recognized by those referring him that Hector had extreme difficulties in attentional deployment and impulse control, and that he was quite hyperactive. In addition, there was some suspicion on the part of the referring parties that Hector had an information-processing problem. His medical history was essentially negative, except for one electroencephalographic examination which was considered to be "mildly abnormal" and suggestive of "mild bilateral disturbance of cerebral function." No specific etiology was suggested on the basis of this EEG recording. In any case, Hector was maintained on relatively small doses of Ritalin, Mellaril, and Dilantin during the course of his residency program.

It was clear that both of Hector's parents were very caring and supportive of him, and that they were highly motivated to learn more effective ways of dealing with his difficulties. During Hector's course of residential treatment, both parents were involved in child management training in order to help them develop those skills necessary to provide the effective and consistent structuring that Hector needed.

It is noteworthy that the therapeutic team was especially concerned with enhancing Hector's problem-solving skills as a means whereby he could learn to control his impulsive response style.

In the testing situation, Hector was extremely distractible and his general level of motoric activity was much in excess of that usually seen in children of his age. Despite this, he was cooperative and talkative, and rapport was easily obtained with him. In general, his motor coordination appeared average. He was reasonably well motivated throughout the day-long assessment, although he refused to complete two tests that involved measures of motor steadiness abilities. The following is a summary of his test results (see Figure 6-3a).

Lateral dominance testing revealed that Hector was exclusively right-handed and primarily left-footed and left-eyed. Strength of grip was slightly deficient with each hand and somewhat better developed with his left hand. Simple motor speed with the upper extremities was average with his right hand and low average with his left hand. Motor speed with the lower extremities was somewhat depressed. He was able to print his name

Figure 6-3a. Neuropsychological test results—Case 6-3 (Hector).

Age	7 yr, 5 mo	9 yr, 3 mo
WISC		
Verbal IQ	97	95
Information	11	11
Comprehension	8	12
Arithmetic	11	7
Similarities	12	10
Vocabulary	9	9
Digit Span	7	6
Performance IQ	94	106
Picture Completion	13	13
Picture Arrangement	8	8
Block Design	12	11
Object Assembly	9	14
Coding	4	8
Full Scale IQ	96	100
PPVT		
IQ	108	95
Mental Age	7–10	8–5
WRAT		
Reading (grade equiv.)	2.6	5.1
Spelling (grade equiv.)	2.1	4.5
Arithmetic (grade equiv.)	2.7	2.9

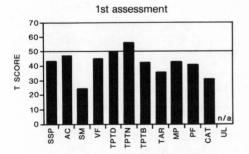

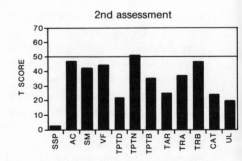

SENSORY-PERCEPTUAL ABILITIES

In the first examination, there was no evidence of simple tactile imperception or suppression. Tests for finger agnosia were essentially negative. There was no evidence of finger dysgraphesthesia or astereognosis for forms. (It should be noted that a great deal of attention is necessary to complete these tasks at this level of proficiency.) In both examinations, there was no evidence of any simple visual or auditory imperception or suppression, and Hector's performances on the Sweep Hearing Test were normal. In the second examination, there were no indications of any tactile imperception or suppression, but he did exhibit some marginal difficulties with the left hand on tests for finger agnosia. He also had very marked difficulties in identifying numbers written on the fingertips of each hand and fairly clear problems in identifying coins placed in each hand. It is probable that the attentional requirements of these tasks were the features that posed particular difficulties for him.

APHASIA SCREENING TEST

There was no evidence of any aphasic disturbance on the first administration of this test (younger children's version). On the older children's version of this test, administered as part of the second assessment, he exhibited one phonetically accurate spelling error, some difficulty in the enunciation of complex multisyllable words, two minor reading errors, and clear difficulties in arithmetic calculation. Otherwise, his performance on this test was unremarkable.

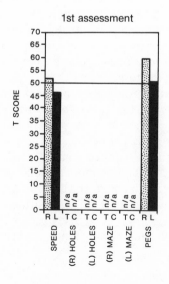

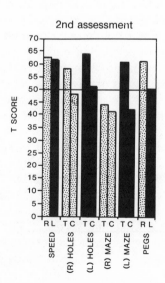

reasonably quickly with each hand, although these productions were quite poor from a qualitative standpoint. Tests for the measurement of motor steadiness in the kinetic and static dispositions were not completed because he would not comply with task requirements. In this connection, it was noteworthy that the quality of his graphomotor performances (drawing and printing) suggested the possibility that he had some motor steadiness difficulties. The Grooved Pegboard Test was performed very well with his right hand and in an average fashion with his left hand.

On the Tactual Performance Test he performed in an average fashion with his right hand, and in a high-average fashion with his left hand. However, it should be noted that he was unable to complete this task any more quickly using both hands than when using only his left hand. Despite his efficiency in completing the various trials of this task, he had much difficulty in remembering the shapes of the blocks used and in designating their correct spatial locations on the drawing of the formboard. The dissociation between his obvious efficiency in learning how to do this task and his poor incidental memory for the shapes and locations of the blocks that he was handling would suggest rather strongly that for him repetition and drill would be quite desirable as aids for memory storage and retrieval. However, his extreme difficulties with attentional deployment suggested that such protracted efforts on his part would be somewhat improbable.

The extreme scatter evident on the Performance section of the WISC would suggest that the Performance IQ of 94 was an underestimate of this boy's visual–spatial analytic and organizational skills. Indeed, the attentional deployment requirements (including focusing, coordination, and shifting) appeared to pose insurmountable problems for Hector on the Coding subtest. Throughout this examination, he tended to do much better on tasks that had uniform and fairly brief response requirements (such as pointing or the uttering of one word), especially when the stimulus array was not complex or multimodal. For example, his mildly impaired level of performance on the Target Test was probably a particular reflection of his problems in attending to changes in sequences of events in both the stimulus and response requirements of the task.

For the most part, Hector was able to reproduce simple geometric forms in an age-appropriate fashion. However, the quality of his performances over repeated trials varied considerably, from quite poor to quite excellent. On one test of visual-matching skills (Matching Pictures) he performed somewhat poorly on a subtest that required some degree of abstraction. On a more straightforward, yet technically more difficult, test of visual-matching skills (Matching Figures), he performed in an age-appropriate fashion; the same was the case with respect to his performance on the Matching V's test. His graphic reproductions of complex geometric forms were somewhat poor with respect to details, although not markedly distorted from a visual–spatial standpoint.

His performances on the Peabody Picture Vocabulary Test, the Verbal section of the WISC, the Speech-Sounds Perception Test, and the Auditory Analysis Test were thought to suggest a good prognosis for the development of word-recognition skills. His relatively poor Digit Span subtest scaled scores is often seen in children suffering from attentional deployment difficulties. He also performed very poorly on the Sentence Memory Test, probably as a result of difficulties in attending to the auditory input requirements of this test. Although there were some borderline indications of problems in enunciation during this examination, his performance was average on the Verbal Fluency Test.

Another instance of his problems in shifting set was his poor performance on the Progressive Figures Test. This test requires the completion of a visual–spatial sequence while utilizing shape and size alternately as cues for direction and orientation. Indeed, this impaired performance was exhibited even though he was given step-by-step directions by the examiner throughout this test.

His moderately deficient performance on the Category Test was not seen as reflecting an outstanding difficulty in hypothesis testing, concept formation, problem solving, or the capacity to benefit from positive and negative informational feedback. Indeed, his good to adequate performances on the Object Assembly, Block Design, and Picture Completion subtests of the WISC, in addition to his obvious capacity to benefit somewhat from experience on the Tactual Performance Test, would argue against such a formulation. Our experience with youngsters such as Hector is that the sounding of the bells and buzzers on the Category Test, in conjunction with the other attentional deployment requirements, serve to depress their scores for reasons quite unrelated to concept formation, problem solving, and the other higher-order abilities that the test was designed to reflect.

The quality of his reading and spelling performances on the Wide Range Achievement Test suggested clearly that he was able to implement his knowledge of sound–symbol relationships when reading and spelling novel words. Even though his WRAT Arithmetic performance was at the 70th centile, it should be noted that he only completed correctly those questions involving simple, single-digit addition and subtraction. We anticipated that he would perform progressively less well in arithmetic calculation at more advanced age levels as the requirements for complex operations, attentional shifting, and sustained concentration increased.

In summary, Hector did not exhibit any deficits in psycholinguistic skill development that could not be explained readily on the basis of his problems in the deployment of attention. His performances on tests involving visual–spatial–organizational skills varied as a function of the extent to which graphomotor skills were required. In addition, his problem-solving and strategy-generation abilities appeared to be intact, although he had considerable difficulty in utilizing these skills in situations that involved many distractors and the necessity for shifting psychological set (e.g., the Category Test). At the same time, it is evident that he would not be expected to direct his behavior well in any sort of novel problem-solving situations that involved such dimensions. Also, his incidental learning was very poor, suggesting strongly that, unless he is directed specifically to particular aspects of learning situations and is kept on-task during these learning situations, he would not be expected to benefit very much from them. For the most part, his other neuropsychological skills and abilities appeared to be intact, and it is clear that he was making adequate progress in reading, spelling, and arithmetic at this time.

Although clearly not diagnostic of any neuropathological condition, these test results were considered to be marginally compatible with mild, chronic impairment at the level of the cerebral hemispheres. The abilities ordinarily thought to be subserved primarily by the prefrontal regions of the brain seemed to be compromised. However, it is clear that the evidence for this hypothesis at this time was not entirely consistent or compelling.

The remedial implications of these neuropsychological test results are very straightforward. These were summarized for his parents and teachers as follows:

1. Hector requires much more external direction and structuring of his behavior than do other children of his age. This is especially the case in novel or otherwise complex situations.

2. In the academic situation, the development of reading comprehension skills should be emphasized. It was thought that his word-recognition skills would advance much more quickly than would his capacities in the area of reading comprehension. Hence, procedures designed to enhance the structure of reading material prior to embarking upon it, as well as focused discussion of the material after it had been read, were encouraged.

3. He would be expected to learn best in situations that involve a minimum of distractors. Hence, a highly structured, small-group situation would be preferred as an academic milieu. In addition, the structuring of play situations in the community and at home in a similar fashion was encouraged.

4. The scheduling of activities both at home and at school such that many expectations in both milieux might become routinized would be desirable. Once again, because Hector has such difficulty in structuring the world around him on his own, environmental manipulation that diminishes the novelty and increases the routine nature of his day-to-day activity was encouraged.

5. It was felt to be extremely important that integration into any new situation (e.g., leaving the residential program for home and a community school) must be done very gradually, with his behavior monitored closely by his teachers, parents, and other caretakers. Continuity of reinforcement

schedules and environmental structuring was felt to be extremely important.

Hector's course in the residential treatment program proceeded very
well. It was the impression of his caretakers that he was much better able
to channel his energy, deploy his attentional skills, and comply with
environmental demands after seven months in the program. However, his
level of hyperactivity was not reduced, and it was felt very strongly that a
great deal of external control and consistency would be necessary if his
behavior were to be predominantly goal-oriented and appropriate. His
discharge from the residential treatment program took place approximately 6 months after his first neuropsychological assessment. It was felt
at the time of discharge that his parents had the capacity and the willing-
ness to follow through with the recommendations of the treatment team.

Unfortunately, the transition from the residential treatment program
to the community school did not go nearly as well as was anticipated.
Indeed, although the parents continued assiduously to apply the recommendations of the treatment team, such was not the case for his caretakers
within the community school situation.

For these and other reasons, a repeat neuropsychological investigation was carried out when this boy was 9 years, 3 months of age. The
referring problems at that time were essentially the same as those for the
initial examination, with the added concern that Hector was doing especially poorly in arithmetic calculation and written test requirements. He
was also seen as an extreme "behavior problem"; he was characterized as
extremely hyperactive by his teachers and other academic caretakers. At
the same time, it was clear that the parents were experiencing no particular
difficulties in controlling his behavior at home, and they were somewhat
dismayed that such "control" could not be exercised in the academic
situation.

During our second examination of Hector, he was very cooperative
and talkative. His levels of hyperactivity and distractibility were very high,
and he exhibited a rather low level of tolerance for frustration. It was
obvious that he was eager to please the examiner by trying very assiduously to complete the tasks that were presented to him, but periodically he
seemed quite unable to focus on these tasks. A summary of the findings of
his second neuropsychological assessment follows.

In this second examination, there were no clear, unequivocal, or
consistent indications of central processing deficiencies evident in Hector's
protocol of neuropsychological test results. There were some tasks that
posed particular difficulties for him; these were usually ones that required
sustained attention for good performance. It is notable that there was no
particular "lateralizing" pattern of performance evident on the motor and
psychomotor measures. However, he did very poorly with his right hand
on the first trial of the Tactual Performance Test. This particular pattern of

performance on the Tactual Performance Test is somewhat similar to that evident in the first examination; it is rather unusual and may reflect problems in maintaining attention and concentration throughout the task. As in the first examination, his incidental memory for the shapes of the blocks used on this task and for their locations on the formboard was quite poor.

His levels of performance were roughly normal on tasks requiring sound blending, memory for sentences of gradually increasing length, and phonemically cued verbal fluency. However, he performed very poorly on the Speech-Sounds Perception Test, which demands more in the way of sustained attention and concentration than do the latter tests.

His grade-equivalent scores on the WRAT reflected advances in word recognition and spelling since the first assessment but, as expected, he made little or no advance in arithmetic calculation. On the Spelling subtest of the WRAT most of his misspellings were of the phonetically accurate variety (e.g., "nacher" for "nature"). On the Reading subtest he was able to read such words as "abuse," "humidity," and "residence." His misreadings suggested that he was capable of using a phonetic word-attack strategy for the decoding of unfamiliar words, but that he may also have adopted a "sight-word/best-guess" approach under many conditions. The latter reflected, in part, his impulsive response style.

As in the first examination, he obtained a very low score on the Digit Span subtest of the WISC. He also did very poorly on the Arithmetic subtest (which requires the focusing of attention on questions delivered orally).

It is noteworthy in this connection that his performance on the Sentence Memory Test was much better than was his performance on the two aforementioned tests on the Verbal section of the WISC. It was apparent from his responses on the Sentence Memory Test that he appreciated the context of the sentences, and there was good reason to believe that this appreciation and understanding was of assistance to him in remembering the words in the sentences.

Attentional deployment problems were apparent on the Trail Making Test. Also, his outstanding difficulties on those subtests of the Underlining Test that require an appreciation for sequenced target items (both verbal and nonverbal) are often seen as a concomitant of attention disorder in children of this age.

His configuration of performances on the Performance section of the WISC was relatively unchanged since our first examination of him. The notable advance of 4 subtest scaled score points on the Coding subtest and 5 points on the Object Assembly subtest may be a reflection of practice with these tasks and, in the case of the Coding subtest, much more practice and proficiency in the use of a pencil.

As in the first examination, he did very poorly on the Category Test. In the second assessment, the older children's version of the Category Test was administered, and he had roughly the same difficulties with the attentional deployment and conceptual shifting requirements of this test as were evident in the first assessment. Overall, he continued to have clear difficulties on nonverbal problem-solving tasks that do not involve the manipulation of concrete stimuli.

In summary, Hector appeared to have the levels of psycholinguistic proficiency that are necessary to make adequate progress in the academic environment. In some senses, he was also seen to have the requisite skills within the visual–spatial–organizational realm to match his progress in the psycholinguistic areas. However, his problems in attentional deployment seemed to have a pervasive negative impact on all aspects of this functioning when consistent, structured approaches to the analysis of information are required. In this connection, he tended to do somewhat better when he could manipulate objects and be actively involved in tasks than when he was expected to sit passively and attend to incoming stimuli in a discriminative fashion.

In conjunction with this second neuropsychological assessment, Hector's mother completed the PIC (see Figure 6-3b). It is clear from this profile, as well as from the parents' responses on the Activity Rating Scale and the Behavior Rating Scale, which they also completed, that they saw Hector as exhibiting a number of acting-out problems (the elevations on the Delinquency, Hyperactivity, and Social Skills scales) in conjunction with some relatively bizarre behaviors (Psychosis scale). This particular profile is very similar to that seen in groups of hyperactive children (Breen & Barkley, 1984). This, in addition to all the other clinical information available to us, suggested very strongly that this boy was in need of a consistent, highly structured program of behavioral modification in his academic program and the continuation of his parents' efforts in the home if his behavior were to be brought under control. Consequently, we recommended placement in a special academic–treatment setting where this sort of consistent structure and patterns of reinforcement could be maintained. He attended this setting for 6 hours each day, Monday through Friday, and there was an opportunity for his parents to meld their own program of intervention in the home with that which transpired in the treatment center. One clear advantage of this arrangement was that Hector was placed in an academic environment that was, in the best sense of the term, "least restrictive" for him, given his extreme difficulties in attentional deployment and motoric control.

We have continued to monitor this situation closely, and there is every indication that Hector is making advances in impulse control, social skills, and academic performance. It is anticipated that he will require this sort of

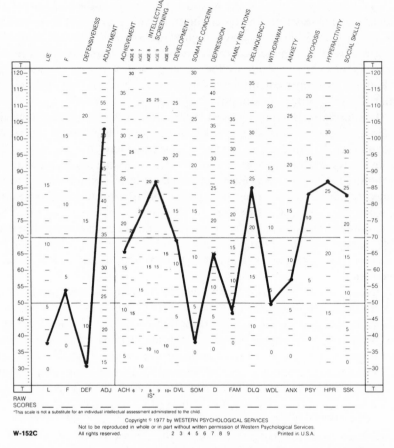

Figure 6-3b. Personality Inventory for Children profile—Case 6-3 (Hector).

setting until the late grade school or early secondary school years, and that even then there will be problems similar to those experienced earlier in the transition from the treatment center to the community school.

In summary, this case illustrates many of the features that we have found to predominate in children who are afflicted with extreme attentional deficits and hyperactivity. It was especially fortunate for Hector that his parents were, and continue to be, a particularly good source of therapeutic efficacy for him. However, even with their well-motivated and well-informed approaches to him, it is clear that he continues to require intensive and extensive programs in the areas of academic and social skill learning. The developmental demands within the two latter areas pose increasingly more difficult obstacles to him and, without the assistance that a well-structured day-care center can provide, Hector would be expected to experience progressive deterioration in psychosocial adjustment.

The particular importance of the neuropsychological assessment results was to demonstrate the dissociations that obtained between his problem-solving skills in different situations, and a specification of the manner in which his higher cognitive skills tended to deteriorate when symbolic shifting and sequencing requirements were increased. That he did not attend well under passive attention conditions was well known prior to our examination of him. What was not known were the situations under which he could deploy his cognitive skills, and indeed whether he had such skills to deploy.

Finally, in contrast to the two previous cases (Patricia and Morrie), it is clear that Hector's basic neuropsychological difficulties (attentional deployment and hyperactivity) had a direct and overwhelming impact on his problems in socioemotional adaptation in the academic and community milieux. Although similar to the first two cases in the sense that his neuropsychological difficulties were essentially independent of his developmental environment with respect to etiology, Hector's continuing problems in adaptation were apparent despite sensitive and intelligent child management by his parents. For Hector, the need for responsible, sensitive, and consistent care was especially apparent in the academic and social environments outside of his home. And one important element of this total treatment program was the information provided in the neuropsychological assessment regarding his particular pattern of information-processing abilities and penchants.

Nonverbal learning disabilities

We turn next to a discussion of a group of children whose pattern of neuropsychological strengths and deficiencies renders them particularly vulnerable to significant, long-term problems in adaptation and personality adjustment. These children, who exhibit outstanding deficiencies associated primarily with nonverbal neuropsychological functions, have been an important focus of our research and associated clinical study since 1971 (Rourke, Young, & Flewelling, 1971). They constitute a particularly significant subtype of neuropsychologically impaired learning-disabled children who are likely to exhibit a largely predictable pattern of personality maladjustment and other adaptive difficulties.

Our interest in the adaptive behavior and personality characteristics of this group of learning-disabled children was a natural outgrowth of early research conducted in our laboratory on the neuropsychological significance of particular patterns of academic performance. The first specific investigation in this series (Rourke & Finlayson, 1978) compared three groups of 9- to 14-year-old children who were selected on the basis of their patterns of performance on the WRAT Reading, Spelling, and Arithmetic subtests. Group 1 was composed of children who were uniformly deficient in reading, spelling, and arithmetic; children in Group 2 were relatively adept (although still impaired relative to age norms) at arithmetic as compared with their performance in reading and spelling; Group 3 was composed of children whose reading and spelling performances were average to above, but whose arithmetic performances were quite deficient. The performances of these three groups were compared on a number of auditory–perceptual, verbal, and visual–perceptual–organizational variables that had been shown in previous research (e.g., Boll, 1974; Rourke, 1975) to be sensitive to the relative integrity and primary functional capabilities of the two cerebral hemispheres in children. The results of this study indicated that children who performed very poorly in arithmetic as compared with their levels of achievement in reading and spelling (Group 3) exhibited generally well-developed auditory–perceptual and verbal skills and somewhat deficient visual–perceptual–organizational skills.

A second study (Rourke & Strang, 1978) compared these same three groups on measures of motor, psychomotor, and tactile–perceptual abilities. It was found that Group 3 children performed normally on measures of simple motor skills, but quite poorly on measures of complex psychomotor abilities and on tests designed for the identification of tactile–perceptual impairments. Specifically, children in Group 3 exhibited bilateral impairments on two measures of psychomotor abilities (Grooved Pegboard Test and Maze Test). Also, they exhibited a normal right-hand performance and an impaired left-hand performance on the Tactual Performance Test. Performance with both hands together for Group 3 children on the Tactual Performance Test was found to be especially impaired. Furthermore, Group 3 children exhibited evidence of bilateral impairment on a composite measure of tactile–perceptual abilities; this tactile–perceptual impairment was more marked on the left side of the body.

In the third study in this series (Strang & Rourke, 1983), performances on the older children's version of the Halstead Category Test by Group 2 and Group 3 children (9 to 14 years of age) were compared. In this investigation, the performance of Group 3 children on this measure was approximately 1 standard deviation below the mean; the performance of Group 2 was average for their age. The Group 3 children performed especially poorly on those subtests which require a substantial degree of "higher-order" visual–spatial analysis.

Based on the results of the Rourke and Finlayson (1978), Rourke and Strang (1978), and Strang and Rourke (1983) investigations and our ongoing clinical study of Group 3 children, we determined that the "classic" neuropsychological symptomatology that best identified and differentiated this group from other groups of neuropsychologically impaired children included the following: (1) well-developed "automatic" or over-learned auditory–perceptual and verbal skills; (2) impaired visual–percep-tual–organizational abilities; (3) impaired tactile–perceptual abilities, more so on the left side of the body; (4) impaired psychomotor abilities, more so on the left side of the body; and, (5) impaired nonverbal concept-formation and related abilities. In addition, a pattern of at least age-appropriate levels of academic performance on the WRAT Reading and Spelling subtests, in conjunction with relatively impaired performance on the WRAT Arithmetic subtest, was found to be a hallmark characteristic of this subtype of learning-disabled child.

We have assessed a number of children who exhibit this classic neuropsychological symptomatology. For example, Laurie, who is de-scribed in some detail in Strang and Rourke (1985a), represents a typical case. At the same time, we have noted that children who exhibit many of the personality and adaptive behavioral characteristics that are typical of Group 3 children may not exhibit all of the "classic" neuropsychological symptoms. In this regard, it would appear that well-developed (basic) auditory–perceptual and verbal abilities in the context of relatively im-paired visual–perceptual–organizational abilities represents the primary identifying neuropsychological pattern. The results of an initial investiga-tion of younger (7- and 8-year-old) children of this subtype (Ozols & Rourke, in preparation) would also support this conclusion.

The wide range of neuropsychological deficiencies exhibited by Group 3 children suggested to us that they might be very much at risk for the development of rather serious general adaptive deficiencies. Moreover, the nature of their neuropsychological strengths in the language realm (including superficially adequate verbal expression and at least age-ap-propriate development of word-recognition and spelling skills) suggested that such children may be doubly handicapped in that the extent and significance of their deficiencies may go unrecognized by their parents and teachers. This hypothesis provided further impetus for study of this type of child because we felt that their needs may not be well understood by those who are in the best position to shape and enhance their development, thus rendering such children at further risk for serious adult adjustment diffi-culties (Rourke, Young, Strang, & Russell, 1986).

Perhaps one of the most outstanding findings in our ongoing clinical investigations of nonverbal-learning-disabled children is their propensity for exhibiting socially inappropriate behaviors. For example, we are re-minded of a 9-year-old girl who, when her mother attempted to kiss her as she returned from an afternoon testing session, blew a bubble with her bubble gum into her mother's face; and of a 12-year-old boy who, while attempting to return to the testing room after having used the washroom (which was almost directly across the hall from the testing room), acciden-tally entered the office of an occupational therapist, and then proceeded to ask her who she was and why she was in his testing room. Eight-year-olds with shoes on the wrong feet, 10-year-olds with their shirts on backwards (without knowing it), inappropriate jokes and use of clichés, poor use and understanding of personal space (e.g., standing almost nose to nose with the examiner)—the cataloging of such inappropriate social interactional behaviors is endless. These findings also contributed to our concerns about this group of children and their need for further study.

It is our estimate that the incidence of this general type of nonverbal learning disability is about 10% of the learning-disabled population, or approximately 10 in 1,000 births. The accuracy of this statement would have to be verified through a careful epidemiological study, which we have not as yet conducted. About one-half of this population is female, which contrasts sharply with most types of language-related (including reading) disabilities, where the ratio is probably closer to 8 to 10 males for every 1 female. We have found that children who exhibit specific and outstanding nonverbal learning disabilities are not typically referred for assessment until about the age of 9 or 10 years, and that most often the referral concerns center on the child's behavior rather than his/her academic difficulties (although the observation of particular difficulty in arithmetic calculation and poor graphomotor skills is quite common).

The PIC was added to our standard neuropsychological assessment battery shortly after it was published in its original form. This allowed us to collect systematic data regarding parental perceptions (usually the mother's) of the child's personality status. Within the last 5 years, we have completed a number of studies that address issues pertaining to the personality status of different subtypes of learning-disabled children. One focus of our concern has been the personality status of the nonverbal-learning-disabled children under discussion. For example, Strang and Rourke (in preparation) compared the PIC profiles of children who exhibited good performance on the WISC Similarities and Vocabulary subtests and much poorer performance on the WISC Block Design and Object Assembly subtests, with two other groups of learning-disabled children, one of which exhibited the opposite pattern of abilities and deficits. These independent variables were chosen in part because this pattern of subtest performances is often seen in the WISC profiles of Group 3 children. We found that the nonverbal-learning-disabled children exhibited a mean PIC profile that was most suggestive of the presence of psychopathology (as compared with the other two groups). The PIC Psychosis scale and in general those scales that constitute the Psychopathology–Internalization factor identified by Lachar (cited in Wirt, Lachar, Klinedinst, & Seat, 1977)—namely, Psychosis, Social Skills, Anxiety, Withdrawal, and Depression—best characterized and distinguished the PIC profiles of the nonverbal-learning-disabled children. When the degree of discrepancy between the groups was increased through a reselection procedure, the

PIC profile differences became more evident. Furthermore, the Psycho-pathology–Internalization pattern became more distinct for the Group 3-like children. These findings fit well with our clinical observations, with the results of other studies (Fisk, Rourke, & Strang, 1985; Ozols & Rourke, in preparation; Rourke, Pohlman, Fuerst, Porter, & Fisk, 1985), and with a recent developmental model of central processing abilities and deficits (Rourke, 1982a).

In this regard, our findings to date (e.g., Strang & Del Dotto, 1985) include the following: poor socialization skills, including poor peer relations; a tendency to gravitate toward younger or older playmates; isolative tendencies in social situations; inappropriate or peculiar behaviors, especially in unstructured social situations; a poor appreciation for social distance, territoriality, and spatial boundaries. When the children are younger (in early school grades) there may be a tendency to act out. Excessive activity, impulsiveness, problems with sustained vigilance, and hyperverbal behavior are often reported in the case histories of the younger children as well. As the children approach adolescence, there would appear to be a shift for most toward internalized personality maladjustment. The children become increasingly anxious and feel out of place in many situations, especially when these are novel or otherwise complex. There is a movement toward more social withdrawal, although the penchant for loquaciousness remains.

An informal study of the developmental histories of specific nonverbal-learning-disabled children whom we have assessed has revealed some common recognizable difficulties in adaptation that first present during infancy. A perusal of their developmental histories, including parental reports and the reports of other caretakers and/or professionals, has revealed the following: There tends to be a lack of effective exploratory play on the part of the child; the onset of clear expressive speech tends to be closer to the "normal" milestones than does independent walking; there is delayed acquisition of basic self-help skills, including the proper use of utensils for eating; there is a tendency toward motoric clumsiness; the children seem to be overly dependent on adults for assistance; and more than the expected number of difficulties arise in peer interactions, especially in unstructured play activities.

Although the linguistic skills of this subtype of neuropsychologically impaired children represent an area of strength for them, adaptive deficiencies associated with ineffective and/or maladaptive communication skills are characteristically identified. In this regard, excessive talking, including tangential verbiage, is often found to be present in the language behavior of this group of children. There appears to be a problem with respect to language content or the pragmatics of their language. Verbal reasoning skills and/or the ability to grasp the larger significance of what may be said to them (e.g., within the context of a social situation) is usually an area of weakness. The interpretation of the nonverbal behavior of others and the ability to convey meaning to others by nonverbal means is a form of communication which is most often sorely deficient in such youngsters.

We have found that the adaptive defiencies of nonverbal-learning-disabled children are in evidence in the home, community, and school settings. While at school (at least at the elementary school level), the following difficulties are most often noted as well: substantial difficulty with mechanical arithmetic and other forms of mathematics; graphomotor problems, including printing and handwriting difficulties; poor reading comprehension as contrasted with their excellent word-recognition skills; and general organizational difficulties (e.g., organizing one's notebook). Some other specific academic difficulties may arise, but the aforementioned represent those which tend to be most prominent.

It should be emphasized that the general adaptive deficiencies that typify nonverbal-learning-disabled children are quite pervasive and raise some serious clinical concern about them. Their principal adaptive deficiencies may be categorized in the following manner.

1. They have communication difficulties, including the following: inappropriate use of language; a general lack of, or ineffective, nonverbal behavior; and an inability to grasp the complete significance of the communications of others, particularly in novel social or other complex situations.

2. There are deficits in basic self-help skills. Their psychomotor and visual–spatial deficiencies contribute to their problems with self-help skills development. It is often noted that there is a lack of appropriate experience and parental expectations in this area, which is in part a reflection of the perceived nature of the child's competencies and deficiencies. Such children are usually perceived as reasonably bright and competent because of their demonstrated verbal skills. This may increase the likelihood that such children will learn to use their verbal skills to avoid those tasks which prove to be problematic for them.

3. There are specific academic difficulties, including problems in arithmetic calculation, handwriting, reading comprehension, and the understanding, organization, and consolidation of more complex subject matter.

4. Finally, there are adaptive difficulties which relate directly to their deficient problem-solving and reasoning skills. One consequence of their limitations in problem solving is the characteristic difficulties that they experience in adapting to change and novel or complex situations.

In our view, the type and range of such adaptive deficiencies render such children vulnerable to serious adjustment problems throughout their development. We present next a case which illustrates this developmental interaction.

Case 6-4: Natalie

Natalie underwent her first neuropsychological assessment at the age of 7 years, 8 months; we followed her for a period of over 5 years after this initial assessment. She does not exhibit all of the neuropsychological symptomatology that is characteristic of Group 3 children, but she certainly fits into the larger subgroup of nonverbal-learning-disabled children. At the same time, the socioemotional and other adjustment difficulties that she experienced serve to illustrate some of the special problems in adaptation that are characteristic of children who exhibit nonverbal learning disabilities.

Natalie's developmental history included a low birth weight (1200 g) following a difficult prenatal period and birth. Shortly after birth, she exhibited respiratory problems that included times at which she stopped breathing. She was incubated for approximately 2 months following her birth to monitor her low birth weight and respiratory problems. Shortly afterward, she contracted pneumonia and was readmitted to hospital. After that period, her mother maintained that she seemed to develop fairly "normally." However, she was an only child and her mother may not have had a firm understanding of age-appropriate expectations when she made this statement.

Difficulties emerged when Natalie entered school. She was identified as exhibiting motor restlessness and distractibility at the kindergarten level. In addition, she tended to be very verbal and it was difficult for her teacher to understand why this seemingly "bright" child was having so much difficulty in completing her work. She did not socialize well with the other children and she was considered by the special education consultant to be at risk for further difficulties in the academic realm. Consequently, she was referred at the Grade 2 level for neuropsychological assessment.

As was pointed out earlier in this discussion, children in our area who exhibit specific nonverbal learning disabilities are typically not referred for neuropsychological assessment until about the Grade 4 level. In Natalie's case, her aggressive behavior toward other children, in combination with her mother's persistence in obtaining appropriate assessments and services for her, led to the referral for neuropsychological assessment at this point in time. It should be noted that Natalie's mother was a highly verbal person who at times seemed to have difficulty staying "on track" when discussing her child's difficulties. In fact, in many respects she exhibited some of the social interactional and linguistic characteristics that we associate with nonverbal learning disabilities.

The examination took place over a 2-day period and was carried out without any great difficulties. Although rapport was easily obtained with her, she sometimes appeared to be uncooperative. She tended to be very talkative and was prone to guess in situations in which it was clear that she did not know the answer. She was attentive when supervised, although there was a tendency toward distractibility. She needed encouragement to complete some of the Performance subtests of the WISC. It was thought probable that we obtained a fairly reliable estimate of her abilities and deficits in this examination. Natalie's neuropsychological test results are presented in Figure 6-4.

Natalie exhibited a well-developed capacity to process auditory–verbal information. An exception to this was her somewhat poor performance on the Sentence Memory Test, which may have been affected adversely by her attentional difficulties and by problems in dealing with the semantic content of the sentences. Fairly outstanding and pervasive difficulties were noted on tests of visual–perceptual and visual–spatial abilities. She exhibited some tactile–perceptual deficiencies that were more evident with her left hand. Her WRAT Reading and Spelling scores were superior, while she performed very poorly on the WRAT Arithmetic subtest. All of these findings are typical of Group 3 children. However, she performed reasonably well, after a somewhat poor start, on the younger children's version of the Halstead Category Test.[1]

Natalie performed in an at least age-appropriate manner on the Maze, Holes, and Grooved Pegboard Tests. In this regard, she performed much better than we would expect of a "classic" specific nonverbal-learning-disabled child. Nevertheless, she did exhibit mildly impaired left-hand performance and markedly impaired performance with both hands on the Tactual Performance Test; she performed in an essentially normal manner with her right hand on the first trial. This pattern of Tactual Performance Test results is quite typical of such children.

In summary, Natalie exhibited most of the features and neuropsychological symptomatology that we have typically seen with specific nonverbal learning disabilities, with the exception that she had better developed psychomotor abilities bilaterally. Her observed limitations in problem solving that were evident during the course of our examination and follow-up work with her suggested strongly that the younger children's version of the Category Test did not reflect adequately the limits of her deficiencies in this area. In fact, Natalie's problems are typical of children of this type in that, even with extensive remedial efforts, she continued to exhibit debilitating deficiencies in the area of social learning and those aspects of practical intelligence that are sometimes termed "common sense."

1. In the Ozols and Rourke (in preparation) investigation, we found that Group 3 children had no particular difficulties with this version of the Category Test. Two interrelated explanations for this finding can be suggested: (1) the younger children's version of this test does not involve the type and degree of conceptual complexity with which Group 3 children have difficulty; and (2) verbal facility is a principal feature responsible for success on it.

Shortly after her assessment, a series of informal clinical studies were arranged to explore further Natalie's information-processing limitations. We were particularly interested in the status and function of her language behavior. For example, when asked informally about "big" words that she knew, Natalie was able to pronounce many multisyllabic words, but she usually had little or no idea of their meaning. When questioned about this, she stated simply that she had heard these words on television or from her mother, and that "they seemed like interesting words."

With this and other information regarding specific nonverbal-learning-disabled children in mind, we hypothesized that her difficulties in novel social interactions may be complicated, and to some extent precipitated, by her tendency to consider in isolation and/or overrate the significance of the language behavior of others. For example, such children may attend to what they hear rather than to what they see when there is competing information available. In any case, we asked Natalie to name words that had to do with feelings such as "sad," "happy," "angry," and so on. Then we had her define these words as best she could; in fact, she was able to do a creditable job of this. We then wrote each of these "feeling" words on separate white cards and had her read them back to us to make certain that she could recognize the words; she also had no difficulty with this task. Then she was systematically exposed to a number of pictures of people who were exhibiting various types of facial expressions. Some were obviously happy, while others were angry or sad, and so forth. Next we had her look at some pictures and tell us what she thought was happening and what people were feeling. We found that her analyses of the situations were quite superficial and that she tended to pick out the most salient feature of the picture (e.g., the man is smiling) and then build her explanation around this isolated finding (confabulation?).

Following this, we showed her other pictures one at a time while casually presenting a card with a directly contrasting "feeling" word printed on it. We found that Natalie performed especially poorly under these conditions. Most often, she simply read the word and seemed to attempt to make the person's facial expression fit what she had read. For example, she was shown a large picture of a very prominent American political figure who exhibited an obviously distraught facial expression. The word "happy" was placed in close proximity to this picture. She was asked how the man was feeling. She said, "I think he is feeling very very happy." When asked about her statement, she said, "He must be happy, it says it right here [pointing to the word]."

Through further research we have identified other factors that may have adverse effects on the social sensitivity of nonverbal-learning-disabled children. For example, the work of Ozols and Rourke (1985) illustrated the difficulty that such children most likely have with the analysis of the

Figure 6-4. Neuropsychological test results—
Case 6-4 (Natalie).

Age	7 yr, 8 mo
WISC	
Verbal IQ	103
Information	7
Comprehension	7
Arithmetic	10
Similarities	14
Vocabulary	14
Digit Span	10
Performance IQ	82
Picture Completion	8
Picture Arrangement	5
Block Design	8
Object Assembly	6
Coding	10
Full Scale IQ	92
PPVT	
IQ	107
Mental Age	8–9
WRAT	
Reading (grade equiv.)	4.4
Spelling (grade equiv.)	3.7
Arithmetic (grade equiv.)	1.8

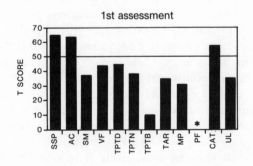

244

SENSORY-PERCEPTUAL ABILITIES
There were no indications of any auditory imperception. However, Natalie's performance on a Sweep Hearing Test raised the possibility of a mild binaural hearing loss. A thorough audiological assessment revealed that she had a mild degree of hearing loss with the right ear across a number of frequencies. There were no indications of any tactile imperception or suppression with the right hand. With her left hand, there were no indications of any tactile imperception, but she did (on two of four occasions) suppress stimuli delivered to the left side of the body under bilateral simultaneous stimulation conditions. She experienced considerable difficulty in identifying symbols written on the fingertips of her left hand.

APHASIA SCREENING TEST
There were no indications of any anomia, spelling dyspraxia, dysgraphia, dyscalculia, body disorientation, or right–left disorientation problems. However, she did rather poorly on tests requiring her to draw simple and complex figures (on this and other tests). Her drawing of a Greek cross was particularly distorted.

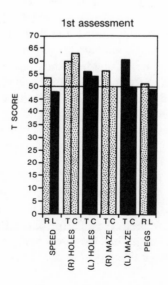

nonverbal behavior of others. In any event, their difficulty in interacting appropriately in novel or otherwise complex social situations, even when they have the benefit of extensive social training, suggests that there is a multidimensional aspect to their difficulties in this area.

Natalie attended a special school for children with learning disabilities from about her eighth birthday until 13 years of age. She developed only superficial relationships with the other children in the program, although she was not disliked by them. Rather, her demeanor was thought to be unusual and she often engaged in behavior, such as making off-handed comments about the adequacy of a language-disabled child's reading skills, that served to alienate her from others. Her social relationships in the community were limited and she did not make a "best friend" during this period. Rather, she spent most of her time at home reading or watching television.

When she was finally integrated into a regular elementary school, she still lacked the practical intelligence to make careful choices of friends and acquaintances. Although there had been extensive efforts in her residential school to prepare her for integration into a regular school program, the skills which she had been taught were not easily or naturally applied by her. Instead, they served as fragmented pieces of information that were most likely to be applied only within the context of the situations in which they were learned (e.g., providing specific answers to certain types of questions).

In addition to these pervasive problems in stimulus and response generalization, Natalie was quite gullible; she was easily involved by unscrupulous age-mates and adults in a variety of nefarious activities. Her problems in social perception and judgment and her failure to appreciate potentially dangerous social situations were such that she was constantly at risk for being induced to participate in antisocial activities. Efforts to deal with this situation were instituted, but it would take us too far afield to go into an explanation of these at this juncture.

Provisions for the care of children such as Natalie should continue through the adolescent years and into adulthood. In this connection, the results of a recent study (Rourke et al., 1986) of eight adult psychiatric adult patients (five women and three men) who were referred to a major hospital in a large metropolitan area are instructive. These cases were referred specifically for neuropsychological assessment and were chosen because of the similarity between their neuropsychological patterns of strengths and weaknesses and those of Group 3 children. In fact, all of these adults exhibited the classic symptomatology associated with specific nonverbal learning disabilities. For example, their WAIS Verbal IQs ranged from 96 to 116, whereas their Performance IQ range was 83 to 100.

Six of the eight patients had post-secondary-school experience and four had undergraduate university degrees. Their socioeconomic status ranged from lower to upper class. Six of the cases were referred because of serious occupational adjustment difficulty, while for two others serious emotional disturbance was part of the clinical picture. For seven of the eight patients, depression was the primary presenting characteristic. Two of the patients were thought to be serious suicidal threats, and two had schizophrenia as part of their diagnostic formulation.

For these patients and those like them, the prognosis for adequate social and emotional adjustment is quite guarded. Individual psychotherapy with the patients in our study was found to be fruitless, since sessions served essentially as crisis interventions, without having any long-range positive effects. Their lack of insight and problems in generalization and transfer of training were seen as primary characteristics by attending health-care professionals. These few observations should serve to make it abundantly clear that early identification and intensive milieu-oriented treatment is necessary if we are to minimize the serious adaptive limitations and long-term adjustment difficulties of such persons.

Summary and conclusions

In this chapter, we have discussed in detail some special problems in adaptation, including difficulties with respect to personality adjustment, that are more or less related to the child's pattern of neuropsychological strengths and weaknesses. The first two cases illustrate that the presence of a neuropsychological handicap (in these cases, lateralized psychomotor deficiency) may, if not appreciated and dealt with adequately by the child's parents, play a role in the setting of unrealistic demands for the child. In turn, the development of secondary personality adjustment difficulties is enhanced. Furthermore, some of the practical adaptive limitations of these sorts of motoric deficiency were illustrated in some detail. The more general point to be made in this context is that caretakers should recognize that such neuropsychological handicaps do involve certain limitations for the child and that these limitations must be taken into account when setting academic, social, and other performance criteria for them. Failure to do so will almost certainly increase the likelihood of untoward socio-emotional behavior in such children.

Furthermore, the cases of lateralized psychomotor deficiency should serve to illustrate that the specific form of emotional disturbance (e.g., "internalized" or "externalized") does not, in such cases, depend on the neuropsychological handicap. Rather, factors relating to the defensive styles of the child's parents, the nature of the expectations placed on the child, and/or other individual circumstances faced by the child (e.g., sex-role stereotyping), appear to be critical determinants in this regard.

The last two cases presented in this chapter were meant to illustrate the rather direct interaction that may obtain between the adaptive limitations imposed by the child's neuropsychological handicap and particular forms of personality maladjustment. In the case of the hyperactive attentional-disordered child (Hector), his parents had taken every possible step to modify their parenting style and expectations of him to meet his therapeutic needs. Furthermore, he had received optimal treatment in a children's mental health center which proved to be quite effective when he was in that environment. Unfortunately, entrance into the community school occasioned a precipitous deterioration in the delicate adjustmental level that he had reached. Maintenance in a day-treatment–academic facility, with continued support and interaction with the parents turned out to be the "least restrictive" milieu in which he could cope.

Finally, the characteristics of specific nonverbal-learning-disabled children were described in some detail. The case presented in this connection (Natalie) serves to illustrate the vulnerability of such children, even when they have received appropriate treatment. The predictable nature of the adaptive deficiencies and personality adjustment problems of such children has been the subject of our research since 1971. Further study of this group of children who would appear to be very much at risk for serious adult adjustment difficulties, is a particular focus of our current clinical and research programs.

References

Barkley, R. A. (1981). *Hyperactive children: A handbook for diagnosis and treatment.* New York: Guilford.

Boll, T. J. (1974). Behavioral correlates of cerebral damage in children aged 9 through 14. In R. M. Reitan & L. A. Davison (Eds.), *Clinical neuropsychology: Current status and applications* (pp. 91–120). Washington, DC: V. H. Winston.

Breen, M. J., & Barkley, R. A. (1984). Psychological adjustment in learning disabled, hyperactive, and hyperactive/learning disabled children as measured by the Personality Inventory for Children. *Journal of Clinical Child Psychology, 13,* 232–236.

Fisk, J. L., Rourke, B. P., & Strang, J. D. (1985). The clinical and research utility of the Personality Inventory for Children (PIC) for learning-disabled children. *Canadian Psychology, 26,* 152. (Abstract)

Fletcher, J. M., & Taylor, H. G. (1984). Neuropsychological approaches to children: Towards a developmental neuropsychology. *Journal of Clinical Neuropsychology, 6,* 39–56.

Ozols, E. J., & Rourke, B. P. (1985). Dimensions of social sensitivity in two types of learning-disabled children. In B. P. Rourke (Ed.), *Neuropsychology of learning disabilities: Essentials of subtype analysis* (pp. 281–301). New York: Guilford.

Ozols, E. J., & Rourke, B. P. (in preparation). Neuropsychological and behavioral characteristics of young learning-disabled children classified according to patterns of academic achievement.

Porter, J. E., & Rourke, B. P. (1985). Socioemotional functioning of learning-disabled children: A subtypal analysis of personality patterns. In B. P. Rourke (Ed.), *Neu-*

ropsychology of learning disabilities: Essentials of subtype analysis (pp. 257–280). New York: Guilford.

Rourke, B. P. (1975). Brain–behavior relationships in children with learning disabilities: A research program. *American Psychologist, 30,* 911–920.

Rourke, B. P. (1978). Reading, spelling, arithmetic disabilities: A neuropsychologic perspective. In H. R. Myklebust (Ed.), *Progress in learning disabilities* (Vol. IV, pp. 97–120). New York: Grune & Stratton.

Rourke, B. P. (1981). Neuropsychological assessment of children with learning disabilities. In S. B. Filskov & T. J. Boll (Eds.), *Handbook of clinical neuropsychology* (pp. 453–478). New York: Wiley-Interscience.

Rourke, B. P. (1982a). Central processing deficiencies in children: Toward a developmental neuropsychological model. *Journal of Clinical Neuropsychology, 4,* 1–18.

Rourke, B. P. (1982b). Child-clinical neuropsychology: Assessment and intervention with the disabled child. In J. de Wit & A. L. Benton (Eds.), *Perspectives in child study: Integration of theory and practice* (pp. 62–72). Lisse, The Netherlands: Swets & Zeitlinger.

Rourke, B. P., Bakker, D. J., Fisk, J. L., & Strang, J. D. (1983). *Child neuropsychology: An introduction to theory, research, and clinical practice.* New York: Guilford.

Rourke, B. P., & Finlayson, M. A. J. (1978). Neuropsychological significance of variations in patterns of academic performance: Verbal and visual–spatial abilities. *Journal of Abnormal Child Psychology, 6,* 121–133.

Rourke, B. P., & Fisk, J. L. (1981). Socio-emotional disturbances of learning-disabled children: The role of central processing deficits. *Bulletin of the Orton Society, 31,* 77–88.

Rourke, B. P., Pohlman, C. L., Fuerst, D. R., Porter, J. E., & Fisk, J. L. (1985). Personality subtypes of learning-disabled children: Two validation studies. *Journal of Clinical and Experimental Neuropsychology, 7,* 157. (Abstract)

Rourke, B. P., & Strang, J. D. (1978). Neuropsychological significance of variations in patterns of academic performance: Motor, psychomotor, and tactile–perceptual abilities. *Journal of Pediatric Psychology, 3,* 62–66.

Rourke, B. P., & Strang, J. D. (1983). Subtypes of reading and arithmetical disabilities: A neuropsychological analysis. In M. Rutter (Ed.), *Developmental neuropsychiatry* (pp. 473–488). New York: Guilford.

Rourke, B. P., Young, G. C., & Flewelling, R. W. (1971). The relationships between WISC Verbal–Performance discrepancies and selected verbal, auditory–perceptual, and problem-solving abilities in children with learning disabilities. *Journal of Clinical Psychology, 27,* 475–479.

Rourke, B. P., Young, G. C., Strang, J. D., & Russell, D. L. (1986). Adult outcomes of central processing deficiencies in childhood. In I. Grant & K. M. Adams (Eds.), *Neuropsychological assessment of neuropsychiatric disorders* (pp. 244–267). New York: Oxford.

Strang, J. D., & Del Dotto, J. E. (1985). *Specific nonverbal disorders in children: Neuropsychological assessment and intervention.* Unpublished manuscript. (Available from authors: Regional Children's Centre, Windsor Western Hospital, 1453 Prince Road, Windsor, Ontario, Canada, N9C 8Z4.)

Strang, J. D., & Rourke, B. P. (1983). Concept-formation/nonverbal reasoning abilities of children who exhibit specific academic problems with arithmetic. *Journal of Clinical Child Psychology, 12,* 33–39.

Strang, J. C., & Rourke, B. P. (1985a). Adaptive behavior of children with specific arithmetic disabilities and associated neuropsychological abilities and deficits. In B. P. Rourke (Ed.), *Neuropsychology of learning disabilities: Essentials of subtype analysis* (pp. 302–328). New York: Guilford.

Strang, J. D., & Rourke, B. P. (1985b). Arithmetic disability subtypes: The neuropsychological significance of specific arithmetical impairment in childhood. In B. P. Rourke (Ed.), *Neuropsychology of learning disabilities: Essentials of subtype analysis* (pp. 167–183). New York: Guilford.

Strang, J. D., & Rourke, B. P. (in preparation). Personality dimensions of learning-disabled children.

Wirt, R. D., Lachar, D., Klinedinst, J. K., & Seat, P. D. (1977). *Multidimensional description of child personality: A manual for the Personality Inventory for Children.* Los Angeles: Western Psychological Services.

7. Summary of principles and future directions

Principles of assessment and intervention

Throughout this work we have tried to emphasize a number of characteristics of neuropsychological assessment that we feel are especially important. In this chapter, by way of summary, we consider the most important of these. In order to highlight each of these issues, we have stated them in the form of principles. Each of these statements is followed by a brief explanation.

1. *The principal aim of neuropsychological assessment is to determine the interaction that obtains between brain lesion(s) and the child's ability structure as this impacts on adaptive behavior.* It should be clear that there is no obvious, clear-cut, or universal relationship that obtains between brain lesions and ability structure in a developing child. These relationships must be determined through the application of a comprehensive neuropsychological assessment. At the very least, such an assessment should include tests and measures that encompass a broad range of complexity and that reflect in a reliable and valid fashion the important sensory–perceptual capabilities, motor and psychomotor skills, attention and memory capacities, psycholinguistic skills, and higher-order conceptual and problem-solving capacities of the child. In turn, this interaction between brain lesion and abilities should be framed in a fashion that sheds light on the immediate and long-range adaptive capacities of the individual child.

2. *Neuropsychological tests and measures should be amenable to a variety of levels and types of analysis.* The assessment data collected should be such that various types of interpretative strategies may be applied to them. For example, one should be in a position to state with some assurance whether and to what extent a particular child's performances approximate appropriate developmental levels. This, of course, presumes that norms are available for each of the tests and measures employed. In addition, the data collected should be amenable to pattern or configurational analysis, since this is often the most powerful interpretative strategy that can be employed. Of course, measures that involve comparisons on the two sides of the body within the sensory–perceptual and motor and

251

psychomotor realms are basic to any neuropsychological assessment regimen. Finally, insofar as possible, the child's performances should be amenable to a qualitative analysis that includes a search for pathological signs as well as other unique characteristics of the individual child's ability profile. Indeed, it is this last dimension of analysis that often holds particular promise for reflecting the information processing capacities and potentials of the child.

3. *The results of a neuropsychological assessment of a child must be seen within the context of the immediate and long-term developmental needs of that child.* An assessment that focuses only on (say) the immediate needs of the child in the formal school situation must, by its very nature, be less than ideal. Assessment results should be evaluated within the context of informal learning situations as well as the various demands for social interaction that the child faces. In addition, it is clear that a focus only on the immediate presenting problems of the child must perforce be limited because of the obvious need to prepare the child for the long-term developmental demands which he/she will face. In addition, as we have often emphasized, it may very well be the case that a young child may benefit greatly from the initiation of "treatment" for problems in skill and ability areas (e.g., social interaction) that though predictable are not yet obvious emergent difficulties.

4. *Prognostications for the child in a variety of relevant adaptive domains should be derived prior to the development of a treatment plan.* Recommendations for various forms of therapeutic involvement are contingent upon the confidence with which one can make short- and long-term predictions regarding the child's adaptive behavior. Such predictions are usually based on the results of a comprehensive neuropsychological assessment as these are interpreted within the context of the natural history of the child's brain lesion and the specific and general requirements of his/her particular environment. Failure to formulate such prognostications would be expected to dilute the effectiveness of program planning. In addition, it is axiomatic that long-term evaluation of such predictions is impossible if these are not formulated in a precise fashion. This latter point is particularly crucial because, if the relative therapeutic efficacy of particular interventions for brain-impaired children is to be evaluated both clinically and experimentally, it is crucial to generate rigorous and testable formulations of predictions. Ex post facto reconciliations of test findings to the changing agendas of parents, teachers, and others are unscientific and invite criterion contamination.

5. *The formulation of the ideal treatment plan for a brain-impaired child should flow directly from considerations relating to the foregoing principles.* The ideal intervention plan for a brain-impaired youngster should bear a logical and clear-cut relationship to the interactions between neuropsychological profile, brain impairment, and developmental de-

mands as previously discussed. Otherwise, there is no rationale for conducting a neuropsychological assessment, seeking knowledge about the
state of the child's brain, or involving developmental principles within a
habilitational or rehabilitational context. If one already has a therapy in
mind, there would seem to be no basis for engaging in any of the latter
pursuits unless one wishes to establish a baseline for the evaluation of a
particular form of therapy. Assessing ability structure and dynamics,
determining relevant brain lesion variables, and considering how both of
these relate to immediate and long-term developmental demands are exercises in which one should engage only if one has not previously decided
upon a course of therapeutic action.

6. *The realistic remedial plan should be formulated on the basis of
the resources that are available in the family and the community.* To this
end, it is necessary that the practicing child-clinical neuropsychologist be
able to assess the resources of the child's family, have an understanding of
programs of intervention that are available in the community, and be quite
familiar with the actual skills and penchants of the therapists who are to be
involved with the child. Failure to make an adequate determination of the
foregoing will almost without exception eventuate in a far less than
adequate impact for the intervention plan. A corollary of this principle is
that the mere enunciation of therapeutic programs for the family and child
without regard to available resources in the family itself and the therapeutic community is tantamount to taking up permanent residence in a
clinical ivory tower.

7. *Prognostications and the effectiveness and current appropriateness of intervention plans should be evaluated through ongoing monitoring of the child's neuropsychological status.* This monitoring may take the
form of abbreviated assessments of particular skill and ability areas, or it
may require a full-scale comprehensive evaluation. In any case, it is clear
that the effects of maturation, ongoing learning experiences, and functional adaptations resulting from processes of recovery and neuropsychological adaptation constitute a dynamic mix that must be subject to
reliable and valid assessment if changes in the treatment plan are to be
made in a rational manner. Fine-tuning, cessation, or intensification of an
original program should not be considered unless and until the interactions between the child's brain lesion, ability structure, and adaptional
potentials are scrutinized within the context of his/her immediate and
long-term developmental demands.

8. *All of the above principles apply to the child who is suffering from
diseases and disorders that have a direct impact on brain functioning but
that are not, per se, alterations of cerebral substance.* As illustrated in
Chapters 4 and 5, a number of diseases have a very direct impact on brain
substance and function that must be taken into consideration by the child-
clinical neuropsychologist. As in lesions of the brain substance itself, the

interactions between these various disease processes, the child's ability structure, and the child's adaptive potential must be assessed within the context of the child's immediate and long-term developmental demands. The formulation of ideal and realistic remedial planning in such cases is usually no less important, but may be considerably more complex. Indeed, this complexity strongly suggests that the frontiers of research in child neuropsychology will be greatly enlarged through the vigorous investigation of children suffering from such diseases and anomalies.

9. *Although never entirely satisfactory, it is necessary to attempt to apply the findings of a neuropsychological assessment even when little or nothing is known about the state of the child's brain.* We see this situation most vividly in children who present with various levels, configurations, and signs that we have come to associate with brain lesions, but whose neurological status is thought to be "negative." That is, although the child may be "neurologically negative," it remains the responsibility of the child-clinical neuropsychologist to deal with all of the foregoing considerations in the formulation of a realistic remedial plan and its implementation and evaluation. Although more may be known in the future about specific brain structures and systems that are damaged or dysfunctional in such cases, this does not mean that the child-clinical neuropsychologist should wait for such information to be available. Rather, it would make good sense to proceed solely on the basis of what is known, and to try to formulate a rational treatment plan that takes into consideration the cognitive and developmental dimensions that are discernible in such cases.

Future directions in neuropsychological assessment: The next frontier

These latter considerations lead very directly to what we view as the next frontier of child-clinical neuropsychology. Traditionally, the focus of concern for child-clinical neuropsychologists has been the elucidation of brain–behavior relationships in children by means of the application of comprehensive neuropsychological assessment methods; the intended goals of such an exercise are primarily diagnostic in nature. Recently, as described in this work, much more attention has been focused on neuropsychological assessment as a means whereby developmental neurocognitive relationships can be specified and their adaptive ramifications understood; the principal clinical aims of this particular approach are the formulation, implementation, and evaluation of habilitational and rehabilitational plans for brain-impaired youngsters.

What is emerging as imperative if this direction is to yield full fruit is the need for new measurement techniques and the modification of old techniques in order to increase the range of applicability of neuropsychological assessment technology and to expand the neurodevelopmental ramifications of the use of such technologies in a variety of clinical settings. The goal of such an exercise is to enhance the formulation, implementation, and evaluation of intervention strategies for brain-impaired youngsters.

What follows is a brief overview of measurement domains and associated measurement instruments that appear to hold considerable promise for yielding information relevant to the treatment aims of the child-clinical neuropsychologist.

Adaptive behavior: The Vineland Adaptive Behavior Scales

The actual activities of daily living and the developmental demands which children face are difficult to measure in a reliable and valid fashion. The best attempt to do this at the time of this writing is that embodied in the Vineland Adaptive Behavior Scales (VABS; Sparrow, Balla, & Cicchetti, 1984). This instrument is an excellent example of the melding of psychometric sophistication with clinical applicability. The principal utility of this instrument for the child-clinical neuropsychologist may very well turn out to be its accurate reflection of ecologically valid behaviors. These in turn can then be related to various information-processing abilities of the brain-impaired child. One would expect that the interactions that would emerge through this comparison would shed considerable light upon the therapeutic requirements of children who exhibit varying levels, configurations, and types of neuropsychological abilities and deficits. In addition, it would be expected that developmental models of neuropsychological functioning would be greatly enhanced by research that seeks to determine these interactions.

Memory

It is clear that considerable advances have been made recently in the understanding of children's memory and meta-memory skills (Flavell & Wellman, 1977). This being the case, the time would appear ripe to attempt to introduce standardized measures of memory that would be applicable to the examination of various types of brain-impaired children.

Excellent examples of attempts along these lines are the measures of selective reminding within the verbal sphere and an analogue of this procedure within the visual sphere that have been developed by Fletcher (1985). Performances on these measures have been shown to differentiate various subtypes of learning-disabled children, and Fletcher and his associates are currently engaged in a series of investigations of frankly brain-damaged youngsters that utilize these and a number of other measures. It would seem most likely that considerable relevant information will be gained from such studies. Within the present context, the relationship between various memory skills as tapped by these and related instruments would be expected to be of particular interest. For example, one would expect that an interaction between developmental level and various rote and novel memory capacities will emerge. This would have implications, not only for theory testing in developmental neuropsychology (Rourke, 1982a), but also for clinical concerns in habilitation and rehabilitation (Rourke, Bakker, Fisk, & Strang, 1983).

Cognition

As noted throughout this work, the dimensions of hypothesis testing, strategy generation, problem solving, concept formation, and reasoning are crucial variables to consider in the assessment of the brain-impaired child. In addition, the child's capacity to deal with positive and negative informational feedback, to shift psychological set in a flexible fashion, and to deal systematically with the analysis of information in novel problem-solving situations are aspects of adaptive behavior that have far-reaching general impact on response to therapeutic intervention. For some time now, developmental theorists (e.g., Flavell, 1979) have stressed some of these dimensions in attempts to understand cognitive development in children. Within the general field of neuropsychology, there has always been an abiding interest in forms of higher-order concept-formation, problem-solving, and reasoning skills. However, there have been relatively few investigations of these important dimensions in groups of children who are of interest to the child-clinical neuropsychologist (Strang & Rourke, 1983). This situation is expected to change rapidly in the next few years. Spurred on by the availability of norms for tests in this area (e.g., Chelune & Baer, 1986), specific test developments (Pajurkova, Orr, Rourke, & Finlayson, 1976; Rourke & Fisk, 1977), and the obvious clinical needs for such measures (Rourke *et al.*, 1983), it is expected that much useful clinical information in these interrelated areas will soon be available.

Personality measurement

Consideration of the dimensions of socioemotional disturbance and personality deviation in children with central processing deficiencies has been a central concern of ours in recent years (Ozols & Rourke, 1985; Porter & Rourke, 1985; Rourke, 1975, 1982b; Rourke & Fisk, 1981; Strang & Rourke, 1985). We have been especially interested in the adaptive significance of deficiencies in social perception, cognition, and sensory-motor skills for emotional, social, and personality development. There are indications that investigations along these lines are intensifying in a number of other laboratories (e.g., Breen & Barkley, 1984), and this trend is expected to continue. The upshot of this effort should be a far clearer understanding of the relationship between varying configurations of neuropsychological abilities and deficits, on the one hand, and patterns of social adjustment and personality development on the other. An understanding of these relationships within a developmental context will aid in the identification of children at risk for problems in these areas as well as in the formulation of early intervention treatment programs designed to forestall such untoward types of development. In this regard, it is clear that associated measurement of adaptive abilities (e.g., with the VABS) would be expected to be particularly helpful.

Behavioral ratings

Advocated by Barkley (1981) for some time, it is apparent that much more in the way of correlative measurement of brain-impaired youngsters with behavioral rating scales and developmental neuropsychological instruments is a fruitful avenue to pursue, especially in the management and treatment of children with "acting-out" problems and those suffering from various forms of attentional deficit. Very often behavioral ratings identify *what* should be treated, whereas neuropsychological assessment information is valuable in determining the most fruitful avenue(s) to follow in delivering relevant information so that behavioral management techniques can proceed efficiently. Failure to appreciate the particular contributions that can be made in these two quite different domains tends, unfortunately, to abound in the general field of child-clinical psychology. We are particularly fortunate to have a number of investigators and clinical commentators in the field of child-clinical neuropsychology who are quite conversant with behavioral methodology, especially as this applies to children with developmental problems. Hence, a fruitful melding of these two modes of approach would be expected to enjoy much further development among those investigators and clinicians whose everyday concerns center around the understanding and treatment of the brain-impaired child.

In discussing future directions, we have attempted simply to indicate those areas of research and development that seemed to be of particular importance for the child-clinical neuropsychologist. The actual mechanics of these developments, embracing as they do burgeoning techniques in psychometrics (e.g., confirmatory factor analysis), neural imaging (e.g., magnetic resonance imaging), and multidimensional subtyping procedures (e.g., cluster analysis) could also have been mentioned. However, we thought it best to accentuate "content" areas in this context rather than to explore in detail these very promising techniques. It remains now for us to bring this work to a close with one final comment on the sociopolitical climate in which our field is developing.

A final note

Throughout this work, we have stressed the importance of an ecological approach to the understanding of the relationship between assessment and intervention. A prerequisite for the full implementation of such an approach is the cooperation of families, educational personnel, and other help-providing professionals in the remediation process. As pointed out in the discussions of Step 5 in our model, it is often found that these resources are much less than optimal. There is an additional consideration that may further complicate the implementation of appropriate interventions for brain-impaired children. This factor, for lack of a better name, we will refer to as the "sociopolitical climate."

At any given time in the history of the treatment of brain-impaired and other disturbed children in Western society, there have been popular forces and factors—some would refer to them as fads—at work that have exerted considerable influence on the sorts of intervention practices and facilities that are made available for such children. For example, there have been periods during the 20th century when children who were "different" in any way were thought to be best served by separating them from "normal" children for the purposes of education and therapy. Currently, we are in the midst of efforts in many North American jurisdictions to effect almost exactly the opposite state of affairs. Often these efforts get lumped under the rubric of "mainstreaming." This concept and its attendant goal of placing the child in the "least restrictive environment" for both education and therapy are themselves products of the sociopolitical climate, and as such may evanesce as quickly as they have arisen.

For these and other reasons, it is incumbent upon the child-clinical neuropsychologist to be abundantly aware of what is "in" and "out" regarding the penchants and proclivities of social policy makers, while at the same time maintaining a reasonable and circumspect clinical position regarding the specific needs of different types of brain-impaired children. The practical corollary of such a position is that the child-clinical neuropsychologist often finds it necessary to use the jargon of the day in order to "package" recommendations and programs that would otherwise be dismissed as either outdated or too radical. The necessity for prudence in such circumstances should not be misconstrued as a counsel for pusillanimity. Indeed, Aristotle's view of prudence as "daring wisely" and his notion that the stance of the prudent person is one that lies in the mean between pusillanimity and foolhardiness would be exactly what we have in mind.

In any case, the crucial variable to bear in mind in this context is the determination of who, in fact, constitutes "the patient." For the child-clinical neuropsychologist, this is, without exception, the brain-impaired child whom we are responsible for assessing and treating. Failure to appreciate this simple fact may lead to the adoption of modes of assessment and intervention that are dictated more by concerns relating to economics, sociopolitical fads, and other irrelevancies rather than by calm, informed, and thoughtful reflection—that is, the qualities that are the indispensable wellsprings of responsible and compassionate clinical practice.

References

Barkley, R. A. (1981). *Hyperactive children: A handbook for diagnosis and treatment.* New York: Guilford.

Breen, M. J., & Barkley, R. A. (1984). Psychological adjustment in learning disabled, hyperactive, and hyperactive/learning disabled children as measured by the Personality Inventory for Children. *Journal of Clinical Child Psychology, 13,* 232–236.

Chelune, G. J., & Baer, R. A. (1986). Developmental norms for the Wisconsin Card Sorting Test. *Journal of Clinical and Experimental Neuropsychology, 8.*

Flavell, J. H. (1979). Metacognition and cognitive monitoring: A new area of cognitive–developmental inquiry. *American Psychologist, 34,* 906–911.

Flavell, J. H., & Wellman, H. M. (1977). Metamemory. In R. V. Kail, Jr., & J. W. Hagen (Eds.), *Perspectives on the development of memory and cognition.* Hillsdale, NJ: Erlbaum.

Fletcher, J. M. (1985). External validation of learning disability typologies. In B. P. Rourke (Ed.), *Neuropsychology of learning disabilities: Esssentials of subtype analysis* (pp. 187–211). New York: Guilford.

Ozols, E. J., & Rourke, B. P. (1985). Dimensions of social sensitivity in two types of learning-disabled children. In B. P. Rourke (Ed.), *Neuropsychology of learning disabilities: Esssentials of subtype analysis* (pp. 281–301). New York: Guilford.

Pajurkova, E. M., Orr, R. R., Rourke, B. P., & Finlayson, M. A. J. (1976). Children's Word-Finding Test: A verbal problem-solving task. *Perceptual and Motor Skills, 42,* 851–858.

Porter, J., & Rourke, B. P. (1985). Socioemotional functioning of learning-disabled children: A subtypal analysis of personality patterns. In B. P. Rourke (Ed.), *Neuropsychology of learning disabilities: Essentials of subtype analysis* (pp. 257–280). New York: Guilford.

Rourke, B. P. (1975). Brain–behavior relationships in children with learning disabilities: A research program. *American Psychologist, 30,* 911–920.

Rourke, B. P. (1982a). Central processing deficiencies in children: Toward a developmental neuropsychological model. *Journal of Clinical Neuropsychology, 4,* 1–18.

Rourke, B. P. (1982b). Child-clinical neuropsychology: Assessment and intervention with the disabled child. In J. de Wit & A. L. Benton (Eds.), *Perspectives in child study: Integration of theory and practice* (pp. 62–72). Lisse, The Netherlands: Swets & Zeitlinger.

Rourke, B. P., Bakker, D. J., Fisk, J. L., & Strang, J. D. (1983). *Child neuropsychology: An introduction to theory, research, and clinical practice.* New York: Guilford.

Rourke, B. P., & Fisk, J. L. (1977). *Children's Word-Finding Test* (Revised). University of Windsor, Department of Psychology, Windsor, Ontario.

Rourke, B. P., & Fisk, J. L. (1981). Socio-emotional disturbances of learning-disabled children: The role of central processing deficits. *Bulletin of the Orton Society, 31,* 77–88.

Rourke, B. P., Young, G. C., Strang, J. D., & Russell, D. L. (1986). Adult outcomes of central processing deficiencies in childhood. In I. Grant & K. M. Adams (Eds.), *Neuropsychological assessment of neuropsychiatric disorders* (pp. 244–267). New York: Oxford.

Sparrow, S. S., Balla, D. A., & Cicchetti, D. B. (1984). *The Vineland Adaptive Behavior Scales; A revision of the Vineland Social Maturity Scale by Edgar A. Doll.* Circle Pines, MN: American Guidance Services.

Strang, J. D., & Rourke, B. P. (1983). Concept-formation/nonverbal reasoning abilities of children who exhibit specific academic problems with arithmetic. *Journal of Clinical Child Psychology, 12,* 33–39.

Strang, J. D., & Rourke, B. P. (1985). Adaptive behavior of children with specific arithmetic disabilities and associated neuropsychological abilities and deficits. In B. P. Rourke (Ed.), *Neuropsychology of learning disabilities: Essentials of subtype analysis* (pp. 302–328). New York: Guilford.

Appendix. Descriptions of tests administered to children (5 – 15 years)

Tests administered to all children (ages 5 –15)

Wechsler Intelligence Scale for Children (Wechsler, 1949)

Full Scale IQ. A composite score derived from the total scaled subtest scores. Indicative of overall "intellectual" functioning.

Verbal IQ. A prorated score derived from the total scaled scores of six Verbal subtests. Indicative of overall "verbal" functioning.

Performance IQ. A composite score derived from the scaled scores of the five Performance subtests (excluding the Mazes subtest). Indicative of overall nonverbal, "visual–perceptual" functioning.

VERBAL SUBTESTS

Information. Thirty questions. Involves elementary factual knowledge of history, geography, current events, literature, and general science. *Score*: number of items correct. *Task requirement*: retrieval of acquired verbal information. *Stimulus*: spoken question of fact. *Response*: spoken answer.

Comprehension. Fourteen questions. Involves the ability to evaluate certain social and practical situations. *Score*: number of items correct. *Task requirement*: evaluation of verbally formulated problem situations. *Stimulus*: spoken request for opinion. *Response*: spoken answer.

Arithmetic. Sixteen arithmetic problems of increasing difficulty. *Score*: number of problems correctly solved, within time credit. *Task requirement*: arithmetic reasoning. *Stimulus*: spoken (first 13 items) or printed (last 3 items) question. *Response*: spoken answer.

Reprinted by permission from *Child Neuropsychology: An Introduction to Theory, Research, and Clinical Practice* by B. P. Rourke, D. J. Bakker, J. L. Fisk, and J. D. Strang, 1983, New York: Guilford.

Similarities: Sixteen pairs of words. The most essential semantically common characteristic of word pairs must be stated. *Score*: number correct. *Task requirement*: verbal abstraction. *Stimulus*: spoken question. *Response*: spoken answer.

Vocabulary. Forty words. Spoken definition of words. *Score*: number of words correct. *Task requirement*: verbal definition. *Stimulus*: spoken word. *Response*: spoken definition.

Digit Span. Repetition in forward order of three- to nine-digit numbers and repetition in reversed order of two- to eight-digit numbers. *Score*: simple total of forward and reversed digit span. *Task requirement*: short-term memory for digits. *Stimulus*: spoken numbers. *Response*: spoken numbers.

PERFORMANCE SUBTESTS

Picture Completion. Twenty pictures of familiar objects, each with a part missing. The missing part is identified from simple line drawings. *Score*: number of missing parts correctly identified. *Task requirement*: location of missing part on the basis of memory of the whole object. *Stimulus*: picture. *Response*: spoken name of missing part.

Picture Arrangement. Eleven series of picture cards. Pictures are sequentially arranged to form a story. *Score*: total credits for speed and accuracy of arrangement. *Task requirement*: manipulation of the order of picture cards to form the most probable sequence of events. *Stimulus*: pictures. *Response*: simple motor manipulation.

Block Design. Ten designs. Arrangement of colored blocks to form designs which match those on printed cards. *Score*: total score for speed and accuracy of block placement. *Task requirement*: arrangement of blocks to match a printed design. *Stimulus*: printed geometric design. *Response*: manipulation and arrangement of blocks.

Object Assembly. Four formboards (puzzles). Parts of each formboard are to be arranged to form a picture. *Score*: total score for speed and accuracy of assembly. *Task requirement*: spatial arrangement of parts to form a meaningful whole. *Stimulus*: disarranged parts of picture. *Response*: complex manipulation and arrangement of parts.

Coding. Ninety-three digits, preceded by a code which relates digits to symbols. Symbols are to be written below digits as rapidly as possible. *Score*: number of symbols correctly written within a fixed time. *Task requirement*: association of digits and symbols by direct visual identification and/or by short-term memorization. *Stimulus*: printed digits and symbols. *Response*: rapid coordination of visual identification with a complex writing response. (For children under 8 years, symbols within common shapes are used; the score is the number of symbols correctly written in 45 shapes within a fixed time.)

Peabody Picture Vocabulary Test, Form A (Dunn, 1965)

Picture Vocabulary, Oral Raw Score, Oral IQ, Mental Age derived from IQ. One hundred fifty sets of four line drawings, with which 150 words of increasing difficulty are to be associated. The words are those of Form A of the Peabody Vocabulary Test. *Score*: total correct picture–word associations. *Task requirement*: selection of picture most appropriately related to the spoken word. *Stimulus*: four visual pictures, one spoken word. *Response*: simple pointing or verbal response. Oral IQ is the transformation of the oral raw score to an IQ score on the basis of test norms.

Wide Range Achievement Test (Jastak & Jastak, 1965)

Reading. Standardized test of oral word-reading achievement. *Score*: centile score based on total number of words correctly read aloud. *Task requirement*: association of printed letters with spoken word. *Stimulus*: printed word. *Response*: spoken word.

Spelling. Standardized test of written spelling achievement. *Score*: centile score based on total number of words correctly spelled. *Task requirement*: written production of spoken word. *Stimulus*: spoken word. *Response*: written word.

Arithmetic. Standardized test of written arithmetic achievement. *Score*: centile score based on total number of correct solutions to progressively more difficult arithmetic problems. *Task requirement*: solution of arithmetic problems. *Response*: written answers.

Personality Inventory for Children (Wirt, Lachar, Klinedinst, & Seat, 1977)

The Personality Inventory for Children (PIC) is an empirically and rationally constructed instrument that seeks to provide comprehensive and clinically relevant personality descriptions of individuals primarily in the range of 6–16 years of age. It is composed of 600 true–false questions regarding the child's behavior, disposition, interpersonal relations, and attitudes, and is to be completed by one of the child's parents.

The PIC contains 33 scales. Of these 33 scales, there are 16 profile scales and 15 supplementary scales. The PIC profile includes all scales judged to be most important. The PIC profile scales can be divided further into three validity scales (the Lie, F, and Defensiveness scales), one screening scale for general maladjustment (the Adjustment scale), and 12 clinical scales. The clinical scales include the following: Achievement; Intellectual Screening; Development; Somatic Concern; Depression; Family Relations; Delinquency; Withdrawal; Anxiety; Psychosis; Hyperactivity; and Social Skills. Score elevations in the positive direction (e.g., $> 70\ T$) increase the likelihood of significant pathology for each of these scales.

Older children's battery (ages 9–15)

Tests for Sensory-Perceptual Disturbances (Reitan & Davison, 1974)

TACTILE PERCEPTION

The child is required to identify correctly (without vision) the hand or face (left or right) which receives tactile stimulation. The stimulus is produced by a light touch. Following this determination of the child's ability to perceive unilateral stimulation, simultaneous bilateral hand stimulation and contralateral hand–face stimulation are interspersed with unilateral stimulation. The score is the number of errors for each hand and each side of the face under all conditions.

AUDITORY PERCEPTION

The child is required to identify correctly (without vision) the ear to which an auditory stimulus is presented. The stimulus is produced by rubbing the fingers together lightly. Following this determination of the child's ability to perceive unilateral stimulation, bilateral stimulation is interspersed with the unilateral stimulation. The score is the number of errors for each ear under all conditions.

VISUAL PERCEPTION

The child is required to identify correctly slight finger movements presented in a confrontation manner to the visual fields. Stimulation is presented first unilaterally and then simultaneous bilateral stimulation is interspersed with the unilateral trials. The score is the number of errors made within the quadrants of the visual fields.

FINGER AGNOSIA

The child is required to identify (without the aid of vision) the finger which has been touched. Each of the five fingers is stimulated four times in a random order. First the right hand and then the left hand is stimulated. The score is the number of errors made with each finger for each hand.

FINGERTIP NUMBER-WRITING PERCEPTION

The child is required to verbalize (without the aid of vision) which of the numbers 3, 4, 5, or 6 has been written on his/her fingertips. A different finger of the right hand is used for each trial until four trials have been given for each finger. The procedure is then repeated for the left hand. The score is the number of errors made with each finger for each hand.

COIN RECOGNITION

The child is required to identify, by tactile perception only, 1-, 5-, and 10-cent pieces placed in his/her right hand, then his/her left hand, and then each coin placed simultaneously in both hands. The order of presentation is unsystematic. The score is the number of errors made with each hand under each condition.

Target Test (Reitan & Davison, 1974)

The child is required to make a delayed response in reproducing visual–spatial configurations of increasing complexity tapped out by the examiner. The score is the number of items out of 20 correctly reproduced.

Trail Making Test (Reitan & Davison, 1974; Rourke & Finlayson, 1975)

The Trail Making Test consists of two parts, A and B. In A, the child is required, under time pressure, to connect the numbers 1 to 15 arranged on a page. The requirements are essentially similar in Part B, except that it is necessary to alternate between the numeric and the alphabetic series. The scores recorded are the number of seconds required to finish each part; the number of errors made on each part is also recorded.

Sweep Hearing Test

The child is required to indicate whether or not he/she can detect a series of pure tones, ranging from 125 Hz to 8,000 Hz. Each tone is presented unilaterally through ear phones. The decibel level of each tone is systematically decreased until the minimal audible level is determined.

Auditory Closure Test (Kass, 1964)

The child is required to blend into words 23 progressively longer chains of sound elements presented on tape. The score is the number of words correctly identified.

Sentence Memory Test (Benton, 1965)

The child is required to repeat sentences of gradually increasing length (from 1 to 26 syllables). These are presented on a tape recorder. The score is the number of sentences correctly repeated.

Speech-Sounds Perception Test (Reitan & Davison, 1974)

The child is required to attend to 30 tape-recorded nonsense syllables and to select the correct response alternative from among three printed choices. The score is the number of sounds correctly identified.

Verbal Fluency Test

The child is required to name as many words as he/she can, within 60 seconds, which begin with the sound "P," as in "pig." This is repeated with the sound "C," as in "cake." The score is the mean number of correct words for the two trials.

Auditory Analysis Test (Rosner & Simon, 1970)

The child is required to repeat a word and then repeat the same word with specific parts of it omitted. There are 40 progressively more difficult test items. The score is the total number of (modified) "words" correctly repeated.

Halstead–Wepman Aphasia Screening Test (Reitan & Davison, 1974)

Naming (Dysnomia). Five items which require the child to name familiar objects. *Score*: number of errors.

Spelling (Spelling Dyspraxia). The child is required to spell orally three spoken words. *Score*: number of errors.

Writing (Dysgraphia). Two items. The child is required to write a word and a sentence which are presented to him/her orally. *Score*: number of errors.

Enunciation (Dysarthria). Three items. The child is required to repeat three increasingly complex words spoken to him/her by the examiner. *Score*: number of errors.

Reading (Dyslexia). Six items. The child is required to read numbers, letters, and words. *Score*: number of errors.

Reproduction of Geometric Forms (Constructional Dyspraxia). Four items. The child is required to copy a square, a triangle, a Greek cross, and a key. *Score*: number of errors.

Arithmetic (*Dyscalculia*). Two items. The child is required to solve two problems: one subtraction (written) and one multiplication (oral). *Score*: number of errors.

Understanding Verbal Instructions (*Auditory–Verbal Agnosia*). Four items. The child is required to demonstrate an understanding of four verbal items. *Score*: number of errors.

Seashore Rhythm Test (Reitan & Davison, 1974)

The Rhythm Test is a subtest of the Seashore Tests of Musical Talent. The child is required to differentiate between 30 pairs of rhythmic patterns which are sometimes the same and sometimes different. The score is the number of errors.

Halstead Category Test (Reitan & Davison, 1974)

This test consists of 168 visual-choice stimulus figures which are presented to the child individually on a milk-glass screen located on the front of the apparatus. An answer panel is provided for the child. This consists of four answer buttons which are individually identified by the numbers 1, 2, 3, and 4. The child's task is to view the stimulus figure and to offer his/her answer by depressing one of the four answer buttons. A pleasant bell sounds after each correct response and a harsh buzzer sounds after each incorrect response. The bell and buzzer, therefore, provide the essential information necessary for determining the concept underlying the stimulus figures. In successive sequences of trials, the abstraction of principles of numerosity, oddity, spatial position, and relative extent is required for successful responding. The final subtest of the Category Test is of a summary nature and therefore does not have a principle to be discerned. The child is told to try to remember the correct answer based on his/her previous observation of the item and to give that same answer again. The score is the number of errors.

Tests for Lateral Dominance (Harris, 1947; Miles, 1929)

HAND PREFERENCE

The child is required to demonstrate the hand used to throw a ball, hammer a nail, cut with a knife, turn a doorknob, use scissors, use an eraser, and write his/ her name. The number of tasks performed with each hand is recorded.

EYE PREFERENCE

The child is required to demonstrate the manner in which he/she would look through a telescope and use a rifle. The eye used for each task is recorded. In addition, the subject is given the Miles ABC Test for Ocular Dominance, in which (without ordinarily being aware of it) he/she has to choose one eye or the other to look through a conical apparatus to identify a visual stimulus. The eye chosen on each of 10 trials is recorded.

FOOT PREFERENCE

The child is asked to demonstrate the manner in which he/she would kick a football and step on a bug. The foot used on each trial is recorded.

Strength of Grip (Reitan & Davison, 1974)

The Smedley Hand Dynamometer is used to measure strength of grip. The child is required to squeeze the dynamometer three times with the dominant hand and three times with the nondominant hand, alternating between hands on each trial. The mean pressure which the hand exerts on the three trials is recorded (in kilograms) for each hand.

Writing Speed (Reitan & Davison, 1974)

The child is required to write his/her name with a pencil as rapidly as possible, first with the preferred hand and then with the nonpreferred hand. The score is the time taken for each hand.

Finger Tapping (Reitan & Davison, 1974); Foot Tapping (Knights & Moule, 1967)

For finger tapping, the child uses alternately the index finger of the dominant hand and of the nondominant hand. Four trials of 10 seconds each are given for both hands. The Foot Tapping Test employs the same principles and instructions, but this time the child uses his/her feet, alternating between the dominant foot and the nondominant foot. Four trials of 10 seconds are given for each foot. The score for both finger and foot tapping is the average of the best three out of four trials.

Maze Test (Kløve, 1963; Knights & Moule, 1968; Rourke & Telegdy, 1971)

The child is required to run a stylus through a maze which has the blind alleys filled and is placed at a 70° angle (on the Tactual Performance Test stand). Three scores are obtained: the number of contacts with the side of the maze, the total amount of time during which the stylus contacts the side of the maze, and the speed (total time from start to finish). These are electrically recorded. There are two successive trials with each hand. The scores are the totals for the two trials with the dominant hand and the two trials with the nondominant hand.

Graduated Holes Test (Kløve, 1963; Knights & Moule, 1968; Rourke & Telegdy, 1971)

The child is required to fit a stylus into a series of progressively smaller holes. The idea is to hold the stylus in the center of the holes for a 10-second period without contacting the edge. Two scores are obtained: the number of contacts with the edge of the hole, and the duration of the contact. These are recorded electrically. The test is performed once with the right hand and once with the left hand.

Grooved Pegboard Test (Kløve, 1963; Knights & Moule, 1868; Rourke, Yanni, MacDonald, & Young, 1973)

The child is required to fit keyhole-shaped pegs into similarly shaped holes on a 4" × 4" board beginning at the left side with the right hand and at the right side with the left hand. The child is urged to fit all 25 pegs in as rapidly as possible. One trial is performed with the dominant hand followed by one trial with the nondominant hand. The scores obtained are the length of time required to complete the task with each hand and the total number of times the pegs are dropped with each hand.

Tactual Performance Test (Reitan & Davison, 1974)

This test is Reitan's modification for children of the test developed by Halstead (1947). Halstead's test was based, in turn, upon a modification of the Seguin–Goddard formboard. The child is blindfolded and not permitted to see the formboard or blocks at any time. The formboard is placed in a vertical disposition at an angle of 70° on a stand situated on a table immediately in front of the child. He/she is to fit six blocks into the proper spaces with the dominant hand, then with the nondominant hand, and a third time using both hands. After the board and blocks have been put out of sight, the blindfold is removed and the child is required to draw a diagram of the board representing the blocks in their proper spaces. In all, six measures are obtained. Scoring is based on the time needed to place the blocks on the board with the dominant, the nondominant, and both hands. A fourth measure is the sum of the time taken with the right, left, and both hands. The Memory component of this test is the number of blocks correctly reproduced in the drawing of the board; the Location component is the number of blocks correctly localized in the drawing.

Children's Word-Finding Test (Reitan, 1972; Pajurkova, Orr, Rourke, & Finlayson, 1976; Rourke & Fisk, 1976)

The test consists of 13 items, each item composed of 5 sentences. Each sentence contains a nonsense word, "Grobnik." The child is required to determine

(10 seconds per sentence) the meaning of the nonsense word through the appreciation of its verbal context. *Score*: total correct. *Task requirement*: verbal problem solving and appreciation of contextual cues. *Stimulus*: spoken words. *Response*: spoken answer.

Underlining Test (Doehring, 1968; Rourke & Orr, 1977; Rourke & Petrauskas, 1977; Rourke & Gates, 1980)

These tests are intended to assess speed and accuracy of visual discrimination for various kinds of verbal and nonverbal visual stimuli presented singly and in combination. In general, the visual stimulus becomes more verbal and more complex with each succeeding subtest. Subtests 1 and 13 involve the same task in order to permit assessment of practice effect. A final test (14) is administered to control for motor speed. A short practice item is given for each subtest.

SUBTEST 1: SINGLE NUMBER

The child is required to underline the number 4 each time it appears on a printed page containing a random sequence of 360 single numbers. An example of the number to be identified is printed at the top of the page. A short practice test is given. *Score*: total numbers correctly underlined minus total incorrectly underlined in 30 seconds. *Task requirement*: locating and underlining a particular number interspersed among other numbers. *Stimulus*: random sequences of printed numbers. *Response*: simple underlining response to identify single numbers.

SUBTEST 2: SINGLE GEOMETRIC FORMS

The child is required to underline a Greek cross with a pencil each time it appears in random sequence among a series of 235 geometric forms, including squares, stars, circles, and triangles, and so forth. The forms are about ¼″ in height. *Score*: total crosses underlined minus total errors in 30 seconds. *Task requirement*: as in previous subtest, but for identification of a geometric form.

SUBTEST 3: SINGLE NONSENSE LETTER

A single nonsense letter is interspersed among 10 structurally similar nonsense letters in a random sequence of 126 letters. *Score*: total correct minus incorrect underlined letters in 30 seconds. *Task requirement*: as in previous subtest, but for identification of a nonsense letter.

SUBTEST 4: GESTALT FIGURE

The figure to be identified is a diamond about 8 mm in height containing a square which in turn contains a diamond. This figure is interspersed among similar figures in a random sequence of 168 figures. *Score*: total correct minus incorrect underlined figures in 60 seconds. *Task requirement*: as in previous subtest, but for identification of a complex figure.

SUBTEST 5: SINGLE LETTER

The letter *s* is interspersed among 360 randomized letters. *Score*: number underlined minus number of errors in 30 seconds. *Task requirement*: as in previous subtest, but for a single letter.

SUBTEST 6: SINGLE LETTER IN SYLLABLE CONTEXT

One hundred sixty-two four-letter nonsense syllables are presented, 47 of which contain the letter *e*. The child is required to underline each syllable containing *e*. *Score*: total correct minus incorrect in 45 seconds. *Task requirement*: as in previous subtest, but for a letter in syllable context.

SUBTEST 7: TWO LETTERS

The letters *b* and *m* are interspersed among 360 randomized letters. *Score*: number underlined minus number of errors in 45 seconds. *Task requirement*: as in previous subtest, but for two letters.

SUBTEST 8: SEQUENCE OF GEOMETRIC FORMS

Four geometric forms (triangle, Greek cross, circle, crescent) are presented in various orders for a total of 65 "syllables." The child is required to underline only the groups with the order triangle, cross, crescent, and circle. *Score*: total groups correctly underlined minus errors in 60 seconds. *Task requirement*: same as in previous subtest, but for groups of geometric figures.

SUBTEST 9: FOUR-LETTER NONSENSE SYLLABLE, UNPRONOUNCEABLE

The child is required to underline a four-letter nonsense syllable ("fsbm") interspersed among 146 four-letter nonsense syllables. All syllables are made up of the consonants *f*, *s*, *b*, and *m*, which renders them unpronounceable. *Score*: total correct minus incorrect in 60 seconds. *Task requirement*: same as in previous subtest, but for nonsense syllables.

SUBTEST 10: FOUR-LETTER NONSENSE SYLLABLE, PRONOUNCEABLE

This task is the same as in the previous subtest except that it involves the identification of a pronounceable nonsense syllable ("narp") instead of an unpronounceable nonsense syllable. This syllable is interspersed among other nonsense syllables made up of the letters *n*, *a*, *r*, *p*. *Score*: total correct minus incorrect in 60 seconds. *Task requirement*: same as in previous subtest but for a pronounceable nonsense syllable.

SUBTEST 11: FOUR-LETTER WORD

The word "spot" is interspersed among 146 four-letter syllables made up of the letters *s*, *p*, *o*, *t*. *Score*: total correct minus incorrect in 60 seconds. *Task requirement*: same as in previous subtest, but for a four-letter word.

SUBTEST 12: UNSPACED FOUR-LETTER WORD

The word "spot" is interspersed among the letters *s*, *p*, *o*, *t*, in various orders, with no syllable spacing. *Score*: total correct minus incorrect in 60 seconds. *Task requirement*: same as in previous subtest, but for an unspaced word.

SUBTEST 13: SINGLE NUMBER

This task is exactly the same as that involved in the first subtest except that the number to be underlined is 5 instead of 4.

SUBTEST 14: SINGLE RECTANGLE

The child is required to underline a series of identical rectangles, approximately 1 cm × .5 cm. *Score*: total number underlined. *Task requirement*: speed of underlining.

Younger children's battery (ages 5–8)

A. The following tests are the same as those administered to children 9–15 years of age:

- The tactile, auditory, visual, and finger agnosia portions of the Sensory-Perceptual Disturbances Tests
- Target Test
- Sweep Hearing Test
- Auditory Closure Test
- Sentence Memory Test
- Speech-Sounds Perception Test
- Verbal Fluency Test
- Auditory Analysis Test
- Lateral Dominance Examination
- Strength of Grip
- Name-Writing Speed
- Finger- and Foot-Tapping Speed
- Mazes
- Children's Word-Finding Test
- Underlining Test

B. The following tests differ somewhat from those administered to children 9–15 years of age:

Fingertip Symbol-Writing Recognition

The procedure is identical to that described above for Fingertip Number-Writing Perception except that X's and O's are used instead of numbers.

Tactile-Forms Recognition

The child is required to identify familiar forms placed in his/her hands. Four forms are used. Each of these is placed in either hand separately. Then, different pairings of the forms are placed in both hands simultaneously. In all, there are eight possible correct identifications for each hand. *Score*: total incorrect identifications in eight trials for each hand. *Task requirement*: recognition of forms by touch only. *Response*: spoken name of object or pointing to a representation of it.

Halstead-Wepman Aphasia Screening Test (Reitan & Davison, 1974)

Naming (Anomia). Four items. Otherwise, the same.

Writing (Dysgraphia). One item written, one item printed. Otherwise, the same.

Reading (Dyslexia). Three items. Otherwise, the same.

Drawing (Constructional Dyspraxia). Three items. Otherwise, the same.

Arithmetic (Dyscalculia). Four items. Otherwise, the same.

Body Orientation. Four items. The child is required to show or point to his/her nose, tongue, eyebrow, and elbow. *Score*: number of errors.

Right–Left Discrimination. Two items. The child is required to put his/her right hand on his/her nose, and his/her left hand on his/her head. *Score*: number of errors.

Category Test

The Category Test utilizes the same general apparatus and procedure as the Halstead Category Test. However, the test consists of 80 stimulus figures divided into five subtests. The answer panel consists of four answer buttons which are individually identified by red, blue, yellow, and green lights. The principles involved are color, quantity, oddity, and color prominence. As in the Halstead Category Test, the final subtest is of a summary nature and therefore does not have a principle to be discerned.

Graduated Holes Test

The procedure is identical to that described above except that only the four largest holes are used.

Grooved Pegboard Test

The procedure is identical to that described above except that only the first two rows (10 holes) are used.

C. The following tests are used only with children 5–8 years of age:

Color Form Test (Reitan & Davison, 1974)

The Color Form Test uses stimulus material of various colors and shapes. Initially, the child is instructed to follow a sequence of progress from one figure to another by shifting between shape and color as stimulus clues. After a sample, in which careful instruction is given, the test itself is administered. The child moves from the initial figure to one having the same shape even though the color is different, next proceeds to a figure that is different in shape but has the same color, and continues to alternate in this fashion.

Progressive Figures Test (Reitan & Davison, 1974)

This test is presented on an 8¼″ × 11″ sheet of paper on which are printed eight stimulus figures. Each stimulus figure consists of a large outside figure (such as a circle) and a smaller figure of another shape inside (such as a square). The child's task is to use the small inside figure as the clue for progressing to the outside shape of the next stimulus figure. For example, if the child is located at a large circle enclosing a small square, the small square would indicate the next move would be to a large square. If the large square then enclosed a small triangle, the small triangle would serve as a clue for the next move. In this way the child progresses from inside figure to outside figure, moving from one stimulus configuration to the next.

Matching Pictures (Reitan & Davison, 1974)

The test consists of five pages, the first of which is a practice page. The task requires the child to match pictures located at the top of the page with their appropriate pairs shown across the bottom of the page. While the practice items require only matching of identical figures, the test progresses in such a way that a limited degree of generalization is required. For example, on one page a picture of a woman must be used to match the stimulus figure of a man, or a girl to match a boy. On another page a horse matches a cow, a chicken matches a rooster, and so forth. The test is so organized that it requires the child to respond in terms of equivalent categories in order to perform the test correctly.

Matching Figures and Matching V's (Reitan & Davison, 1974)

The child is asked to match figures printed on little blocks with the same figures printed on a single card. These figures become progressively more complex along the card. The little blocks are presented to each subject in a standardized manner. The score is the time in seconds required to complete the task, and the number of errors.

Drawing of Star and Concentric Squares (Reitan & Davison, 1974)

The child is required to copy the figure presented to him/her. The examiner points out specifically how the figure is made up. The score is the time in seconds required to complete each drawing, and the number of errors in each drawing.

References

Benton, A. L. (1965). *Sentence Memory Test.* Iowa City, IA: Author.

Doehring, D. J. (1968). *Pattern of impairment in specific reading disability.* Bloomington: Indiana University Press.

Dunn, L. M. (1965). *Expanded manual for the Peabody Picture Vocabulary Test.* Minneapolis, MN: American Guidance Service.

Halstead, W. C. (1947). *Brain and intelligence.* Chicago: University of Chicago Press.

Harris, A. J. (1947). *Harris Tests of Lateral Dominance, Manual of Directions for Administration and Interpretation.* New York: Psychological Corp.

Jastak, J. F., & Jastak, S. R. (1965). *The Wide Range Achievement Test.* Wilmington, DE: Guidance Associates.

Kass, C. E. (1964). Auditory Closure Test. In J. J. Olson & J. L. Olson (Eds.), *Validity studies on the Illinois Test of Psycholinguistic Abilities.* Madison, WI: Photo.

Kløve, H. (1963). Clinical neuropsychology. In F. M. Forster (Ed.), *The medical clinics of North America.* New York: Saunders.

Knights, R. M., & Moule, A. D. (1967). Normative and reliability data on finger and foot tapping in children. *Perceptual and Motor Skills, 25,* 717–720.

Knights, R. M., & Moule, A. D. (1968). Normative data on the Motor Steadiness Battery for Children. *Perceptual and Motor Skills, 26,* 643–650.

Miles, W. R. (1929). *The A-B-C Vision Test.* New York: Psychological Corp.

Pajurkova, E. M., Orr, R. R., Rourke, B. P., & Finlayson, M. A. J. (1972). Children's Word-Finding Test: A verbal problem-solving task. *Perceptual and Motor Skills, 42,* 851–858.

Reitan, R. M. (1972). Verbal problem-solving as related to brain damage. *Perceptual and Motor Skills, 34*, 515–524.

Reitan, R. M., & Davison, L. A. (1974). *Clinical neuropsychology: Current status and applications.* Washington, DC: V. H. Winston.

Rosner, J., & Simon, D. P. (1970). *Auditory Analysis Test: An initial report.* Learning Research and Development Center. University of Pittsburgh.

Rourke, B. P., & Finlayson, M. A. J. (1975). Neuropsychological significance of variations in patterns of performance on the Trail Making Test for older children with learning disabilities. *Journal of Abnormal Psychology, 84*, 412–421.

Rourke, B. P., & Fisk, J. L. (1976). *Children's Word-Finding Test* (Revised). University of Windsor, Department of Psychology, Windsor, Ontario.

Rourke, B. P., & Gates, R. D. (1980). *Underlining Test: Preliminary norms.* University of Windsor, Department of Psychology, Windsor, Ontario.

Rourke, B. P., & Orr, R. R. (1977). Prediction of the reading and spelling performances of normal and retarded readers: Four-year follow-up. *Journal of Abnormal Child Psychology, 5*, 9–20.

Rourke, B. P., & Petrauskas, R. J. (1977). *Underlining Test* (Revised). University of Windsor, Department of Psychology, Windsor, Ontario.

Rourke, B. P., & Telegdy, G. A. (1971). Lateralizing significance of WISC verbal–performance discrepancies for older children with learning disabilities. *Perceptual and Motor Skills, 33*, 875–883.

Rourke, B. P., Yanni, D. W., MacDonald, G. W., & Young, G. C. (1973). Neuropsychological significance of lateralized deficits on the Grooved Pegboard Test for older children with learning disabilities. *Journal of Consulting and Clinical Psychology, 47*, 128–134.

Wechsler, D. (1949). *Wechsler Intelligence Scale for Children.* New York: Psychological Corp.

Wirt, R. D., Lachar, D., Klinedinst, J. K., & Seat, P. D. (1977). *Multidimensional description of child personality: A manual for the Personality Inventory for Children.* Los Angeles: Western Psychological Services.

Author index

Abrams, H. S., 144, 155
Adams, K. M., 12, 13, 15, 36, 38, 39, 143, 154–156, 204, 249, 260
Alexander, K. M., 137, 156

B

Bachman, K. M., 85, 120
Badian, N. A., 28, 36
Baer, R. A., 256, 259
Bakker, D. J., 1, 36, 38, 39, 46, 57, 58, 120, 249, 256, 259, 261
Balla, D. A., 255, 260
Barin, J. J., 85, 120
Barkley, R. A., 25, 28, 37, 130, 155, 233, 248, 257, 259
Bash, M. S., 67, 116, 119
Bawden, N. N., 31, 39
Becker, L., 199, 204
Becker, W., 199, 204
Benson, D. F., 164, 204
Bentler, P. M., 142, 156
Benton, A. L., 5, 18, 28, 31, 37, 38, 76, 120, 161, 204, 249, 259, 265, 275
Black, F. W., 123, 155
Black, P., 86, 119
Blashfield, R., 15, 37, 158, 204
Blumer, D., 86, 119
Boder, E., 158, 204
Boll, T. J., 38, 236, 248, 249
Breen, M. J., 25, 37, 233, 248, 257, 259

Bresman, M. J., 135, 156
Brown, G., 86, 119
Brust, J. C. M., 149, 154, 155
Bruyn, G. W., 119

C

Camfield, C., 107, 119
Camfield, P. R., 107, 119
Camp, B. W., 67, 116, 119
Carmine, L., 199, 204
Carter, S., 149, 155
Chadwick, O., 76, 77, 86, 119, 120
Charney, S., 137, 155
Chelune, G. J., 256, 259
Cicchetti, D. B., 255, 260
Corbett, J. A., 96, 119
Craft, A. W., 76, 119

D

Davis, D., 144, 156
Davison, L. A., 14, 17, 19, 38, 120, 248, 264–269, 273–276
Delaney, C. R., 155
Del Dotto, J. E., 239, 249
Dennis, M., 3, 14, 17, 37
Derons, M. P., 100, 120
deWit, J., 38, 249, 259
Dixon, R., 199, 204
Doehring, D. G., 19, 37, 158, 204, 270, 275

277

Subject index